R.D. BUJ

ANIRUDHA BHATTACHARJEE, an alumnus of IIT Kharagpur, works with IBM as a SAP consultant. He is an amateur musician with a flair for films, quizzing and puzzles. He lives in Kolkata.

BALAJI VITTAL is an alumnus of Jadavpur University, Kolkata. He works for The Royal Bank of Scotland. He shuttles between New Delhi, where he works, and Hyderabad, where his family lives. He contributes regularly to the *Hindu Metroplus*.

R.D. BURMAN

The Man, The Music

Anirudha Bhattacharjee
Balaji Vittal

HarperCollins *Publishers* India
a joint venture with

New Delhi

First published in India in 2011 by
HarperCollins *Publishers* India
a joint venture with
The India Today Group

HarperCollins *Publishers*
A-53, Sector 57, Noida 201301, India
77-85 Fulham Palace Road, London W6 8JB, United Kingdom
Hazelton Lanes, 55 Avenue Road, Suite 2900, Toronto, Ontario M5R 3L2
and 1995 Markham Road, Scarborough, Ontario M1B 5M8, Canada
25 Ryde Road, Pymble, Sydney, NSW 2073, Australia
31 View Road, Glenfield, Auckland 10, New Zealand
10 East 53rd Street, New York NY 10022, USA

Typeset in 11/15 Bell MT at
SÜRYA

Printed and bound at
Thomson Press (India) Ltd.

*To Basudev Chakravarty, Manohari Singh, Maruti Rao Keer
and R.D. Burman*

*We're sure they are sitting together somewhere
composing music*

Contents

Book Three: SUN IN GEMINI

Foreword

At the outset, I would like to thank Balaji Vittal and Anirudha Bhattacharjee for this endeavour. I'm afraid, more often than not, an artiste's persona and the nuances of his work get lost in the fog of time because as a nation we are poor at keeping records. I think this kind of history is precious, important for coming generations. Today, when someone decides to make a documentary on a great film-maker like Bimal Roy, there are hardly any people around who have had first-hand experience of working with him. In the course of their work, these masters often say and do things off the cuff, almost casually at times, which offer an insight into their minds and their crafts. These pearls of wisdom need to be documented, preserved and handed over to the next generation. But more often than not, these get lost. It is desirable and imperative that we talk to people who have worked with these masters, who know how they functioned, who understood the basic texture of their personality, what it was that made them what they were. That is how we can relate their art to them and them to their art. It makes me happy that in this book the authors have given space to the people who were fortunate enough to work with this maestro called R.D. Burman. They have made the effort to go beyond the songs, talked to people who were present when the songs were being composed and recorded. And in the process they have given us a wonderful account of the work of a genius.

What can I say about R.D. Burman? Some people become successful at a given point in time. And as time passes, vogues and fashion and styles change, these people either die or wither away and new people come. The only ones we remember are those who were not just successful, but who did something unprecedented; who took their art to a whole new level and whose contribution changed their field of craft for coming generations. RD introduced a new sound, with a new sensibility, new beats, new ways of using existing instruments, and brought new musical instruments too. The technical facilities we take for granted today were not available in the 1960s or '70s. Yet Pancham's music remains as fresh, it sounds as contemporary as it did three decades ago. And he had the genius to create sounds out of everyday things, for example, placing something in front of a big fan and recording. It was a strange, yet unforgettable experience seeing him at work.

His compositions in films like *Chhote Nawab* and *Teesri Manzil* were unprecedented. Those songs did not remind you of the songs of yesteryears. I think it took a little time for Indian listeners to get attuned to the new music. But once it took hold of the listeners' attention or aesthetics, it remained there. That is why contemporaries of RD, who were no less successful if not more, are not remembered today with the kind of reverence that you see for RD. New musicians like Shankar–Ehsaan–Loy or Vishal–Shekhar have great respect for RD, and you can see that in their work they take his tradition forward. Obviously, they are no less talented; they are adding things to his legacy, they are updating, but somewhere you can see that it is the same chain of aesthetics, of musical sensibility that is being carried forward by the next generation.

I have been very fortunate, and I am very proud of the fact that I had a long association with him. My first film with Pancham was *Saagar* and the very first song that we recorded together was *'Jaane do na'*. I remember I was writing the dialogues for *Saagar* at a hotel in Khandala and I had to come back to Bombay to attend a music sitting for a particular situation in the film. He had given me the tune. I tried to write the song to that tune and there was a particular line that I was very keen to bring into the song, but the metre was not allowing me. So I put the tune aside and wrote the song on my own. From Khandala I went directly to his music room, where Ramesh Sippy and others were waiting for me, and I said, 'I have written the song, but please don't get upset – I have not written the song to the tune you gave me because whatever I wanted to say was not fitting the metre.' So RD said, 'Okay, let me write down the song.' He took a pen and paper, and I started dictating the song. By the time he finished, in some part of his brain he had already made the tune – while jotting down the song! As soon as he finished writing the last word, he opened the harmonium and started singing. That is how *'Chehra hai ya chand khila hai'* was born.

After that we did quite a few films, and there came a time when . . . I suppose in this film market and in the commercial market of music, people don't appreciate your talent; people appreciate your last film's success; that's about all. And, unfortunately, some of his films did not do well in spite of his good work. Then, perhaps, failure may have disenchanted him; it may have affected his work for a while too. There came a time when the closest of his close colleagues dropped him; he had no work. Maybe because his films were not doing well, things were not going right. Perhaps he did not concentrate the way he should have on the quality of his work; after all, he was a human being. But instead of inspiring him, instead of cajoling him to the standards he was capable of, his associates preferred to move away. But my faith in him never wavered. I was convinced he was a genius; one didn't have to be a Sherlock Holmes to see that.

We did some films at that time, like *Gardish, Gang*, one film by Ram Gopal Varma, *Drohi*, if I am not mistaken, and *1942: A Love Story*. These were his last films. I have been an admirer and I had unshakeable faith in his talent. Everyone goes through a lean patch and I knew that it was only a matter of time. With *1942* he knew it was now or never, and he had to prove to the world that he was R.D. Burman.

I remember, one evening I went to his music studio and he was sitting alone. He had his headphones on and was listening to something. He gave the headphones to me and said, 'I have dubbed Kumar Sanu once again for "*Kuch na kaho*". Listen to it now.' Then he played the song for me which all of us listen to now. And I could see that he was confident; there was a kind of amused expression on his face and he said, 'Yeh music release hone do.' It did, and obviously it was a major hit; it became a milestone, but he was not there to see this.

Most of his tunes that you appreciate, like '*Ek ladki ko dekha*', were created in five to six minutes. That was the level of his creativity, the energy he had. Today, modernity and dignity have become an either/or matter, you are either modern or you are dignified. It's a bad choice! But you don't have that in RD's music. His music is modern, cool and has a certain dignity; there's nothing cheap about it. It is sophisticated. You don't feel that this sound belongs to an uncouth person; there is something very decent about his compositions. And this combination of modernity and dignity has become very rare.

He was a master with background music too; he knew the role it plays in cinema. One has to just think back on the awesome background score of *Sholay*, with its many elements, to realize how developed his sensibilities were as far as sound was concerned. It makes me immensely happy to note that the authors mention this in quite some detail. Although some of the background and interlude pieces of Shankar–Jaikshan are well known and you can recognize them in an instant, I feel that till RD came along, sound was not as important as the composition as far as musicians were concerned. RD gave equal importance to sound. He paid equal attention to his orchestration, whether it was background music or during the song.

Time works in a strange way. However successful you may be, if your success is only a matter of chance or circumstances, not based on real talent, it will not stand the test of time. But if you are really great, you become greater with time. And time makes a bigger and bigger idol of you. And that is what is happening to RD. Because time is kind to great people. And R.D. Burman was great.

This book – with its insightful analysis of RD's songs, inputs of his team members and other people who worked with him, and the obvious love the authors have for the subject – makes an honest and welcome attempt at understanding what it was that made him great.

Javed Akhtar

Introduction

Despite having 'Dev Burman' as a last name, Pancham had to wait for seven years before he tasted success. He was in no apparent hurry. Rather, he seemed to savour the wait. But that is how it is with the truly and perennially talented. They expect the best to happen and they know that the best takes its time to come by. They are patient with their destinies.

In my interactions with Pancham during the making of *Teesri Manzil*, I figured out the span of genres of music that the boy had exposed himself to – jazz, Latino, folk. I suspect that he had been appreciating and absorbing all of these from his childhood solely as a keen student of music; forms he would subsequently use to paint his music with. Apart from lovely melody and a fascinating sense of rhythm, his other contribution to Hindi film music was his ability to generate supporting music from anything that produced sound – that was his differentiator. To me, Pancham was an enthusiastic chef who enjoyed the unexplored exotica; and not just an efficient cook. Pancham's primary identity was that of an exceptionally gifted musician; music direction could not have been possible otherwise.

Pancham was the music director for both my directorial ventures, *Manoranjan* and *Bundalbaaz*. We also worked closely in numerous other films in which I acted and for which he composed the music. During our association over the years, I got to know him progressively better as a person too. He was a nice boy.

Film-based light music is exposed to a constant layering down by newer albums that appeal to newer sensitivities (perhaps shallower ones). Today, I observe Pancham's inspiration among young composers, a sign of *his* legacy. His achievements need to be documented. His story needs to be told.

This is the Pancham story.

Shammi Kapoor

Authors' Note

At the outset, we need to mention that we did not quite want to write a biography. There are people better qualified to do that, people who knew him closely. What made R.D. Burman (aka Pancham) fascinating for us was his music – and the era in which he composed it. This then is the story of R.D. Burman and his music – what it was about, the era in which it was composed, the factors that influenced it and the difference it wrought in a medium that today connects Indians across the globe. This book is about Pancham's mystique, his differentiator. About why his compositions, once considered counterculture, continue to thrive, either in the original or in remixed versions, even four decades after he composed them. *R.D. Burman – The Man, The Music* is about why his innovations, recording techniques, mixed rhythm patterns, use of brass and sound mixing are discussed on web forums as frequently and as passionately as they are; why his creations, uploaded on various online video sharing sites, have logged eyeball hits in millions; why his fan count outstrips that of all his contemporaries put together.

Pancham's music was contemporary, largely Western in form, and featured instruments not widely used in India before he entered the scene. He blended chord-based arrangements with familiar forms of melody to produce music that was light on the ears and easy to pick up, but which sounded contraband, and gelled more with leather jackets and sports cars than with the traditional bullock cart. It was music that was the well-thought-out handiwork of a maverick.

Like his music, he looked different from the traditional dhoti-kurta or the pyjama-kurta clad musicians one was accustomed to seeing. Dressed in plain, light-coloured shirts and trousers, his shirtsleeves rolled up, Pancham, with his oddly round face and Mongoloid features, was the living representation of his own music – easy, invigorating, young and refreshingly unique. In an age of black-and-white images, Pancham was a medley of colour.

And though we are unabashed fans of his music, it is our endeavour to ensure that we don't do a hagiography. As such, we also focus on the mistakes he made. No man is above making errors, and Pancham made quite a few. God blessed him with less than the normal share of shrewdness and strategic forethought required for long voyages. He took too long to correct his course, provided he figured out the right one at all.

This book is also a homage to the team members from whom Pancham was able to extract the best by giving them due credit for their contribution. And they, and their families in turn, loved and admired both the teddy bear of a gentleman and the musician in Pancham.

This is about a composer whose legacy outlives the person many times over.

Anirudha Bhattacharjee and Balaji Vittal

The RD Team

ASSISTANTS	INSTRUMENT
Bablu Chakravarty	Violin
Basu Chakravarty	Cello
Deepan Chatterjee	Sound recordist
Manohari Singh	English flute, Alto sax, Clarinet, Mandolin
Maruti Rao Keer	Tabla, percussion
Sapan Chakraborty	—

MUSICIANS	INSTRUMENT
Aashish Khan Debsharma	Sarod
Abani Das Gupta	Dhol, Khol
Abdul Kareem Khan	Dholak
Adesh Srivastava	Drums
Amrutrao Katkar	Tabla and secondary percussion
Arvind Mayekar	Sitar
Ashok Sharma	Sitar
Babla	Conga, Bongo
Bahadur Singh	Xylophone
Bhanu Gupta	Mouth organ, Rhythm guitar
Bhavani Shankar	Pakhawaj
Bhupinder Singh	Guitar (lead mainly)
Blasco Monsorate	Trombone
Brajen Biswas	Tabla
Burjor Lord	Drums, Vibraphone

Bursingh Punjabi	Trombone
Castro	Trumpet
Cawas Lord	Bongo, percussion
Chandrakant Satnak	Tabla, Dholak
Charanjit Singh	Transicord, Guitar (lead, bass)
Dakshina Mohan Tagore	Taar Shehnai
Deepak Naik	Tabla
Devi Chakrabarty	Percussion
Devichand Chauhan	Dholak, Tabla
Dilip Naik	Lead guitar
Emil Issac	Bass guitar
Franco Vaz	Drums
Gajanand Karnard	Violin
Ganpat Rao Jadhav	Dhol, Chanda
George Fernandes	Trumpet
Hari Prasad Chaurasia, Pandit	Flute
Homi Mullan	Duggi, Accordion, secondary percussion
Indranath Mukherjee	Tabla
Indru Atma	Matka
Iqbal Khan	Tabla, Dholak
Ivan Muns	Trombone
Jairam Acharya	Sitar
Janardan Abhayankar	Tabla, percussion
Joseph Monsorate	Trumpet
Kartik Kumar	Sitar
Kersi Lord	Accordion, Drums, mallet-based percussions
Kishore Desai	Mandolin
Kishore Sodha	Trumpet
Leslie Godinho	Drums
Louis Banks	Keyboards
Maniya Bharve	Percussion
Mike Machado	Piano
Nandu Chavathe	Violin
Nitin Shankar	Conga, Bongo
Prabhakar Jog	Violin
Pradipto Sengupta	Mandolin
Pramod Sane	Tabla
R.K. Das	Rhythm guitar

Raj Sodha	English flute, Soprano saxophone
Rajendra Singh	Violin
Ramakant Habsekar	Tabla
Ramesh Iyer	Guitar (lead mainly)
Ramu	Mridangam
Ranjit 'Kancha' Gazmer	Madal
Rashid Khan	Banjo
Ravi Gurtu	Tumba
Ravi Sundaram	Mandolin
Ronny	Organ
Ronu Majumdar, Pandit	Flute
Samta Prasad, Pandit	Tabla
Sharafat	Tabla
Shiv Kumar Sharma, Pandit	Santoor
Shyam Raj	English flute, Tenor sax, Soprano sax
Soumitro Chatterjee	Rhythm guitar
Sudarshan Adhikari	Dholak, Khol
Sultan Khan	Sarangi
Sumant Raj	English Flute
Sunil Kaushik	Guitar (lead mainly)
Tony Vaz	Bass Guitar
Trilok Gurtu	Drums
Uday Kumar Dubey	Dholak
Ulhas Bapat, Pandit	Santoor
Uttam Singh	Violin
Vancy D'Souza	Drums
Vijay Indorkar	Pedal Matka, percussion
Viju Rao Katkar	Tabla, percussion
Zarine Daruwala (Sharma)	Sarod

অকস্মাৎ প্রতিভার প্রভাবেই আসে অপ্রত্যাশিত,
স্বসময়ে আকস্মিক প্রত্যাশার সৃষ্টি করে,
আবার চলে যায় অপ্রত্যাশিত,
সুগম্ভীর খরাকে রসে রসাব্রিত করে
উর্বর করে শুকে স্বরস্বায় হয় নির্গমিত,
ভবিষ্যৎ হয় উদ্ভাসিত ॥

Salil Chowdhury, on the death of R.D. Burman

He arrives unexpectedly, unanticipated,
Begets expectations enormous, implausible,
Gratifies the thirsty earth with his creative flair,
Showers it green and fertile
And then goes away one day,
As unexpectedly as he had appeared,
With the future lit up by the halo of his prominence ...

Translated by Supratik Gangopadhyay

Prologue

Marylands Apartments, 20 April 2009. A Fiat, BMC 1139, stands forlorn in the parking lot. We go up to Flat number 101 on the first floor. The light in the narrow corridor bounces off the door's varnish, giving the corridor an eerie look. The brass nameplate says 'R.D. BURMAN'. We ring the bell . . . ring it again. Do we hear shuffling footsteps approaching the main door? Will it open?

1

Bombay, Monday, 3 January 1994. He was living through the climax of the film. Having discussed every little detail with the producer–director in their two-and-a-half-hour-long meeting, he was finally satisfied. He had been waiting for the familiar taste of success for quite a while. 'This will be a masterpiece,' he prophesied. He had a dinner to attend at a friend's place in Santa Cruz. As a rule, he seldom went out without taking a quick bath. The visitor left. It was 9.30 p.m. The host too had to leave soon.

2

Tuesday, 4 January 1994. It was a cool winter morning, the northern winds making the city cooler than what the Santa Cruz weather monitoring station had predicted. Not much smog, noticed Malay Mozumder as he looked out from his apartment on 15th Road, Santa Cruz West. It was just 6.30 a.m. and the streets were silent, devoid of traffic. Mrigendranath Lahiri, Mrs Mozumder's bachelor uncle who had his meals at the Mozumder household, was expected for breakfast in half an hour. The doorbell rang. Unusual, Mr Mozumder thought, as the milkman and the newspaperman had already delivered their goods for the day.

It was the Mozumders' sixty-one-year-old neighbour.

'Pancham is no more,' Bhanu Gupta managed to say, his throat choked, the wrinkles under his eyes soggy.

3

Pancham had returned home around 12.30 a.m. from the party at Shakti Samanta's house in Santa Cruz. He had tipped the building watchman fifty rupees for towing his car into the garage. He was watching the BBC news broadcast on his forty-inch National TV set when, at around 2.30 a.m., he began sweating and his chest constricted with pain. He rang the bell for his servants. Sudam, who rushed into the room, found Pancham with his tongue protruding. He prised his mouth open and sprayed Sorbitrate into it. Ramesh Maharana, the chauffeur, frantically called for an ambulance, while Bharat Ashar, Pancham's secretary, who was informed over the phone, rushed in with a doctor who gave Pancham an emergency cardiac massage. By the time an ambulance, scything through the silence of the night, pulled up outside his door, Pancham had collapsed. It was 3.40 a.m. Time moved on, now without R.D. Burman.

At the pink-blue streak of daybreak, the physician officially pronounced Rahul Dev Burman, fifty-four, dead. In the hours that followed, the news plunged music lovers into a chasm of disbelief first, and then into a deeper abyss of despair.

Sudam Jana, Manu Pal and Ramesh Maharana, Pancham's three men Fridays, were dumbfounded. Mrs Meera Dev Burman, Pancham's mother, was spared the shock of her son's death. Alzheimer's insulated her from the truth. Till her own demise in October 2007, she believed that Tublu was in London, composing music.

4

As was his daily ritual, Mr Lahiri, who had been Pancham's local guardian in Calcutta from the late 1940s until the mid-1950s, walked into Mr Mozumder's flat for breakfast. Moments later, the septuagenarian rushed to Pancham's apartment in Marylands in Santa Cruz. As he stepped into the hall of the first-floor flat, he found, among others, Asha Bhonsle, Madhu Behl and Jaya Bachchan sitting beside 'Tublu'. Composers Jatin and Lalit sat by Pancham's feet, their heads bowed, oblivious to the activity around them.

Shakti Samanta, Gogi Anand, Jackie Shroff, Aamir Khan, Sanjay Dutt, Gulshan Bawra, B.R. Chopra, Majrooh Sultanpuri and many others were part of the silence that hung about the bereaved house. Alka Yagnik and Kavita Krishnamurthy stood by the staircase, tearfully holding each other's hands. This silence in Pancham's house would have been unfamiliar for old comrades like Basu Chakravarty, Manohari Singh, Maruti Rao, Pandit Ulhas Bapat, Kersi Lord and Shailendra Singh. Mahmood sat on a chair, looking unwell. Gulzar stood by his side, talking to him, trying to comfort him.

'Uh?' was all Amit Kumar could say when Leena Ganguly gave him the news that morning. Guitarist Ramesh Iyer, after repeated attempts to get through over the phone, had hurried to Amit's bungalow on Juhu Tara Road. Pancham and Amit had spoken just the day before. 'Let's sit and compose. Let's start again! Come over to my place tomorrow,' Pancham had said. 'I broke down later,' recalls Amit.

5

In Calcutta, Achyutananda Bhattacharya's (better known as Badal Bhattacharya) mind wandered back to what had been one of his last telephone conversations with his childhood friend on

14 December 1993. Pancham had invited Badal and his wife
Maitrayee (aka Mili) to accompany Asha Bhonsle on her way
back to Bombay from a performance at Ranchi. Pancham had
been down with malaria for almost two weeks prior to the
conversation. He had talked enthusiastically about recovering,
of his hopes for his latest film, *1942: A Love Story*, and about his
plans to organize the Saraswati Puja in a big way the coming
spring. Badal-babu's hand baggage aboard the Bombay-bound
Indian Airlines flight that fateful morning contained a Kali Puja
gift for Pancham – a hand-stitched kurta from French Tailors
located in the busy lane adjoining Globe Cinema in central
Calcutta. The kurta would now have to serve as a funeral
offering.

6

Grief has different ways of affecting people. Some withdraw
into absolute silence; others seek relief in remembrances. While
most bystanders stood quietly, Anu Malik kept talking
animatedly about the R.D. Burman of yore, humming some of
his favourite refrains to a young Goldie Behl.

Sandip Ray was dumbstruck by the news passed on to him by
Sromona Guha Thakurta, daughter of noted singer Ruma Guha
Thakurta. Sromona was like a daughter and sister to Pancham
and had last called up Pancham-da on New Year's Day to wish
him. Unable to believe what had happened, she went into a daze
and was unable to go to office. It would be a month before her
stubborn stoicism collapsed. At a live show by Suman
Chattopadhyay (now Kabir Suman), a particular song, 'Gaanwala'
(the Music Man), brought forth the reality of Pancham's absence.
Finally, she wept.

'How can a person so young and lively die?' was classical
vocalist Pandit Ajoy Chakrabarty's first reaction to the news

conveyed to him by singer Chhaya Ganguli. His association with Pancham was still growing – their plans for an album together had just been drawn. So was the case with S.P. Balasubrahmanyam, whose fascination for Pancham-da's music was flowering with the frequency of his interactions with him. Among others, Pancham-da's statement during the recording of *Aaja meri jaan* – 'You $&8#, that is why I have called you all the way from Madras. You can do it!'– echoed again and again.

7

The preparations for Pancham's final journey were under way. He had been dressed in a new dhoti and kurta that Raakhee Gulzar had brought.

Apart from Pancham's closest chums like Randhir Kapoor, Gogi Anand and Gulshan Bawra, the funeral procession included most musicians and luminaries of the film world. Almost like a thumb rule in filmdom, the convoy also included people who went about extending commiserations but had never used him in their productions like Yash Chopra, Prakash Mehra and Subhash Ghai.

For Dev Anand, it was the end of a two-generation association with the Dev Burmans. He had seen both father and son rise and shoulder his Navketan Films. Dev's shoulders would be needed today.

Amrish Puri walked with the cortege to the Shastri Nagar crematorium in Juhu, reciting verses from the Bhagavadgita.

In deference to the choice of the film fraternity and the musicians who had worked with Pancham, Mr Lahiri lit the pyre, bidding farewell to the boy he had mentored forty-eight years ago in Calcutta when S.D. Burman had moved to Bombay to pursue a career in music.

8

Salil Chowdhury was in a contemplative mood. Shocked at the sudden loss of a person he had described as the 'only musical phenomenon in the last twenty years of our film era', he wrote a poem as a tribute which was published in the Bengali daily, *Aajkaal.*

Ashim Samanta wondered if things would have turned out differently had Pancham stayed back for the night as Shakti Samanta had suggested. Pancham had averred at the party that *1942: A Love Story* would be the beginning of his second innings and that there would be no looking back. He had sounded very confident that evening.

9

On 5 January, music lovers nationwide woke to the news of Pancham's demise on the front page of leading dailies. The *Times of India*, Bombay, dedicated an editorial to him, perhaps the first for a composer of popular film music.

'In the death of Rahul Dev Burman, the world of music in particular and the world of cinema in general has suffered a great loss,' stated K.P. Singh Deo, the then Information and Broadcasting minister. Jyoti Basu, chief minister of West Bengal, too mourned the passing away of R.D. Burman, adding that Indian music had suffered a great loss.

The East Bengal Club, a premier sporting club in Calcutta, announced a musical soirée in memory of Pancham as part of their fund-raising programme. Pancham had been a life member of the club.

Amit Kumar and Ramesh Iyer announced their latest album *Surer Raja* as a dedication to 'Boss'.

The electronic media, sensing the potential of the story, shifted its focus to his last (still unreleased) work, *1942: A Love*

Story. The print media too caught up quickly, as contributors and critics rushed in to file their stories. Amazingly, within days, *1942: A Love Story* went from being an unheard-of album to being imprudently lauded as 'R.D. Burman's greatest work'. The music of the film had not even been released.

'Life is a real bitch,' fumed Vidhu Vinod Chopra, on the sets of *1942: A Love Story* at Film City, depressed and unable to shoot. In another forty days, the music would have released and 1994 would have ended up as Pancham's year. Pancham had worked hard for nearly two years, going over every minute detail of the film's climax with Vidhu in the two-and-a-half-hour meeting at Marylands Apartments just six hours before his death. 'Pancham-da seemed to be passing on a baton,' recalls Vidhu.

As per Asha Bhonsle's wishes, Pancham's ashes were carried in an earthen pot to Nashik by Badal Bhattacharya, Gogi Anand and Sapan Chakraborty to be immersed in the Godavari.

On the fourth day following Pancham's death, Asha Bhonsle performed the Chautha. The ceremony was attended by musicians, film stars and friends of Pancham.

Starting 4 January, an eleven-day Bhagavadgita paath was organized at Marylands. It was conducted by devotees from ISKCON.

Mr Lahiri performed the Shraddh ceremony at his residence on the eleventh day of Pancham's death. It was attended by most of R.D. Burman's associates. With the shock now over a week old, the prevalent mood was of grief mingled with nostalgia. Once the rituals were completed, and after the mourners had partaken of the meal, the musicians gathered around and hummed, sang and exchanged anecdotes about their recording days, the post-work laughter, the eating and drinking together. They clung to those memories, reliving those irretrievable moments.

10

Pancham was gone. But, energy, they say, is never lost in the universe. It merely morphs from one form to another. And from musician to musician, fan to fan, follower to follower, composer to composer, remixer to remixer, from one millennium to another ... Pancham would live on.

Book One

ASCENDANT IN LEO

A fine white bull, grazing in the shade of a large tree which stands in a park . . .

The person denoted by this degree will lead a quiet and successful life, and be born into large estates. In character, the native will be steadfast, firm, independent, very reserved, benevolent, yet outwardly forbidding, patient, and cautious. This degree is one of advantage.

1

The Chhote Nawab

In the early 1960s, early-morning walkers on Red Road, near the Maidan in Calcutta, ploughed through the wintry mist, bundled in warm clothing that had been rescued from their attics and dry-washed at Band Box dry cleaners. The Bengali babu draped in his customary shawl, and the British-Indian settler in his heirloom jacket, treaded the same grass on the Maidan, now awash with overnight dew. The distant honking of the occasional Plymouth or the Standard cars and the clanging of the foot bell by the tram drivers apart, the mornings were quiet, yet invigorating. A little later, over a cup of steaming Darjeeling tea, Britannia Thin Arrowroot biscuits and a copy of the *Statesman*, the gentlemen ordered their servants to get their suits and dinner jackets steam-pressed in preparation for the champagne evenings at Skyroom, Trincas and Blue Fox on Park Street, at Firpo's, and at Princess on the Chowringhee. Uniformed bearers and stewards, in black bow ties and contrasting white shirts, waited to receive their patrons and the 'memsahibs', both original as well as the English-tutored ones, as they alighted from their gleaming motor cars.

Walking into one of the restaurants or nightclubs, one expected a musical fare imported directly from the West to go with the continental cuisine and Black Label whisky on offer. Eddie Calvert and Frank Sinatra numbers were as popular as the cakes that disappeared from the counters at Flury's across the road; as was 'Moon river' by Johnny Mercer and Henry Mancini that had won the Academy Award recently. Fans in downtown Calcutta, like thousands of others across the world, enshrined Elvis 'The King' in their hearts while dancing to Chubby Checker's twist and Harry Fox's foxtrot.

Hindi music, especially Bombay film music, frowned upon by the intelligentsia in Calcutta, was avoided conscientiously by artistes and patrons alike. Even after more than a decade of Independence, people prided themselves on flaunting their colonial bearings, their tastes parroting foreign trends. The occasional Salil Chowdhury or Sachin Dev Burman folksy number was fine as long as it was played in the privacy of their living rooms. Shankar–Jaikishan, O.P. Nayyar, C. Ramachandra, even Madan Mohan, were names that were taboo, at least in the daily lives of the vintage rich who had been brought up on a diet of the West, Rabindranath Tagore, and cursorily understood (but knowledgeably head-nodded to) Indian classical music.

Therefore, starched shirtsleeves fluttered, and stiff upper lips pursed in embarrassment when the musicians at one of these establishments played – after the time slot for Indian music was over – an instrumental version of the Hindi film song 'Matwali ankhon wale' one evening in January 1962. That India had just trounced England at Eden Gardens thanks to an amazing display by Chandu Borde did not quite justify this lapse of taste. This was no noisy Barabazaar or Park Circus Maidan where working-class men coated in the dust of their honest labour flocked around Murphy radio sets outside tea stalls to listen to such music.

The song in question was a mix of various genres. It started with castanets and the acoustic guitar being played flamenco style for the first twenty-five seconds. It then cut to a forty-one-second-long Arabic-style high-pitched humming by Mohammad Rafi. Finally, guitar and castanet took centre stage again, and the intro tapered off with a violin ensemble after a full one minute and twenty-seven seconds. It was, and still is, considered an unconventional prelude, given that even the most Western of Hindi film songs then followed the same pattern: guitar solo, with the bongo following it on a 2/4 or 3/4 beat. The main melody toed the line of the prelude; a duet between Lata Mangeshkar and Mohammad Rafi, where the rhythm was maintained on a secondary percussion instrument, the resso resso.

The song was from the film *Chhote Nawab* which had released a few months back. The composer was a debutant – Rahul Dev Burman – who, according to Kersi Lord, contributed to the song with his foot tapping and clapping too. The first line, '*Matwali ankhon wale*', was in a way 'written' by Rahul himself. These words were his dummy lyrics while composing the metre that was retained in the final recorded version.

In the song, Lata Mangeshkar breezes through her lines, amplifying and vocalizing Helen's on-screen sensuality as she swings between the mukhra and the antara, connecting them using a drawn-out hum, like a trapeze artist. In contrast, Mohammad Rafi appears to be caught slightly off-guard, perhaps in his attempt to sound overly open-throated. The flamenco and the gypsy feel are woven into the song and, unlike the normally appalling picturization of Hindi film songs, Helen dancing with castanets in her hands, gives the visual a semblance of reality.

In April 2009, on hearing '*Matwali ankhon wale*' after a gap of
almost five decades, Kersi Lord instinctively called up composer
Pyarelal who, along with Laxmikant, was an assistant for the
film's music. 'It is so fresh, sounds like a song of 2009,'
complimented Kersi.

2

Sayyed Ali Akbar was a directorial assistant and a member of
the struggling Bombay film fraternity. Suave and charming, his
smooth talk won him the trust of comedian Mahmood Ali, his
sisters Zubeida and Meenu Mumtaz, and their mother
Latifunnisa. Everyone, including Mahmood, believed that Akbar
was in love with Zubeida; so it came as a rude shock when
Akbar abruptly broke off his relationship with Zubeida and
expressed his wish to marry Meenu instead. With Meenu
agreeing to the proposal, the engagement was held.

Professionally, Meenu was more successful than Akbar who
came within touching distance of success when he was offered
an assistantship to director Nasir Husain in the Shammi Kapoor–
Asha Parekh hit *Dil Deke Dekho* (1959). But while the film's
success catapulted the lead pair's careers to great heights, it did
nothing to further Akbar's. It was to prop his brother-in-law's
then sagging career that Mahmood Ali started his own film
production company.

The script for the film he planned (about the son of a Nawab,
a man-child) was already there: a one-act skit that Mahmood
had performed at Fatima Devi English High School in Bombay.
The name of the play was *Chhote Nawab*. The film marked the
debut for all three – Akbar as director, Mahmood as hero in his
first home production, and Pancham as composer. Composing
for films featuring debutants was to become a distinguishing
feature of Pancham's career.

3

William 'Willkie' Collins's timeless *The Woman in White*, published in 1859, is one of the first mystery novels to have been written. Almost a hundred years later, in 1958, Guru Dutt decided to adapt the novel for the screen with Waheeda Rahman and Sunil Dutt in the lead. Impressed by his work as assistant in *Pyaasa* (1957), Dutt also signed on the nineteen-year-old Rahul Dev Burman as composer, an act that reportedly upset S.D. Burman, who feared that it was too soon for his son to take on projects independently. Titled *Raaz*, the film, to be directed by Guru Dutt's assistant Niranjan, was featured along with *Chaudhvin Ka Chand* (1960) as a forthcoming attraction from the house of Guru Dutt in the publicity booklet for *Kaagaz Ke Phool* (1959).

Chhote Nawab was also the first film of Mahmood's son, Lucky Ali, who played one of the toddlers. The year 1961 saw the emergence of another important personality in the capacity of a composer, somebody who was to share an inseparable relationship with Pancham later – Kishore Kumar, whose career as composer took off with *Jhumroo*.

The song in *Chhote Nawab* that has connoisseurs in raptures, and is regarded as one of the finest of Pancham's oeuvre, was the Lata Mangeshkar solo '*Ghar aaja ghir aaye*.' Music historians consider this as Pancham's first composition. Interestingly, it was conceived three years earlier for a different film.

After filming a few reels, Guru Dutt replaced Sunil Dutt with himself and re-shot the scenes, only to abruptly shelve the film. Perhaps he had lost interest in the project following the withering of *Kaagaz Ke Phool*. Pancham's first venture as music director thus came to an untimely end.

In the meantime, a Hemant Kumar–Geeta Dutt duet, based on the theme tune of Charlie Chaplin's *Limelight*, had been recorded for *Raaz*. Guru Dutt often gave his composers foreign tunes, and it is likely that he suggested the tune of *Limelight* to Pancham. It was later recorded by Kishore Kumar and Lata Mangeshkar for S. Ramanathan's *Bombay to Goa* (1972) as *'Tum meri zindagi mein'* but was left out in the final version of the film. The tune was remodelled and finally used in *Mukti* (1977), as *'Main jo chala peekar'* and as the Bengali song *'Ki kore jaanle tumi'* released in actor Victor Banerjee's film titled *Debotaa* (1991).

The Woman in White served as inspiration for *Woh Kaun Thi* (1964). It was directed by Raj Khosla, Guru Dutt's assistant. Madan Mohan's haunting music was in tune with the supernatural elements of the script and has stood the test of time, unlike the film which seems quite dated now.

Some more tunes were composed during the making of *Raaz* but not recorded then. One of them was used in *Chhote Nawab* as *'Ghar aaja ghir aaye'* and is hence considered Pancham's first officially completed composition. Based on Raga Malgunji, the song was picturized on Sheila Vaz, who appeared in a cameo as a courtesan in the film. It is said that this song marked Lata Mangeshkar's re-entry into Sachin Dev Burman's bungalow, 'Jet', as Lata and SD weren't on talking terms, following a misunderstanding during the making of *Miss India* in 1957. This soft, semi-classical number too had its share of detractors and there have been insinuations that Pancham was given the raw material for composing *'Ghar aaja'* by his father. This is extremely debatable since, rummaging through SD's repository of Bengali compositions till then, one comes across just a solitary compostion in Raga Malgunji titled *'Manju rate aaj tandra keno he priyo'* (unpublished, performed in the Senate Hall of Calcutta University in December 1934). The structures of the songs are poles apart. The SD composition is on Teentaal, a 4/4 rhythm form and begins with Ma (the fourth note). Pancham's composition starts with the flat seventh note, Komal Nishaad, and is on Tewra, a 7/4 beat played on the tabla by Maruti Rao Keer. Its muted notes and ephemeral silence contribute more to the rhythm of the song than the use of augmented sounds. The use of percussion (in this case, a ghungroo) acting as a connecting device between lines became one of the features of Pancham's arrangement later.

Interestingly, Pancham hardly ever used Raga Malgunji again. Malgunji is a synthesis of two other ragas, Rageshri and Bageshri, neither of which ranked among Pancham's favourites. However, Khamaj thaat (Western equivalent: scale), the umbrella for Raga Malgunji would find liberal usage in Pancham's compositions later.

Apart from *'Ghar aaja ghir aaye'* and *'Matwali ankhon wale'*, there were six other songs in *Chhote Nawab*. Among them, *'Ilahi tu sunle hamari dua'*, sung by

Which of the three Lata solos of *Woh Kaun Thi* – '*Jo humne dastaan apni sunayi*', '*Naina barse rimjhim*', '*Lag ja gale*' – was conceived to fit the situation for which '*Ghar aaja ghir aaye*' was originally designed is difficult to guess. Notwithstanding the sheer elegance and simplicity of Pancham's first film song, it does pale in comparison with the three Lata solos from *Woh Kaun Thi*. Incidentally, *Woh Kaun Thi* was Madan Mohan's first silver jubilee hit in his then fourteen-year-old career as an independent music composer. Pancham's journey had just started. His time would come. Eighteen years later, Pancham went out of his way to help Sanjeev Kohli, Madan Mohan's son, secure an interview with Mohammad Rafi. This was Pancham's way of acknowledging the respect he had for the Ghazal King. The venue for this interview was Film Centre, the studio where Pancham recorded most of his songs since the late 1960s – as did Madan Mohan in the 1970s.

Mohammad Rafi, was reportedly the first one that Mahmood approved. Part devotional, part mournful, the song uses instruments like bells, guitars and organ and reaches a crescendo with a violin ensemble. *'Aaj hua mera dil matwala'*, sung by Lata and Rafi, stands out as a racy number where the accordion, the brass section and the rhythm section had a major role to play in the different metres for the mukhra and the antara. Pancham once mentioned that he had composed a tune for *Chhote Nawab* while driving to Taloja for a plate of biryani. It might be an amusing coincidence if *'Aaj hua mera dil matwala'* turned out to be the song in question, since it was filmed on the lead pair while on a drive. Curiously, Pancham gave Rafi only one stanza in the entire song; he often reserved a solitary stanza for male singers in later years too.

Extended intro music, secondary percussions like the castanet, bells and ghungroo, differential intra-song rhythm patterns, innovations like synchronized clapping-cum-foot tapping, flamenco-style acoustic guitar, the use of brass – *Chhote Nawab* acted as a preview of what would evolve as Pancham's musical differentiators in the times to follow.

The film also marked the beginning of what became a long working relationship between Manohari Singh and Pancham. Singh, a Nepali from the outskirts of Calcutta, had already established himself as a saxophone and clarinet player in Calcutta. He had debuted in Mumbai under Salil Chowdhury and S.D. Burman, playing the flute in the background for Bimal Roy's *Madhumati* (1958) and for songs in Shakti Samanta's *Insaan Jaag Utha* (1959). He played the flute in *'Ghar aaja ghir aaye'* too. Before long, Manohari Singh was the acknowledged king of wind instruments in the industry and subsequently went on to become one of the most important of Pancham's friends and colleagues.

Information is rather vague about why Mahmood chose

Pancham as the music director for *Chhote Nawab*. Pancham had attributed his selection as composer to his proximity with Mahmood, courtesy the car rallies they used to attend together. It is also part of film lore that Mahmood was bugged with Pancham's fingers persistently drumming Mahmood's car. Business, more so film-making, is about money-making. Drumming fingers do not make a business case. Somewhere, there must have been some synergy;

Being a Dev Burman meant that Rahul could engage the services of a few key musicians who had been playing for S.D. Burman, like Cawas (Kaka) Lord who played the castanet in '*Matwali ankhon wale*'; Jairam V. Acharya, the coveted sitarist; Basu Chakravarty, cello specialist and arranger who became Pancham's strings assistant; and Maruti Rao Keer who also played the resso in '*Matwali ankhon wale*' and went on to be crowned RD's chief rhythm assistant.

Mahmood, the entrenched comedian, and Pancham the happy-go-lucky boy-next-studio. Moreover, S.D. Burman had rejected the offer to compose for *Chhote Nawab* even before the storytelling session and Pancham came on-board on the rebound. Even if Mahmood could not be sure of the horse winning in its first race, he knew it could run all right. The pedigree was never in doubt.

No loud announcements, no debutant's dream tee-offs marked Pancham's arrival. *Chhote Nawab* was the first, low-key step in Pancham's career. The movie, as well as its music, was moderately successful with '*Matwali ankhon wale*' occupying the fifth position in the year-ending charts of the long-running radio show, *Binaca Geet Mala*, on Radio Ceylon. The unusual structure of the song was lauded by musicians and, more importantly, by those who played Western instruments. However, the other songs in the film did not strike a chord in the hearts of the people back then. Remarkably, the freshness of these songs takes music veterans by surprise even five decades later.

Pancham, reclusive by nature, went back to assisting his father, choosing not to advertise himself by using either *Chhote Nawab* or his father's name as a jumping board.

The result was a four-year hiatus before his next break as composer.

2

Musical Legacy and Beyond

Despite the moderately successful launch of his career, Pancham was unable to leverage the clout that his surname carried in the rather conservative film fraternity of Bombay. Also, producers wanted S.D. Burman. Nobody was willing to experiment with his son.

Even SD's access to the domain of popular music composition might have remained a pipe dream if, according to plan, his father Nabadwipchandra Dev Burman had inherited the throne of the princely state of Tripura.

Nabadwipchandra Dev Burman was the younger son of Ishanchandra Dev Burman Manikya Bahadur, raja of Tripura. Ishanchandra died young in August 1862, soon after cholera claimed his elder son Brajenchandra. Though Nabadwipchandra was the heir to the throne, the court declared Birchandra, Ishanchandra's brother, the king, based on an *aadeshnama* by

Ishanchandra that cited Birchandra as the Yuvaraj. Nabadwipchandra Dev Burman retreated to Comilla (then part of undivided Bengal, now in Bangladesh) with his family. Kumar Shachindra Deva Varma (aka Shachindra Dev Burman / Shachin Dev Burman / Sachindra Kumar Dev Burman / Kumar Sachin Dev Burman / Sachin Dev Burman / S.D. Burman/ SD / Dada / Karta) was born on 1 October 1906, the youngest of nine siblings.

Sachin Dev Burman inherited his musical DNA from his mother, Nirupama Devi, and more so from his father who was a sitar player, a proficient Dhrupad singer, painter, sculptor and Sachin's first music teacher. He also found a mentor in his elder brother Kiran Kumar who tutored him on the nuances of music. When Kiran died in an accident at the age of forty-three, Sachin lost his sounding board. The singing skills of the two household hands, Madhav and Anwar, also influenced the young musician greatly. SD admits to being captivated by Madhav's spontaneous rendition of the Ramayana. Anwar's dexterity in singing traditional Bhatiyali songs with a dotara as the accompaniment was SD's introduction to the world of folk music. SD also built a repository of folk songs from Saheb Ali, a fakir with a striking voice and an enviable inventory of Sufi songs. Prior to emerging as a vocalist of repute, SD's knock on the door to fame was as a flautist, playing the Tripura flute. Around 1922, he also rubbed shoulders with Kazi Nazrul Islam in Comilla. The relationship grew with time. In addition to these associations, his mingling with the commoners of Comilla, its simple earthiness, the undulating landscape, the boatmen on the river Gomti, the itinerant Bauls frequenting the area, saw the gradual infusion of folk into SD's repertoire.

Abbasuddin Ahmed, a folk singer of substantial standing, claimed to have taught SD the art of 'voice breaking', a feature which became the trademark characteristic of SD's wailing voice.

Graduating from Victoria College in Comilla at the age of eighteen, Sachin Dev became the first graduate in the Tripura royal family. He relocated to Calcutta to pursue a master's degree in English literature in 1925, only to drop out in 1926. His father then enrolled him in a law course, but Sachin's patience with the copious, stern-looking hardbound legal treatises soon wore thin. Nabadwipchandra's plans to send his son to study in the United Kingdom also fell through as Sachin started sculpting a career in music. In 1925, he had begun training under the blind singer Krishna Chandra Dey, Manna Dey's uncle. In the mid-1930s, he also trained under Ustad Badal Khan, Shyamlal Khetri and Pandit Bhishmadev Chattopadhyay, among others. In 1926, he sang for Dacca (now Dhaka) Radio and his first income came from the Indian State Broadcasting Service (renamed All India Radio in 1936), Calcutta. However, there is some controversy regarding the exact time when SD might have got his first salary. Jayati Gangopadhyay, in the article 'Shono Go Dokhino Hawa' in the *Centenary Commemorative* published by the Government of Tripura, dates it to some time in early 1930.

In Calcutta, SD began assisting his gurus on the tanpura even as he continued to build his reputation as a music tutor. In 1932, he got his first major break: an opening to record his songs for Hindustan Records (Hindustan Musical Products, later INRECO). He had been rejected by HMV earlier because of his 'thin and nasal' voice and signed the contract with Hindustan upon being persuaded by family friend Naru Thakur. A similar fate had befallen the greatest playback singer of pre-independence India, Kundan Lal Saigal, who, like SD, had failed the HMV audition on grounds of his voice being nasal.

But while Saigal enjoyed the patronage of New Theatres, the largest film studio in Calcutta, SD was not so fortunate. Neither his guru K.C. Dey nor his friends P.C. Barua and Devki Bose campaigned for him with New Theatres. B.N. Sircar, the business baron who ran the studio, also knew of SD's talents, but remained indifferent to him, as did R.C. Boral, the leading composer of the time. Hemendra Kumar Roy, poet, author, and incidentally, lyricist of SD's first recorded song *'Daakile kokil roj bihaney'* (1932), got SD to compose for two plays, *Satitirtha* and *Janani*, but the kind of exposure needed to enter mainstream cinema eluded him. Sporadic brushes with playback and acting came infrequently while SD worked as co-composer for a few films with Pandit Bhishmadev Chattopadhyay.

According to musicologist Suresh Chakrabarty, Bhishmadev's disciple and biographer, SD's first solo assignment as composer in films was earned by undercutting Bhishmadev, a fact that deeply hurt the veteran musician (reference an article by Suresh Chakrabarty in the book *Bhati Gang Baiya* edited by Tarapada Chakrabarty, Akshar Publications, Tripura, 2001). Though SD escaped the wrath of the media at that time, getting hit below the belt was something his son would suffer badly from later.

In 1937, SD met Meera Dhar Gupta, granddaughter of Justice Kamalnath Dasgupta. Initially his student, she later trained in classical music under Pandit Bhishmadev Chattopadhyay. She had also learnt kathak from Amita Sen at Santiniketan, and Rabindra Sangeet from Anadi Dastidar. Sachin and Meera were married on 10 February 1938.

Since he had defied convention by marrying a non-Kshatriya, Sachin and his bride were denied the customary family welcome by the ladies of the royal household during the couple's visit to Agartala. This upset SD considerably, and he gradually severed ties with the Dev Burmans of Tripura royalty. He deliberately avoided the royal palace in subsequent trips, till he stopped going to Tripura altogether after 1946.

A few months before the Second World War broke out, Rahul was born to Meera and Sachin Dev Burman at 9.29 a.m.

on 27 June 1939, at Hindustan Road, near Gariahat, south Calcutta. He was nicknamed Tublu.

The nickname 'Pancham' came some years later. Apparently, as a child he wailed at the fifth note of the Saptaswara. There is another story: Rahul would invariably sing the note Pa whenever his father sang the note Sa. Thespian Ashok Kumar thus gave him the name 'Pancham' (as per multiple interviews by Pancham). Incidentally, the number five proved lucky for him in his early career – *Teesri Manzil* (1966), his first major hit, was Pancham's fifth film as a composer.

Rahul did not bring luck to the Burman family immediately, though. SD continued singing in stage shows and in films, but the success for which he had forgone the career his father had charted for him continued to elude him. In 1942, Chandulal Shah from Ranjit Studios invited SD to join his group in Bombay, but SD resisted, hoping for the tide to turn in Calcutta. However, when Sasadhar Mukherjee and Rai Bahadur Chuni Lal – barons of Filmistan – called, SD did not have the heart to refuse them. Thus, in 1944, his family in tow, Sachin Dev Burman headed to Bombay, hoping to find success as novelist Saradindu Bandyopadhyay and actor Ashok Kumar had done before him. Assurances had also come his way from Sushil Mazumdar, his friend who was then a part of Filmistan.

In Bombay, SD's first two projects, *Shikari* and *Eight Days*, were released in 1946. It is believed that the studio had to enlist the help of composer C. Ramachandra to arrange the music for *Shikari*, a claim that became a source of debate in later years in *Filmfare*. The music for *Eight Days* – a film for which Ashok Kumar had specially requested Saadat Hasan Manto to write the story – particularly the solo '*Umeed bhara panchhi*', was lauded by the highbrow, but rejected by the film-going commoner.

Around that time, SD sent Pancham back to Calcutta to

study in Ballygunge Government School, an institution rooted in Indian tradition but which operated almost in the manner of an English convent. Among its other famous alumni are film-maker Satyajit Ray and dramatist Shombhu Mitra. Till some years back, the school held a 'Rahul Dev Burman Memorial Singing Competition' as part of its alumni celebrations.

Young Rahul was chubby, agile and uncannily brave. During a trip to Gopalpur-on-Sea, a place in Orissa, a snake coiled around his legs while he was taking a dip in the sea. Without any discernable hesitation, Rahul unwound the serpent from his legs and killed it. Probably the only animal he was dead scared of was the house lizard – a phobia which remained all his life. Like many of his age, he indulged in outdoor activities like cycling, badminton and water sports. He even received a prize for a cycling competition from his father, who was the chief guest for the occasion. Swimming, though, was his favourite sport. It not only helped him get rid of his asthma, but enabled him to develop immaculate breath control too. His other passion, food, was captured in the film *Bhoot Bangla* (1965) in which he played a cameo as somebody who opened his mouth either to eat or to deliver the iconic line: 'Main kha raha hoon'. With his near-Mongoloid features, he could have been mistaken for a Nepali. He was, according to his friends, a natural sportsman who had no love lost for textbooks. As a result of his extreme reluctance to pursue academics, he failed his annual exams in 1948 and then again in 1951, and had to leave Ballygunge Government School subsequently.

S.D. Burman obviously attached far more importance to Rahul's extra-curricular activities than to his academic accomplishments. He presented his son with a Raleigh bicycle the day the boy failed his exams.

2

To one side of Deshapriya Park in south Calcutta, across the tram road, near Ballygunge post office is Tirthapati Institution, a primary and higher secondary school that was instituted on 4 January 1931. Though the school boasts quite a few luminaries including litterateur and accountant Buddhadev Guha among its alumni, unkind couplets abound: 'Jar nei kono goti, shei jaye Tirthapati' (One who has nowhere to go, goes to Tirthapati). Inside a cobwebbed records office, one of the brittle pages from a dusty stack of student registration files shows a name – Rahul Dev Burman. Pancham now rode his new bicycle to Tirthapati Institution after securing a transfer certificate from Ballygunge Government School.

Not too surprised by his son's lack of interest in academics, SD followed his hunch and initiated his son into music. The grind started with RD's tutelage under the blind tabla player Brajen Biswas, the creator of the Brajataranga. His training in tabla continued almost lifelong, in bits and pieces. Pandit Samta Prasad was also one of his gurus in Bombay during the late 1950s. Rahul was also enrolled to learn sarod at the Ali Akbar Khan School in Gariahat, Calcutta. However, the maestro could not devote much time to his pupil and his son Aashish Khan (now Aashish Khan Debsharma) was Rahul's companion during the practice sessions. Pancham also spent long hours watching jugalbandis between Ali Akbar Khan and his brother-in-law, sitar player Ravi Shankar. It gave him enough food for thought and also a working knowledge of Indian classical music. RD acknowledged that he learnt the virtues of humility from Ali Akbar Khan Sahab.

Aashish Khan recounts: 'Rahul was impatient and not a very serious student. But he was innately musical, and could grasp the fundamentals fast. He also attended musical soirées of my father and other greats of his time, and that probably helped him understand the grammar and feel of Indian music better.'

The hip environment of south Calcutta, where the Dev Burmans resided, inevitably influenced Rahul's taste in music, resulting in a partiality towards jazz and Cuban Big Band music. Melody, the famous record shop on Rashbehari Avenue, was where Pancham became familiar with Western music. The owner of the shop was originally from Comilla, and hence, its doors were always open to the Dev Burmans.

Kersi Lord was also instrumental in Pancham's introduction to Western music. When he travelled down to Bombay during his vacations, Pancham listened to Kersi's collection of long-playing records of jazz, Latin American, European and Middle-Eastern music. 'Pancham would listen to every type of music, except Western classical, for which he did not have much patience,' remembers Kersi Lord.

Incredibly for someone who came to be associated with making Western beats and rhythms a fad in Hindi film music, Rahul never formally learnt to play any Western instrument, though his musicians did guide him occasionally. His mastery of the mouth organ was self-taught. One of his achievements early on was to play the harmonica in a floating position in a water ballet at Anderson Club, near Calcutta's Dhakuria Lake. Pancham was cast in the role of Gautam Buddha in the water ballet titled *Discovery of India.*

It was in 1951 that Pancham, as a visitor to the studios in Bombay, met Lata Mangeshkar and Kishore Kumar. In an appearance on the radio show *Meri Sangeet Yatra*, Pancham said that his first meeting with Lata was during the recording of 'Thandi hawayen' (*Naujawan*, 1951). Around that time, SD was composing for Navketan's *Jaal* (1952), directed by Guru Dutt. According to Raju Bharatan, music chronicler, twelve-year-old Pancham had questioned his father's use of a Tagore tune in the interlude of a song where the backdrop was the Goan coast. Since Bharatan mentioned two different songs, *'Kaise yeh jaagi agan'* and *'Pighla hai sona'*, in separate articles, the veracity of the statement is questionable. Nevertheless, while *'Pighla hai sona'* does sound thematically similar to the Tagore song, *'Neel digante oi phuler aagun laaglo'* – the import of the words of *'Neel digante'* might have been the foundation for the opening line of *'Pighla hai sona'* – the tune is definitely a take-off from the state song of Louisiana, *'You are my sunshine'*, made famous by various artists from time to time.

Taking recourse to Rabindra Sangeet for inspiration was not new for SD. Tagore's tunes have an appeal which is hard to ignore and, interestingly, they fit almost all situations, irrespective of the milieu. There is a certain modernity and universality in Tagore's music, making it acceptable beyond the boundaries of its origin. And though Pancham inherited this attribute from his father, he put his stamp all over the songs that inspired him, and rewrote the entire orchestral pattern.

After he somehow managed to clear the stumbling block of school, Pancham, against his grandmother's wishes, was permanently taken to Bombay by his father in 1955. In Calcutta, he had started a music group called Melody Chimes. The Bombay skyline would be much wider.

Calcutta-based composer Dipankar Chattopadhyay who was Pancham's contemporary and part of the same friend circle, recollects some hitherto-untold stories regarding Pancham shifting to Bombay: 'Pancham, during his days at Tirthapati, had become slightly reckless. In the sense that we found him cycling to a pot joint near Kasba. He had already started smoking, and this was a phase where he was gradually being lured into pot. In as much, we had to persuade him not to go to the joint and in turn forced him to indulge in adda near the lake where he would play the harmonica very energetically. His

father was perturbed no less by Pancham's attitude towards life
and almost "schemed" the plot for moving him to Bombay. He
already had him enrolled at the Ali Akbar School of Music in
Gariahat. From the early 1950s, Ali Akbar was getting more
assignments in Bombay and was planning to set up his school
there. SD took that as an opportunity to ask Pancham to
accompany him to Bombay as his music guru was shifting base.
Pancham was reluctant, but before he could realize, he had been
"tricked" to shift to Bombay. This shift gave his career an
almost 180-degree turn.'

Over the next several years, Pancham, as an assistant to his
father, played a key role in many of SD's compositions, beginning
with the Mala Sinha motif (the tune that was played in the
background on the harmonica whenever she appeared on screen)
in Guru Dutt's *Pyaasa* (1957).

When very young, Pancham had composed a tune, which, to
his chagrin, he heard in *Funtoosh* (1956). The film credited S.D.
Burman for the music of '*Aye meri topi palat ke aa*'. When
confronted, SD explained that he 'wanted to judge how [the]
tune sounds when played'. One is not sure whether it was the
father or the guru speaking. Since then, various archives,
interviews, trivia discussions, film and music quizzes, debates
and special interest forums have acknowledged R.D. Burman as
the rightful creator of the song.

While working as an assistant to his father on *Pyaasa*,
Pancham composed the tune that eventually became '*Sar jo tera
chakraye*' which occupied the second spot in that year's *Binaca
Geet Mala*.

Pancham also played the sarod for the Bengali song '*Ghum
bhulechi nijhum*' composed by SD, who later used the tune in
Kaala Pani (1958) as '*Hum bekhudi mein tum ko*'.

Pancham's skill with the harmonica featured in many songs
composed in the 1950s, the most famous of which remains '*Hai*

apna dil to awaara' sung by Hemant Kumar in *Solva Saal* (1958).
The film credits Pancham as 'music assistant'. He played the
harmonica for the title track of the film as well.

Thus, from the age of sixteen, Pancham had started living in
the world that was to become his, participating in and learning
about it from the closest range possible, in the company of the
best in the business. During the making of *Raaz* in 1959,
Manohari Singh and Pancham thought of composing as a team,
but the idea fell through. As did the film.

The *Chhote Nawab* chapter passed by in 1961, virtually
unnoticed by the people who mattered.

In the context of the Hindi film industry, four years of
inactivity is long enough to generate an inertia that is hard to
recover from. Trends, ephemeral in the best of times, change
even faster when one is on the fringe of things. While even the
best struggle to resurface, for most others it is a downward
spiral.

The four-year hiatus after *Chhote Nawab* was, for Pancham,
wrought with the risk of possible oblivion. During this period,
he assisted his father on several films – *Bandini, Tere Ghar Ke
Samne, Benazir, Meri Surat Teri Ankhen, Ziddi, Guide* and *Teen
Deviyan*. Often, there would be the one odd song that was
completely unlike the others in the film. The Asha Bhonsle solo,
'*Dil ki manzil kuch aisi hai manzil*', in *Tere Ghar Ke Samne* (1963)
is one such song where the influence of the younger Burman is
visible in the use of various Western music patterns, especially
cancan, an apt fit for the dance sequence in the song.

In 1963, producer Tarachand Barjatya of Rajshri Productions
signed up Satyen Bose to direct *Dosti* (1964), a film about two
unfortunate young boys from different backgrounds who run
into each other by chance. Low on cash, high on talent, they
lean on one another, struggling against adversity, striving
towards success.

This is not just the story of Ramu and Mohan in *Dosti*, but also of Laxmikant Kudalkar and Pyarelal Sharma, of the true-life friendship that developed behind the scenes and lasted till Laxmikant's death in 1998. Despite the acclaim they received for their work in *Parasmani* (1963), Laxmikant and Pyarelal were in such dire straits that they agreed to compose for *Dosti* for a measly Rs 10,000. L-P, as they were popularly known, needed a harmonica player for the songs of *Dosti* as one of the characters played the harmonica. It was on the recommendation of Laxmikant's sister Vijaylaxmi that R.D. Burman was roped in to play the harmonica in *Dosti*. Pyarelal, in interviews, has acknowledged Pancham's skill with the harmonica as unparalleled, calling him the best in the industry. The delectable harmonica pieces in the songs, especially in *'Jaane walon zara mudke dekho'* creates a mood of sorrow, torment and anguish, which may have mirrored Pancham's internal suffering. Pyarelal Sharma remembers: 'Pancham played the harmonica in all the songs of *Dosti*. In fact, he had offered to play the harmonica for the background score as well, but we did not want to take advantage of Pancham. The harmonica for the background score was played by Milon Gupta.'

According to scriptwriter Sachin Bhowmick, before his alliance with Pyarelal, Laxmikant had wanted to team up with Pancham, but fate had decreed something else.

Director–composer–singer Kishore Kumar also hired Pancham to play the harmonica in *Door Gagan Ki Chhaon Mein* (1964). 'Pancham played the tune of the title song *"Rahi tu mat ruk jana"* on the harmonica in a background piece [in the film] recorded at Bombay Labs,' recalls Amit Kumar.

Throughout this four-year period, another partnership was growing steadily, often alluded to, always popular, invariably accepted, yet not recognized as a brand.

3

Traditionally, in Indian cinema, the credit for a good composition goes entirely to the composer, not to the team. The lack of published data on the specific contributions of the assisting team members does not help matters much. In the case of a composing duo like Shankar–Jaikishan or Laxmikant–Pyarelal, while the individual composer's fans may choose to debate who should be given credit for the tune, the composition would, officially, still be acknowledged as a Shankar–Jaikishan or a Laxmikant–Pyarelal song, because, at the end of the day, they were a team.

Interestingly enough, unlike the S-J or the L-P fan, there was never anything called the Burman fan. There was either the S.D. Burman devotee or the R.D. Burman buff. This absence of a common Burman fan has generated some rather superfluous arguments – courtesy the two fan groups polarized by their own choice – over the genesis of particular tunes and the credit being given to *either* S.D. Burman *or* R.D. Burman. This either/or approach, it appears, is based on various factors, like the extent of emotional attachment of the assessor with the composer's music and the decade to which the assessor belonged. This idea is also perched on the precarious ledge of SD being considered a representative composer from the 'Golden Period' of music, and RD being regarded, by a certain section, as one of the causes leading to the collapse of the same. Who vested whom with the authority to define the 1950s as the 'Golden Period of Indian Film Music' and the basis for such definitions are questions that have, unfortunately, never been asked. Also, statements like 'SD was divine and RD modern' have often germinated from a half-boiled understanding of either divinity or modernity (or both) in music. Even at the age of sixty, SD was, in Pancham's words, 'more modern' than his son. Pancham's compositions in films like *Amar Prem* (1971) or *Aandhi* (1975) are no less divine than anything SD composed. Also, what has not received the attention it deserves is that, during the 1960s, the Burmans functioned like a musical family, where father and son might have been crafting a tune over dinner at home.

There are tales aplenty of the two Burmans often disagreeing while composing together. One such incident relates to Pancham suggesting changes to the rhythm pattern of *'Ab ke baras bhej bhaiya'* (*Bandini*, 1963) only to be rebuked by SD. Another time, Pancham insisted on using Manohari Singh's alto sax strains in the interlude of *'O jane wale ho sake to laut ke aana'* (*Bandini*, 1963), which resulted in SD walking out of the recording. Upon his return, to his delight, SD was told that the version without the sax had been recorded. It is likely that RD's ideas had been overruled by the recordist, who was faithful to the elder Burman!

While direct credit for a lot of compositions in his avatar as SD's assistant between 1955 and 1965 may have eluded Pancham, it also gave him immunity from failure and allowed him to experiment and build his repertoire. It would not be incorrect to say that some of the music from the S.D. Burman camp during this time did point to influences pioneered by Pancham, and his trusted comrades Basu and Manohari, principally in the areas of orchestration, preludes, interludes, rhythm patterns and antaras.

Background music was an aspect where SD engaged his own musical wisdom to a much lesser degree (even in his early days, he used to request directors to summon the help of his guru Bhishmadev Chattopadhyay). Brass and wind, more specifically, trumpet and sax, creeping in perceptibly into his range, presented a more modern S.D. Burman, indicating the increasing influence of his son. With *Guide* (1965), SD's magnum opus and his breathtaking return to mainstream cinema after a heart attack in 1963, and *Teen Deviyan* (1965), it appeared that Pancham's baton was turning

Indubala Devi's song *'Mohe panghat pe nandalal'* can be considered the mother
of the traditional Gara used in films in the 1960s. Composer Naushad was the
first to refashion the gem, which he did without deviating much from the
original, in *Mughal-e-Azam* (1960). However, this is not cited as an example of
plagiarism by Internet forums and websites engaged in discussing the issue.

---

quite active even in the songs. For example, *'Tere mere sapne ab
ek rang hai'* (*Guide*), a Raga Gara-based SD composition, finds
Manohari Singh's alto sax as the main instrument,
complementing Mohammad Rafi's voice. The second antara of
'Din dhal jaye' too had an exquisite piece of sax, as did the first
and third interlude of *'Gaata rahe mera dil'*, a song which RD
supposedly ghost-composed.

Apart from the shift towards Western instruments, there
were other parameters – like the use of long-drawn notes in
'Gaata rahe mera dil' and *'Kaaton se kheench key yeh aanchal'*, and
the use of the large orchestra in *'Piya tose naina lage re'* and
'Mose chhal kiye jaye' – that suggested a deeper involvement of
the younger Burman in his father's music room. *'Piya tose naina
lage re'* incidentally has a touch of Raga Manj Khamaj, one of
Pancham's favourite ragas. According to Pt. Shiv Kumar Sharma,
Pancham coaxed him into playing the tabla for *'Mose chhal kiye
jaye'* though he had given up the instrument in favour of the
santoor, the hundred-stringed instrument to which he (Shiv
Kumar Sharma) added another twenty-five.

Badal Bhattacharya asserts that the music of *Teen Deviyan*
was mostly Pancham's handiwork. No wonder that Pancham's
signature is heard in the background music, in the jazz and
swing pieces embedded throughout.

The Gara from *Guide* morphs into Khamaj and rubs into *Teen
Deviyan* as *'Aise to na dekho'*. The offbeat rhythm with the
interplay of the voice and the tabla subtly suggests Pancham's

influence, though composer Anil Biswas believed the inspiration
for the tune was the Tagore song *'Ami tomaye joto shuniyechhilem
gaan'*. Twenty years later, Bappi Lahiri composed *'Chanda dekhe
chanda'* in *Jhoothi* (1985) on a similar progression.

In 2009, Dev Anand disclosed the existence of an English number sung by Ram Chattopadhyay for *Teen Deviyan* that was written by Ram's father, Harindranath Chattopadhyay, but which hadn't been included in the film.

The re-entry of Kishore
Kumar – who teamed up with
Dev Anand for his first solo
since *'Hum hain rahi pyar ke'*
(*Nau Do Gyarah*, 1957) – into
the Dev Anand camp with
'Khwab ho tum', also suggests the involvement of the son.
Pancham's harmonica in the song acts not only as an interlude,
but also as a livewire. The Kishore–Asha duet *'Arre yaar meri'*
with its complicated interweaving of instruments is again in the
Pancham mould.

According to some musicians and music aficionados, the basic tunes for three
songs – *'Hum bekhudi mein'* (*Kala Pani*), *'Tere mere sapne'* (*Guide*) and *'Kahin
bekhayal hokar'* (*Teen Deviyan*) – were originally created by Jaidev, who was
SD's assistant for a prolonged period of time, but the credit went to S.D. Burman.

Thus, the four years after *Chhote Nawab* turned out to be a
significant period for Pancham the assistant, the musician and
the younger, unacknowledged half of a duo. In 1965, he got his
second film as a composer. It was the Mahmood connection
again. Coincidental, almost spooky.

3

Mango and Cadbury Uncle

The area between 34th Street and 59th Street and from 8th Avenue to the Hudson River in Manhattan is known as Hell's Kitchen. To its south is the West Side.

In 1957, Jerome Wilson Rabinowitz, aka Jerome Robbins, an American Jew and a college dropout conceived, choreographed, and directed a Broadway musical with Hell's Kitchen as the focal point. Titled *West Side Story*, it was made into a major movie by Robbins and Robert Wise in 1961. A modern-day musical version of Shakespeare's *Romeo and Juliet*, *West Side Story* was reincarnated as Tapan Sinha's *Apanjan* (1968), and eventually as Gulzar's *Mere Apne* (1971). Prior to these films, inspired by Guru Dutt's visuals – his distinct use of the interplay of darkness and light which had taken iconic shape in *Pyaasa* – and the cinematic grandeur of Hell's Kitchen as depicted in *West Side Story*, Mahmood decided to stylize the picturization of a street fight in a film he was directing in 1964.

2

'The huge mango tree in the backyard of Lino Minar, the house next to ours, became our favourite meeting place ... we ruled the trees, squealing and giggling ... some atop the tree, some swinging on its branches and some standing below with our skirts held up to catch the mangoes,' Anasua Banerjee and Anindita Roy recall an incident from their childhood. 'Suddenly, one day, we froze. A fat, fair man in his mid-twenties, in loose red shorts and a yellow T-shirt, framed the doorway of the kitchen that led into the backyard. We had been caught red-handed. We stopped laughing. The man unexpectedly broke into a loud, hearty laugh and instructed his servant: "Badri, give these children all the mangoes they want." He then called us inside the house and asked us to sing, and then gave us giant slabs of Cadbury's chocolates. He also sang for us a song from a movie that was just going to be released.'

The mango and Cadbury uncle was Pancham.

The still-to-be-released film was *Bhoot Bangla*.

The song: '*Jago sonewalo*'.

Bhoot Bangla (1965) was dedicated to Guru Dutt – whom Mahmood acknowledged as his friend, 'phylospher' (yes, spelt with a 'y') and guide – and was released almost eight months after Dutt's premature demise. Produced by Mahmood's brother Usman Ali, it was a movie of many firsts: Mahmood's first directorial venture, Pancham's first movie donning grease paint, and the first time Kishore Kumar and R.D. Burman worked together.

For Pancham, the composition of '*Jago sonewalo*' was a test, chiefly because he had been out of (acknowledged) work for quite some time. 'People had no confidence in me. "Baap ne diya hoga music" they'd say,' Pancham said reflectively in an interview for *Showtime* in July 1992.

The song was almost operatic. It mandated a large orchestra, a chorus, a long prelude and long interludes, and a sharp and powerful voice – and consequently brought together Pancham and Kishore Kumar. The result was a C-minor-based progression, a heavily emphasized string section, a minute-long prelude that tapered off with a yodel, an eerie effect created with the harmonica, a chorus that contributed to the countermelody, and the minor chord to major chord shuffle, a Pancham trademark. Abani Dasgupta played the duggi, an important rhythm instrument in Pancham's music, and Mike Machado did the honours on the piano. 'The tune for the antara was contributed by my father,' recollects Amit Kumar, and adds: 'Pancham was receptive to ideas that others around him gave.' Incidentally, twenty years later, director Rahul Rawail came up with a similar setting in *Arjun* (1985), à la the gang fight in *West Side Story*, and Rahul Dev Burman created 'Mammaya kero mama'.

Bhoot Bangla had a song – 'Kahan aa kar lo hum dono' – sung by Mahmood and Pancham. It was a little longer than a minute and was sandwiched between the unearthly wails of 'Bhooooot Banglaaaaa ...' This songlet, arranged by Manohari Singh, could be termed as Pancham's first experimentation in the blues scale. Pancham used songlets to great effect subsequently, including vastly popular ones like 'Doston se pyar kiya' (*Shaan*, 1980) and 'Mera naam hai Shabnam' (*Kati Patang*, 1970).

The song 'Pyar karta ja', shot on a grassy highland surrounded by tall mountains in the distance, is a fine example of Pancham's keen understanding of picturization. The scene mandated a natural echo as part of the song. According to Kersi Lord, Pancham incorporated the 'hey' by chorus using the echoplex instrument, a rarely used innovation those days.

In a picnic scene featuring Tanuja, 'Matwali ankhon wale' can be heard playing on a tape recorder in the background. It is not uncommon for a composer to use a tune from an earlier movie. Pancham had few options; he was after all, only one film old.

'*Aao twist karen*', the most popular song from the film, was slated for another singer, till Pancham's obstinacy resulted in it being awarded to Manna Dey. Not only did Pancham admit to Manna that he had been inspired by the Chubby Checker number '*Let's twist again*', he also made him listen to it in order to imbibe the spirit of the song. Manna Dey admitted that he just replicated the style in which Pancham sang it to him. '*Let's twist again*' reached the second spot in the UK music charts in 1961, while '*Aao twist karen*' shot to the same position in *Binaca Geet Mala* on Radio Ceylon in 1965.

Unfortunately though, *Bhoot Bangla*, intended as a ghostly film, turned out to be a ghastly film. The 'Adults Only' certification further shrunk the target audience. Adults rejected it and children, who may have enjoyed a laugh or two looking at Mahmood and Pancham dancing with the ghosts, were kept out in most places. Pancham's cameo as the brave glutton, Stocky, was an embarrassment.

The press came down harshly on both the film and its music. Father consoled son. Getting reviewed by the press was important, SD advised the twenty-six-year-old.

Pancham's second disappointment in as many ventures. The most critical moment in a failure comes the morning after, when one looks in the mirror and either wills oneself to move on or lets the nightmare take over. Guru Dutt, to whom *Bhoot Bangla* was dedicated, opted for the latter when *Kaagaz Ke Phool* bombed.

Pancham, it appears, just smiled back at the rotund face in the mirror.

3

Director Mohammad Hussain was known for his economy-grade action flicks which starred the stock duo of Dara Singh

and Mumtaz. However, Hussain's *Shikari* (1963) had somehow
contrived to corner a better share of success than usual. It
featured the odd pair of Ajit as hero and Helen as heroine,
where the 'loin' sets out in search of a murderous gorilla named
Otango but decides that Helen is a far more attractive and safe
pursuit. Hussain followed up *Shikari* with three action films,
each with a different composer – G.S. Kohli, Laxmikant–Pyarelal
and Robin Banerjee. It wasn't surprising then that his next film
would have yet another music director.

Teesra Kaun (1965), by a numerical coincidence, became RD's
third film. Starring Feroz Khan and Sachin Bhowmick's first
wife Kalpana, it was directed by Mohammad Hussain. The film
brought Pancham and Asha Bhonsle together for the first time
with '*O dilruba tu muskura*'. The song has a sharp skid from
B-flat to F note, and it gives a preview of the Asha–Pancham
chemistry to come in subsequent years. '*Achcha sanam kar le
sitam*', the other song they did together in the film, did not
emphasize any feature of Pancham's style of composition; it was
sweet, fast paced, hummable and aridly predictable. The Suman
Kalyanpur solo in the film, '*Meri saheliya biyahi gayi*', sounds as
though it was out of a book of north Indian folk. In effect, the
song was very tradition-bound and almost in line with what the
average public and the director would demand.

The song that made its way into the popularity charts was
the Mukesh–Lata Mangeshkar duet, '*Pyar ka fasana*'. This was
the first time that Pancham asked Mukesh, a Salil Chowdhury
and Shankar–Jaikishan favourite, to sing for him. Pancham and
Mukesh collaborated only on nineteen songs (including '*Pyar ka
fasana*') throughout their careers, though an overwhelming
number of these became very popular.

The rhythm pattern in the interlude of '*Pyar ka fasana*' was
maintained on the bongo, coupled with the damped strokes on
the guitar – a progression that Pancham used on several

occasions, with varied degrees of success, an example being
'*Pehle pehle pyar ki mulaqatein*' (*The Great Gambler*, 1979).

The same year, another film which repeated the *Chhote Nawab*
combination of Usman Ali, S.A. Akbar and Pancham was released.
Starring Sanjeev Kumar, Nanda, Mahmood and Mumtaz in the
lead roles, this film named *Pati Patni* could be questioned for its
lack of sanity, barring the music score which found Rahul Dev
Burman in a mood to experiment in his favourite area – rhythm.

4

Bossa nova is a form of music which finds its inspiration in the
Brazilian samba. It is played mainly on the classical guitar with
gut or nylon strings, and uses unconventional and complex
chords which add colour to the basic jazz-based patterns. The
style was developed by musician João Gilberto and composer
Antonio Carlos Jobim, and was lapped up by North American
musicians and popular singers. Frank Sinatra was one of the
first white singers to record songs based on bossa nova. The
genre quickly transcended borders and, though the movement
lasted only six or seven years, it has stayed in the consciousness
of the public and musicians alike for more than four decades.

Exposed to Latino music in Calcutta, Pancham, over the
years, had developed a fondness for its vibrancy. He soon made
the bossa nova form his very own, literally bringing it halfway
across the globe, from the beaches of Rio to the studios of
Bombay where he dovetailed it with a pentatonic tune to create
a song in *Pati Patni* (1966). Sung by Asha Bhonsle, and picturized
on Shashikala playing a seductress, '*Maar dalega dard-e-jigar*'
was not a colossal hit, not even a modest hit during that time,
but has since become an icon for its novel structure. Unlike a
majority of songs in popular Hindi cinema at that time, it is not
easily hummable. It is, however, notable for the Indianization of

the Brazilian genre by Pancham, who stripped bossa nova of the complicated chords while incorporating the rhythm. The song had the feel of an Indian melody, as well as a fragrance that was distinctively foreign but not alien. Asha Bhonsle, in an interview with scribe Girija Rajendran, mentioned that this song made her wake up to a thoroughly new rhythm and metre – the essence of which took time to permeate.

Pancham also used the bossa rhythm in the interlude of '*Allah jane main hun kaun*', a comic number sung by Manna Dey. In the first and third interlude, the beat is fused with brass notes which sustain the melody, and in the second interlude the notes of the harmonica are arranged to the beat of the bossa to give additional colour to a song on a normal 4/4 beat. It appears that Pancham was trying out the feel of the bossa with time-tested elements like Manohari's sax and his own harmonica. The ability to break down patterns in known and accepted forms of rhythm and seamlessly infusing them into popular Indian film music was to become one of Pancham's greatest strengths. Today, the bossa nova is a part of any synthesizer and there are songs being composed on the same.

Pancham's personal favourite in *Pati Patni* was probably the passionate '*Kajre badarwa re*', sung by Lata Mangeshkar. He played this number during an appearance in the long-running radio show for army men, *Jaimala*. '*Kajre badarwa re*' was Pancham's second experiment at a distinctively eastern melody, after '*Ghar aaja ghir aaye*'. With a prominent use of Raga Bhairavi, it featured Nanda enjoying the monsoon winds and permitting herself a smile at the blooming romance in her life.

It was around the time *Pati Patni* was being signed, in 1964, that Nasir Husain conceived of a new venture, starring Dev Anand, to be directed by Vijay 'Goldie' Anand. A whodunnit set in Mussorie. There was high drama long before the movie was released. Drama, suspended from three storeys above, it seemed in retrospect.

5

Hindi cinema habitually promotes cliques, often at the expense of innovation. Actors, producers and directors are generally unwilling to meddle with a winning combination, irrespective of the subject of the film. In the 1960s, this was particularly noticeable in scriptwriting, story selection, dialogue writing and playback singing. Some of the commonly used combos were Raj Kapoor–Mukesh, Shammi Kapoor–Mohammad Rafi and Manoj Kumar–Mahendra Kapoor/Mukesh. While the desire to create a combination and to promote a unique identity is understandable and often welcome, it drastically reduces the inclination to experiment and to diversify. So, in most cases, mediocrity ruled supreme as films hardly broke out of set themes and proven formulae, specially when creating escapist entertainment.

The partnerships, for better or for worse, naturally extended to hero–composer as well. Thus, when Nasir Husain signed Dev Anand for *Teesri Manzil* (1966), the natural choice for music director was Sachin Dev Burman. But SD was not well at that time. So, Majrooh Sultanpuri, Husain's long-time associate, proposed SD's son Rahul's name to him.

Nasir Husain had used three music directors in his last four ventures and was willing to experiment once again, having heard and liked some of Pancham's songs in *Chhote Nawab.* Goldie too had no problems endorsing Pancham. In any case, he had Pancham in mind for *Jewel Thief* (1967) (it eventually went to S.D. Burman). SD, too, was keen on the Anand brothers giving Pancham a break in what was thus far an unremarkable career trajectory. Things began to fall apart when Dev dropped out of the production as he found straddling *Teesri Manzil* and, his own production, *Guide*, difficult. In walked Shammi Kapoor. It is said that Nasir Husain practically kidnapped Shammi from H.S. Rawail's house, in the middle of a game of cards.

Surfing on the success of films like *Kashmir Ki Kali* and *Rajkumar* (1964), while working on *Jaanwar* (1965), Shammi Kapoor was referred to as the king with the animal charm. He was acknowledged to be at the top of the pecking order, the man with the power to mesmerize his leading ladies with his charisma and attractive looks. He moved in the industry as if he owned the place, and few had the nerve to question him. Like a king, he was surrounded by his ardent cluster of followers. And like all royalty, he expected the best of everything.

Shammi's favourite composers were industry favourites Shankar–Jaikishan and O.P. Nayyar, who had helped build his image by churning out colossal musical hits for the star. It was no surprise then that he would have none other than S-J or Nayyar for *Teesri Manzil.* Not only were they tried-and-tested, they were also familiar with the genre of music the film needed. The fact that '*Jaan pehchan ho*', one of the songs that S-J had composed for Raja Nawathe's adaptation of Agatha Christie's *Ten Little Niggers / And Then There Were None, Gumnam* (1965) (a film which was offered to SD but he had to opt out of due to his illness), followed the style needed for many of the *Teesri Manzil* numbers only strengthened Shammi's case.

Pancham, therefore, had to clear the hurdle that was Shammi Kapoor. Well-wishers Jaikishan and screenplay writer Sachin Bhowmick came to Pancham's aid, requesting Shammi to give Pancham an opportunity to showcase his skills.

In what was one of the most decisive auditions of his life, and of Hindi film music for that matter, Pancham lost serve in the first game. He had just sung the first two lines of a Nepali tune, which was later remade as '*Deewana mujhsa nahin*', when Shammi interrupted him, completed the rest of the lines '*Deotara mattali oina*', and said nonchalantly: 'Another one. I will give this number to Jaikishan.' It was quite common for actors to request composers to create songs for them based on tunes they (the actors) had heard and liked.

Shattered nerves gave way. Flabbergasted, Pancham left the room. After a couple of perfunctory puffs on a cigarette, Pancham re-entered the music room and played the tunes he had reserved for the occasion: '*O mere sona*', '*Aa ja aa ja*', and '*O haseena zulfon wali*'.

Shammi Kapoor stopped him abruptly and said, 'You've passed. You are my music director.'

In hindsight, Pancham needn't have been unduly anxious. According to Manohari Singh, '*O haseena zulfon wali*' had been recorded even before Shammi Kapoor's arrival at the studio, at the behest of Nasir Husain.

4

The Pancham Manzil

The thriller or mystery film as a genre has never quite taken off in India. Just around Independence, film baron S.S. Vasan had caustically remarked that the average age of the Indian film-going audience was twelve years. And it remained so for decades after. Such an audience demanded romance, melodrama and song 'n' dance as part of the mix in every film. As such, for film-makers, the idea of making a suspense drama without musical frills was unthinkable. Needless to say, in the labyrinth of six mandatory songs and scenes involving social and romantic melodrama, the element of thrill or surprise so essential to a film in this genre was lost. It is thus a telling pointer to the storytelling skills of a few film-makers that they have surmounted these inherent inadequacies of the standard Hindi film narrative to make films that have managed to thrill within the parameters dictated by the box office. India is probably the only nation that has seamlessly blended the musical with the film noir, in the process creating a genre all its own, the musical thriller. Kamaal Amrohi's *Mahal* (1950), Biren Naug's *Bees Saal Baad* (1962), Raj Khosla's *Woh Kaun Thi* (1964) are examples of this quintessential Indian genre; films that give you the chills, even as they have you humming. Vijay Anand's *Teesri Manzil* (1966) too falls in this category.

As you watch the film, you realize the source of Vijay Anand's inspiration, the master no less, Alfred Hitchcock. Anand freely incorporated many elements of Hitchcock's works in *Teesri Manzil*: intercutting between the legs of two passengers on a railway platform (à la *Strangers on a Train*), using binoculars and zooming on the face (à la *Rear Window*), a climax involving characters precariously perched atop a roof and the ubiquitous cliffhanger moment (à la *To Catch a Thief*).

But even if Hitchcock himself were to make *Teesri Manzil*, a true-blue thriller with an unexpected twist in the tail, he would probably not have managed to do so without songs. More so because the film was produced by Nasir Husain – known for his musical extravaganzas like *Tumsa Nahin Dekha* (1957) and *Dil Deke Dekho* (1959) – and starred the swinging star of the 1960s, Shammi Kapoor.

So even as Vijay Anand was conjuring up the thrills, Pancham was designing his personal blend of rock, jazz, Latino and twist to create a sound, the likes of which was unheard of in the then thirty-five-year history of Hindi films. *Teesri Manzil*, according to musicians, was an instrumentalist's dream. From the violin to the cello, from the vibraphone to the chime, from the sax to the trumpet, from the drums to the conga, and percussion like the triangle and castanet, it had everything, arranged with a perfection that other musicians would only strive to achieve in the years to come.

Immediately after he passed the audition, Pancham had received a call from Jaikishan. 'You must make it terrific,' the gracious composer had said, 'so that people can say, "Haan bhai, baap ka beta hai.'" According to Pancham, SD too felt that if his son continued to assist him, he would follow his style. Father encouraged son to do things differently. As Pancham put it, 'Kuch hat ke karne ki zaroorat hai.' This was the sentiment that drove him while designing the music for *Teesri Manzil.*

In those days, the usual pattern was to play sixteen bars on the violin, then the flute, following which the antara would start on cue. Inspired in part by Henry Mancini, Pancham decided to break from tradition in *Teesri Manzil.* In his interview to the *Sunday Observer* on 31 May 1992, he said, 'In the endeavour to do something different, I was helped by people like Kersi Lord and Manohari Singh. They felt that my father had adapted folk music and I should do something different. We decided that we should bring upfront the brass section of the orchestra.'

Brass it was. Full blast. For the Rafi–Asha duet '*O haseena zulfon wali*', Pancham laid out a variety fare ranging from the drums and the violins for the main course of dominant sounds, the triangle and the trumpet for the side dishes of supporting sounds, and the acoustic guitar and sax in the bossa nova-style interludes. Filmed in multiple crane shots (Hitchcock's *Psycho* – in which crane shots were used aplenty, perhaps in deference to the fact that the heroine was named Marion Crane – thrown in for good measure) with fleeting close-ups and cuts introduced only when switching between characters, '*O haseena*' would set the standard for the portrayal of lively music and dance in Indian cinema.

Anasua and Anindita, who lived next door to Sur Mandir (Lino Minar having been renamed so), remember walking into Pancham's room one afternoon. When he saw the girls, Pancham asked them to sing. Anindita sang '*A north country maid*', a song she had learnt at school. Pancham sat upright, excited. He had found the piece to fill up a blank space, the tune for the line '*Woh anjana dhoondti hoon*'.

Those were the days when songs were recorded live, with musicians playing alongside, unlike the tracking system used today. In *'O haseena'*, around eighty musicians were used; of whom close to forty were violinists. The task of managing the crew itself would have been very difficult, not to speak of the challenges of arrangement and orchestration, given the rapid change of notes and beats in the song. This was no one-dimensional lullaby with a hundred-piece orchestra.

The second Rafi–Asha duet, *'Aja aja main hun pyar tera'*, was Pancham's favourite song in the film. Its highlight is a fourteen-second guitar lead, played thrice at a frenetic pace in the seventy-seven-second prelude. Guitarist Soumitra Chatterjee, who played with Pancham during the second half of the 1980s, remarked: 'So intense and characteristically different was the guitar lead, played by Dilip Naik, that the piece was used by Asha Bhonsle to audition new guitarists who dreamt of playing with her.' Even today, seasoned guitarists find it difficult to reproduce the lead properly during stage shows.

Despite obvious talent which pointed to a great future, Dilip Naik somehow contrived to slip into oblivion in the next few years when he decided to try his luck in the US and migrated, only to end up doing odd jobs.

Apart from the ear-catching guitar, the infectious rhythm, the feverish chants of *'Aja aa aa aja'*, the sporadic touch of the bossa nova, the staccato use of the vibraphone and the piccolo, and the infectious coda designed on alto sax infused with a chorus, it is the tune which leaves you gasping, asking for more, an effect fashioned by Pancham by using the flat seventh note, Komal Ni, as the last note in the antara. There have been discussions galore about how Salil Chowdhury's use of the seventh chord created wonders in *'Aja re pardesi'* (*Madhumati*, 1958). *'Aja aja'*, by the same token, was no less an experiment; but given that the tune was fast paced, it failed to catch the attention of music critics for whom any melody which is not solemn and sombre is tantamount to noise.

In what was a generous compliment to Pancham, Shammi Kapoor said that the song would go on to become a trendsetter. In an interview much later, Pancham admitted that he was not completely satisfied with Rafi's initial rendition and took time to perfect it. He added that Asha Bhonsle had sought the guidance of her elder sister Lata Mangeshkar prior to the recording.

In both *Tumne mujhe dekha* and *O haseena*, the silhouette of the drummer behind the curtain was of the musician who played the drums for the songs, Leslie Godinho. On stage, Salim Khan played the drummer in *O haseena*.

In a *Vishesh Jaimala* radio show, Asha said that the song was recorded in the third take.

In the third stage number, the Rafi solo *Tumne mujhe dekha*, the antara starts on the fourth note (Ma), thus creating a shift-in-scale experience. To get the mood right, Pancham used the notes of the first line of the antara as the prelude of the song.

The song was being filmed when Shammi Kapoor received news that his wife Geeta Bali, then suffering from smallpox, had passed away. Crestfallen at this huge loss, Shammi went into exile. It took a lot of patience and perseverance on Goldie's part to persuade Shammi to face the camera again. Shammi Kapoor wrapped up the sequence in two takes, recovering his lost confidence in the process. But for Goldie's persistence, *Teesri Manzil* might have joined the long list of films that get shelved.

The Nepali folk-based Rafi solo *Deewana mujhsa nahin* was shot in Mahabaleshwar masquerading as Mussorie. The other outdoor song, the Asha–Rafi duet *O mere sona re*, was a Pahadi tune that Pancham married with a jazz-cum-bossa-nova piece, *Song for my father*, by Horace Silver. Pancham used the

tune as a guide to fashion the first line of '*O mere sona ré*',
and did away with the bossa beat, giving it a folksy rhythm
instead. This was one of the first songs to use the electric
organ, played by Kersi Lord. The tempo was maintained on the
cabashe by Devichand Chauhan, the master of rhythm, especially
the tabla.

The tune had originally been composed for another film,
Pramod Chakraborty's idea of a romance in the Orient titled
Love in Tokyo (1966). S.D. Burman was supposed to score the
music for the film, but sickness intervened and Shankar–Jaikishan
took over. Given the fluidity of relationships in the Bombay
film industry, Pramod Chakraborty was back with SD for *Naya
Zamana* (1970) and *Jugnu* (1973).

'*Dekhiye sahibon*', another Asha–Rafi duet, featured the leading
pair on a giant wheel with the hero trying to negotiate with a
crowd in an attempt to win the girl. The rhythm in this vintage
Pancham creation keeps varying between stanzas; 4/4, bossa
nova, pizzicato, and even offbeat. A chorus chips in with a '*Hah
hah*', Asha teases with additional inflexions '*Aye haye haye*' in the
stanzas, and Rafi hurries up to the end of the antara much like
the free fall of the giant wheel. Bhanu Gupta, playing for
Pancham for the first time in this song, went on to become his
chief rhythm guitarist. Their bond went beyond the confines of
recording studios.

The title score is a critical component in any suspense or
action thriller and Pancham made the most of the opportunity
in *Teesri Manzil*. The opening scene shows an attractive young
woman drive up to a hotel in the dead of the night, walk up
three floors and fall to her death. Murder or suicide? Why does
Helen warn Shammi against rushing to the dead body while
shocked onlookers watch blood seep from the victim's smashed
skull? What secret is she hiding? And who is the man, peeping
through a window above, quietly watching the scene unfold?

All this with the film's credits in the foreground and R.D. Burman's pulsating score in the background. One thing was obvious: Pancham had made his mark in the movie even before the song tracks began.

Kersi Lord has given up trying to figure out how the electronic sounds were produced. More than four decades later, when asked about the track in July 2009, he said, 'What Pancham and his team did was unbelievable.' Interestingly, the Lord family – Cawas, Kersi and Burjor – were integral to the 'unbelievable' music score of *Teesri Manzil*.

The film was a huge hit, and its music score is considered one of the principal reasons for its success. It set the Nasir Husain– R.D. Burman combination rolling and provided the Kapoors an alternative to Shankar–Jaikishan and Nayyar. In fact, Shammi got Pancham to compose for the two films he directed in the 1970s.

One career-defining partnership Pancham cemented during *Teesri Manzil* was with Basudev Chakravarty and Manohari Singh, his assistants since *Bhoot Bangla*. For the next two decades, the duo, known as Basu–Manohari, transcribed Pancham's brilliance into notations, arranging the musicians and directing them in their respective notes. Another crucial relationship that Pancham shared was with his chief rhythm architect, Maruti Rao Keer, who worked on stylizing the rhythms Pancham envisaged.

Gulshan Bawra, a lyricist who wrote some popular numbers composed by Pancham, recounted: 'I think this was when Pancham's *Teesri Manzil* or *Pati Patni* had been released; I can't recall now. I had a chance meeting with Jaikishan-ji of S-J fame. They were at the top at that time. I casually asked him who among the new breed he considered a threat to their popularity, and rattled off names like Kalyanji–Anandji, Laxmikant–Pyarelal, Ravi Saab, etc. Jai-ji replied that he was not scared of any of them since he felt that all of them were, in some way, trying to copy the S-J style. The biggest threat he sensed was from Sachin-da's son, a boy named Rahul Dev Burman. I was blissfully unaware of Pancham's music then, and this came as a big surprise. Jai-ji continued, saying that this boy was mixing sounds in such an elegant and unique fashion that he would become a trendsetter in his own right and would rule the industry, forcing others to change their styles.'

2

One of the indicators of an Indian composer's success, till the early 1990s, was the number of solos he/she created for the queen of playback, Lata Mangeshkar.

After a tepid start in *Chhote Nawab*, Rahul's association with Lata was limited to one solo in *Bhoot Bangla* and two solos in *Pati Patni*. The opportunity to build on that association came to him in the form of another Nasir Husain film, *Baharon Ke Sapne* (1967).

Nasir had penned the story of *Baharon Ke Sapne* when he was a student in Lucknow. Set in a daily-wage-earning textile mill labour union in a small industrial township in the suburbs of Bombay, it weighed the relative merits of non-violence over violence, portraying what Nasir believed could be the way to engineer social reforms. The theme may have been influenced by his maternal uncle, freedom fighter Abul Kalam Azad. The film also tried to present debatable messages like communists (depicted in an indirect way by a character named Das Kaka) resorting to violence at the slightest provocation. Unfortunately, with a disappointing treatment of the story and a flip-flop message, the film turned out to be neither art nor commerce. It was rejected by the masses, who found no masala in the film, as well as the classes, who found the message irrelevant. Dedicating the film to the memory of Mahatma Gandhi appeared contrived and phoney too. Had Nasir retained the original ending, where the heroine dies, it might have managed to give the storyline some semblance of realism. Apart from some wonderful black-and-white photography by Jal Mistry, the cinematographer from Navketan, and some realistic romantic interludes between a young Rajesh Khanna and Asha Parekh (who, surprisingly untainted by Eastman colour, looked fresh and lovely), this film had only one element to remember – its music.

The song that became the first showcase for the Lata–Pancham duo, 'Aaja piya tohe pyar doon', was in all likelihood intended for another film.

3

The tune of 'Aaja piya tohe pyar doon', played on the santoor by Shiv Kumar Sharma, is the background score for a scene in *Teen Deviyan*. The instrumental piece also includes the initial bars of the first interlude, the part being played then by Hariprasad Chaurasia on the flute. It is generally accepted that the background music for *Teen Deviyan* was the handiwork of Pancham and his men Basu and Manohari, and that they might have been using the tune experimentally. However, the fact that Majrooh Sultanpuri was the lyricist in both films lends credence to another theory: that the song and its lyrics had been conceived for *Teen Deviyan*, but were left out for want of a proper sequence; only to be used in *Baharon Ke Sapne*.

In *Baharon Ke Sapne*, the song was used to introduce Geeta (played by Asha Parekh) and Ram (played by Rajesh Khanna), whose childhood affection had blossomed into romance.

The strength of the song lay in its innate simplicity. The mukhra used very few notes, arranged almost in a cyclic manner: *Aaja piya* (Sa-Re-Ga), *tohe pyar dun* (Ma-Ga-Re), *Gori baiyaan* (Sa-Re-Ga), *toh pe vaar dun* (Ga-Re-Sa). Bridging the

Baharon Ke Sapne had Mansoor Khan, Nasir Husain's son and director of films like *Qayamat Se Qayamat Tak* (1988) and *Jo Jeeta Wohi Sikandar* (1992), playing a young Rajesh Khanna, and his sister Nuzhat (Irrfan Khan's mother) playing a young Asha Parekh.

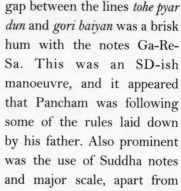

gap between the lines *tohe pyar dun* and *gori baiyan* was a brisk hum with the notes Ga-Re-Sa. This was an SD-ish manoeuvre, and it appeared that Pancham was following some of the rules laid down by his father. Also prominent was the use of Suddha notes and major scale, apart from touching upon the flat seventh note, Komal Ni – a feature that gradually became a fixture with Rahul.

The tune was used generously in the film as a series of heart-wrenching notes on the alto sax, and during a romantic scene just before another Lata solo 'O more sajna, o more balma'. It might not be an exaggeration to say that though the film fell flat on its face, 'Aaja piya', by virtue of its simplicity and uncluttered orchestration – the rhythm was mostly on the secondary percussion: the double bass, the guitar, the flute and the santoor – touched many a heart. The other Pancham–Lata nugget in the film was 'Kya jaanu sajan'. This dream-sequence song, shot in colour, was probably the first, along with 'Baithen hai kya unke paas' (*Jewel Thief*, 1967), to have twin-track recording in India, long before the technology was actually imported from the West. HMV has credited this track to Lata and Usha Mangeshkar, but both the primary and overlapping voices were that of Lata Mangeshkar, confirms Manohari Singh. 'Kya jaanu sajan' would be lauded as the quintessential Pancham number, with its minor scale and slow changes of notes.

Baharon Ke Sapne found Pancham bubbling with ideas, which often went into designing the preludes and the background score as well. In 'O more sajna', the prelude was a glut of tunes varying in emotional content and rhythm, while the number itself sounded rather plain in contrast to the complex build-up. Filmed innovatively in a salt yard, the song succeeded in communicating the passion between the characters, and was one of the few moments where the film looked like a piece of Dresden art. '*Do pal jo teri aankhon se*', a duet featuring Asha Bhonsle and Usha Mangeshkar, was another of Pancham's experiments. The sixty-seven-second prelude had a brass band playing notes on the blues scale, which was later used by Pancham as '*Maine dil abhi diya nahin*' (*The Train*, 1970). The origin of this prelude can be traced back to the second interlude of the Asha–Kishore duet '*Aankhon mein kya jee*', in one of Pancham's uncredited assistantships with Navketan, *Nau Do Gyarah*.

With *Baharon Ke Sapne*, for the first time in his career since *Chhote Nawab*, Pancham got to weave his music around lyrics with depth and meaning. Without Majrooh's firebrand romantic poetry, '*Chunri sambhal gori*', the Manna Dey–Lata duet, might have remained just a tuneful song with a catchy rhythm and a ninety-something-second-long prelude, peppered with experimental beats including the pronounced usage of a variety of drums. But with verses like '*Kirne nahin apni, toh hai baahon ki mala / Deepak nahin jin mein, un galiyon mein hain humse ujala / Aree dhul hi pe chandni khil jaye*' it became a rallying cry representing the spirit of the oppressed.

The Mohammad Rafi solo '*Zamane ne maare jawan kaise kaise*' was recorded in two versions, one with hope wrapped in deep sorrow, and the other expressing resignation. The song was representative of Pancham's ability to keep sentimental pain from spiralling down to maudlin melancholy.

Baharon Ke Sapne was the definitive step in Pancham's evolution from an enthusiast who loved to experiment, into a creator of melody-based compositions that deserved to be treated with lyrical care rather than being considered just as complex sequences of notes and beat patterns.

The media attributed the failure of *Baharon Ke Sapne* to the
new, admittedly boring, role Asha Parekh had been cast in.
Stylish and upmarket, she was something of a fashion statement,
her roles hitherto as 'gang leader' lending her a tinge of
tomboyishness. A monochromatic sari and a plain high-necked
ghagra–choli were not what the public expected to see her in.

4

Another film that RD composed for shared the box-office fate
of *Baharon Ke Sapne* that year: the Dharmendra–Meena Kumari
starrer *Chandan Ka Palna* (1967), directed by Ismail Memon.

Pancham claimed in an interview that *Chandan Ka Palna* was
the second film he had signed, after *Chhote Nawab*. While the
ability to recall film titles and chronology was definitely not
one of Pancham's strengths, he may have been correct in this
case. Meena Kumari looks prim in parts and plump and puffed
up around the cheeks and chin in others, suggesting the
possibility of a significant time lag between the beginning and
end of the making of the film. Going by the numbers of the 78
RPMs, it appears that most songs of *Pati Patni* and *Chandan Ka
Palna* were published simultaneously. The 78 RPMs of *Teesri
Manzil* were cut earlier, but the film was released after *Pati
Patni* and before *Chandan Ka Palna*.

With a storyline that bordered on the impossible and a
screenplay brimming over with sappy melodrama, it wasn't
surprising that the movie-going public gave *Chandan Ka Palna*
a wide berth.

The music of the film was, by all standards, average, at best
experimental. Bossa nova was used again, this time too, not for
the first couplet but as part of the antara in the Asha Bhonsle–
Manna Dey duet, '*Mastaana hoye parwaana hoye*'. Pancham, in an
attempt to popularize the bossa nova, used the word in the

antara: '*Bossa nova bossa nova suno*' in the song '*Baat karte ho baat karna naheen aata*', another Asha Bhonsle–Manna Dey duet.

One song from the film did bring Pancham some acclaim. He was nominated for the Sur-Singar Samsad Award for the use of classical music in Hindi cinema. Pancham described his unintentional effort at classicality thus: 'I was sitting at Outram Ghat, on the banks of the Ganga in Calcutta with my friend Badal Bhattacharya. Badal asked me if I could compose something on the river flowing under our feet. The outcome was "*O Ganga maiyaa, paar laga de meri sapno ki naiya*". The next day, when I was in Bombay, Mahmood hurriedly wanted a tune on the river Ganga and this fit the bill.'

Thus was created the theme song for *Chandan Ka Palna*. According to the convenors of the Sur-Singar Award committee, which included scribe Raju Bharatan, the first two lines of the song are based on the chalan (systematic develoment of the raga) of Raga Jogiya. This was not the first time Pancham had used Jogiya, having used it in the songlet '*Vinti karun Ghanshyam*' in *Pati Patni* earlier.

However, according to Raju Bharatan, Pancham was not conferred the award because the committee decreed it blasphemous that Rahul Dev Burman be considered for an award in the Indian classical music category. The award went to Madan Mohan for his Raga Pilu-based Lata Mageshkar solo '*Maine rang li aaj chunariya*' from *Dulhan Ek Raat Ki* (1967), inspired by *Tess of the D'Urbervilles*.

As a postscript, one might question the committee's claim that the composition was in Raga Jogiya, for Ga (the third note), which is used extensively in the song, is absent in the raga. However, the progression does sound like Raga Kalingra which uses both Ga and the notes of the Jogiya. The pakad (a phrase which captures the essence of the raga) of Kalingra is also similar to the tune of '*Paar laga de*'.

Years later, Pancham did receive a special award from the committee for twenty-five years of contribution to music.

To be fair, the music of *Dulhan Ek Raat Ki* was superior to that of *Chandan Ka Palna*. Apart from '*O Ganga maiya*', the remaining songs of *Chandan Ka Palna* were not comparable to '*Kai din se ji hai bekal*', '*Sapnon mein agar mere*', '*Ek haseen sham ko*' or the award-winning '*Maine rang li*'. But the fact that neither *Teesri Manzil* nor *Baharon Ke Sapne* was even nominated for the Filmfare Awards was questionable judgement on the part of the awards committee. That *Guide* lost to a mediocre *Suraj* (1965) was cold comfort.

5

Goldfinger

The three men in the Fiat spotted her with minutes to spare. Light blue sari, sunglasses, flowers in her hair and white handbag; she stood by the entrance of Regal Theatre at the Colaba Causeway, just as the voice over the phone had said she would. Two of the men slipped out of the vehicle, leaving the third to park the car in the basement, a rare feature in buildings back in 1965. Then they watched from a distance as the third approached the mystery woman, exchanged a few words and disappeared into the complex with her . . .

The movie playing at Regal that afternoon was *Goldfinger*, the third film in the James Bond series and the first one to be directed by Guy Hamilton. The plot that had brought Rahul and his friends Manohari and Sachin Bhowmick to Regal was no less intriguing.

A few days earlier, Pancham, accompanied by composers Laxmikant and Pyarelal, had been to Darjeeling for a vacation. A group of college girls, also from Bombay, were holidaying there. One of them met Pancham and asked for his autograph. On his return to Bombay, Pancham received a phone call from a girl who introduced herself as the autograph hunter and asked him if he would like to watch the matinee show of *Goldfinger* at the Regal with her. Pancham agreed. This would be his second viewing of the film.

When they met outside the theatre, the girl introduced herself as Rita Patel.

The interiors of Regal were designed to create an impression of airiness, coolness and size, in harmony with the modern simplicity of the exteriors. However, Pancham sensed a chill in Rita's initially polite demeanour once they entered the auditorium. This turned to discomfort as she excused herself and left while the commercials were playing.

Rita did not return even when the signature gun barrel sequence of the film began. Sensing something amiss, Pancham got up from his seat and rushed outside, only to find Rita trailing off in a black Ambassador. He hurried down to the basement, hoping to follow her in his car, but by the time he drove onto the road, the Ambassador had vanished.

Meanwhile, CIA Agent Felix Leiter waited on Miami Beach, Florida, with a message from M for James Bond: 'Watch out for Auric Goldfinger.'

At Colaba, Manohari Singh, Sachin Bhowmick and Rahul Dev Burman chalked out a plan to find the mystery girl. There were fewer Ambassadors than Fiats in the city, narrowing down the list of 'suspects'. Rita Patel had also left behind one clue: she frequented Nirmala Niketan, a home science college in the Churchgate area. Pancham knew the area well. Like composer Jaikishan, he too was a regular at Gaylord restaurant in that area.

After a few days' surveillance, Rita was spotted coming out of Nirmala Niketan and driving her car near Bombay's Churchgate

Railway Station. Tailing her, the troika arrived at the posh six-storeyed Cosmopolitan Building off Marine Drive on Chowpatty Road. Their next step was the relatively easy search for a Patel in Cosmopolitan Building, Chowpatty Road. The Bombay Telephone Directory showed three Patels. The phone call to the third Patel household was answered by Rita herself. Scared as she was when Pancham introduced himself, she did agree to meet him.

It turned out that Rita had waged a bet with her friends in Darjeeling that she would get the young composer to go out with her. Her friends, seated inside Regal, had given her the wager amount once they saw her walk in with Pancham. Having won the bet, Rita had not waited to see whether Goldfinger's plot of irradicating the US gold supply at Fort Knox succeeded or not.

Over the next few months, the friendship between Rahul and Rita bloomed into courtship and finally marriage. 'Pancham and Rita had got married secretly at a friend's place in Malabar Hills. I was a witness to the wedding, which was conducted according to Hindu rituals,' recounts Sachin Bhowmick. 'Dev Anand went and broke the news to SD saying that Rita was a nice girl. I too spoke to SD and Meera, his wife, as did Majrooh's wife. Meera boudi accosted me as to why I had not told them despite knowing about it. Then SD and Meera consented and insisted on another wedding ceremony at Turf Club. It was a grand affair.'

Sachin Bhowmick adds, 'Meera boudi refused to let the couple enter "Jet" saying that another flat at 15 Cross Road had been readied for them. This came as a shock for Rita despite the fact that the house was well done up and furnished.' The newly-weds thus began their life together at the 15 Cross Khar residence, known as Sur Mandir, where Pancham was already a temporary resident. Interestingly enough, the music school

where Pancham's parents' courtship had blossomed was called
Sur Mandir as well.

   'Sachin-da used to visit them at Sur Mandir on his evening
walks and stopped by for tea as he himself felt lonely. Meera
boudi rarely visited that place,' points out Bhowmick. 'Sushma
Kohli, niece of Dev Anand, was considered a possible match for
Pancham by her [Sushma's] mother, but Pancham never
reciprocated.' Sushma later married Vijay (Goldie) Anand, her
maternal uncle.

2

In the initial months of the marriage, Rita and Rahul entertained
friends, dined out and were invited to parties. But given the
finite nature of the honeymoon phase, differences began to crop
up, beginning with food preferences, of all things. Pancham, the
quintessential Bengali and a decent cook with a penchant for
chillies, was fond of non-vegetarian food, whereas for Rita, a
traditional Gujarati, anything that was not vegetarian clashed
with her religious considerations. Though Rita finally decided
to try her hand at non-vegetarian cooking, Pancham had begun
eating everywhere but home. This drove the first wedge into
their marital life. And when Rita was unable to conceive despite
medical aid, the wedge dug deeper.

   The film industry is characterized by odd working hours
and impromptu working sessions. Family support – read
tolerance – is critical. While Pancham had been raised in the
environment of film-making, Rita had only seen the three-hour
silver-foiled output, the film. Living on the manufacturing floor
and witnessing its production-stage grime and sweat were hardly
appealing to her. Pancham's bohemian lifestyle did not help
matters either. His late nights in the music room gradually led
Rita to embrace the great taboo of middle-class families then –

liquor. 'Pancham used to come very late, around 2 a.m. He also told Rita that he was okay with her having a drink or two. But she could not control her drink. She would call me up and ask me to get brandy along. I objected to Pancham on this *Saheb-Bibi-Ghulam*-ness of the whole affair, saying that it was up to him to control his wife,' recalls Bhowmick.

It didn't help that the mother-in-law and daughter-in-law did not get on well. 'Rita would use foul language against her mother-in-law when drunk,' says Bhowmick.

During a wedding reception party thrown by a friend, Rita arrived dressed in a simple sari, with no make-up and only with a bindi on her forehead. Her mother-in-law's curt remark about her inappropriate attire sent Rita flying into a rage and Pancham was obliged to devote his entire evening to calming her. Anindita Roy adds, 'There were instances when mother-in-law and daughter-in-law came to fist fights.'

Pancham's neighbour and childhood acquaintance in South End Park, Kolkata, Birajmohan Das recalls: 'In 1966, I went to Bombay on my way to Germany. Pancham was supposed to meet me at the airport, but he gave it a miss. Later, I heard that he and his wife were having problems and this could have been a reason why he did not turn up.'

Marital blues had arrived in Pancham's world. Predictably, Pancham turned to music to relieve his suffering, and the musical genre he chose was, surprisingly, the blues. It may have been the music of pain, the music of the oppressed that gained recognition in the civilized world, courtesy a few bands in New Orleans. But for Pancham, the blues was fun. The coloured man's song, born out of the wedlock of depression and repression, found a patron in Pancham who espoused the scale and retrofitted it into Indian music.

3

S.D. Burman had only two releases in 1965 – *Guide* and *Teen Deviyan*. Due to persisting health problems, SD did not accept any assignments that year and consequently had no releases in 1966. He then teamed up with Navketan for Goldie Anand's *Jewel Thief* (1967). With its unusual plot, Hitchcockian red herrings and the McGuffin (the non-existent dual identity of the lead character kept secret till the end), Dev Anand once again romancing multiple women, the return of Ashok Kumar in a negative role and a riveting music score spanning romantic to cabaret to folk, the film was simply value for money. This was probably the only instance in Hindi cinema where the assistant music director's photograph also adorned the back cover of the LP, subtly pointing to the fact that Pancham was there in the film in a larger capacity than usual. And this showed.

There was quite a sizeable canvas for Pancham to experiment with: the background score; and he did it in style. The music of the sequence where Dev Anand waits for Helen while she steps out to the anteroom to change is an example of Pancham's experimentation using the hexatonic blues. The crisp piece of background music, played on a variety of instruments including the vibraphone, the trumpet and the guitar, added depth to what was the most suspenseful portion of the film. Pancham loved this piece of work, and used it in bits and pieces throughout the late 1960s and '70s. The progression of the last notes, Teevra Ma–Ma–Komal Ga–Komal Ni–Sa, became an obsession that would surface repeatedly in his work.

Before him, composers like C. Ramachandra, O.P. Nayyar, S.D. Burman, and Jaidev, among others, had sporadically used genres such as the foxtrot, polka, boogie-woogie and the rock 'n' roll. But without proper documentation, it is difficult to establish precisely when the blues scale coloured Indian film music. Pancham can be credited with establishing and popularizing blues in Hindi films.

The climactic song of *Jewel Thief*, '*Hothon mein aisi baat*', sung by Lata Mangeshkar, with Bhupendra humming in the beginning and then chipping in with '*O Shalu*' between stanzas, saw the introduction of a style of beats which came to be known as the chapki beat. Bhanu Gupta points out: 'This style was given another name after its inventor ... the Pancham Beat.'

According to Amrut Jaisinghrao Katkar (known as Amrutrao), Pancham's favourite percussionist, the chapki beat involves playing taut notes on the duggi or on the tabla with the palm rather than the fingers. He also reveals the chapki beat as a sound that Pancham fashioned by inserting a thin metal foil between the baddhi (the belt that runs laterally across the length of the dholak/khol) and the main instrument.

Bhanu Gupta narrates an interesting story about the genesis of the chapki beat. One morning, a household help was rubbing a piece of newspaper against the floor with her foot to remove stains. The act of rubbing at a particular pace resulted in a different kind of sound, which aroused Pancham's interest. He summoned the household help to continue generating the sound, which he recreated in the studio by rubbing a piece of aluminium foil on a khol (a tribal leather instrument used widely in Bengal) which SD specially procured for the song. The khol was played by Sudarshan Adhikari, confirms Amrutrao.

Music, it is said, is universal. Folk music is regarded as the mother of all music. Blues music, said to represent the folk song of the oppressed man, could have an Indian counterpart in classical or folk forms of music. The pentatonic blues scale has a direct mapping to Raga Dhani in Indian classical music. The move to the Komal Ni note before terminating on the Sa note on the lower octave in hexatonic blues is similar to the progressions used in Assamese folk music, the Bihu.

The cabaret number *'Baithen hain kya unke paas'* finds bossa nova in SD territory, along with the Pancham-esque twin track. Even today, theories abound among Pancham's team and contemporaries about how much of *'Raat akeli hai'* belonged to SD and how much to RD! In the radio programme *Meri Sangeet Yatra*, Pancham mentioned their 'joint effort' in composing *'Ye dil na hota'* based on Colonel Bogey's tune from *Bridge on the River Kwai* (1957).

4

What can one say about the movie *Padosan* (1968)? The average Indian has seen it many times over, laughing harder each time he watched Kishore Kumar (in his real-life maternal uncle Dhanajay Banerjee's avatar) with his immaculate dhoti–kurta and thick curling moustache, mouth dripping betel syrup, singing, as he and the venerating 'chamchas' of his 'nautanki' party try to beat Mahmood, the quintessential south Indian classical music teacher in his veshti, in wooing the buxom young lady across the street.

Mahmood had first offered the role of Bhola to Pancham opposite Shikha Biswas, daughter of composer Anil Biswas. He thought that Pancham, one of the two people who invariably made him laugh, had a great career as a comic actor; but Pancham was focused – he was in Bombay to compose, not act. Unlike most of Pancham's previous films for Mahmood where songs were a respite from a flagging script, music was integral to *Padosan*. Lyricist and screenwriter Rajendra Krishan based the screenplay for the film on a Bengali story, Arun Chowdhury's *Paasher Badi* (which was made into a film by the same name in Bengali in 1952 and had music by Salil Chowdhury) and, with uncanny sense, designed the songs around the film.

Padosan boasts of a song loved across generations, the Manna

Dey–Kishore Kumar duet *'Ek chatur naar karke shringaar'*. Kishore Kumar – yes, even he – balked at the sheer difficulty of the number in which some of the vocal trapeze acts had to be left out in the final take, says Bhanu Gupta. The song was one of the most challenging in the careers of Manna Dey and Kishore. Before the nine-hour-long rehearsal, Manna was confidence personified since the song demanded a fight between two classically trained singers. He was perturbed too, since he was supposed to lose the battle to Kishore who was not trained in classical music. Eventually though, he accepted that Kishore had got under the skin of the character and had so mastered the song that 'losing' to him was no longer improbable. Kishore also played his pranks, improvising during the recording. His sudden outburst of *'O tedhe, seedhe ho ja re'* took Manna by surprise, but Pancham signalled that they carry on.

'Ek chatur naar' is actually a cleverly mixed, not-so-obvious medley of songs. The first line is from a song sung by Ashok Kumar in Raga Jhinjoti in *Jhoola* (1941). The line *'. . . dekhi teri chaturayi'* was a parody of the bhajan *'Van chale Ram Raghurai'* by Vishnupant Pagnis. *'. . . Kala re ja re ja re'* was derived from the Raga Chayanat-based Lata Mangeshkar solo *'Chanda re ja re ja'* from *Ziddi* (1948). Combining these elements, Rajendra Krishan and Pancham remodelled the sources to merge flawlessly, resulting in the genesis of probably the greatest comic-war song ever.

In *'Mere saamne wali khidki'* Pancham kept the background music to a bare minimum, limited only to guitar and a few other percussion instruments like the resso, played by Amrutrao in the prelude, allowing the song to fulfil its purpose and stamp the authority of Bhola's 'voice'.

The first few lines of the Lata solo *'Bhai battur'* were part of Mumtaz Ali's contribution to the film. According to guitarist Ramesh Iyer, the lines *'Bhai battur ab jayenge kitni door'* had been used by Mahmood as part of the one-act skit *Chhote Nawab* which preceded the film of the same name. Mahmood is even seen humming the first two lines in the film *Gumnam* (1965). This song, featuring Saira Banu, celebrates the mood of a teenager on the threshold of womanhood.

'*Sharm aati hai magar*' was another Pancham–Lata number remembered for its saccharine flavour, peppered with Pancham's trendy beats. The Lata–Asha duet '*Main chali, main chali*' left viewers gaping as the young women cycled their way across the screen. Homi Mullan, who had debuted for Pancham in *Chandan Ka Palna*, rang the cycle bells to complement the visual. A Calcutta boy, Mullan started his musical career at the age of sixteen, moving to Delhi, then Madras and finally to Bombay, where he became one of the key percussionists in Pancham's team.

'Guess how many accordions are playing?' Kersi Lord asked us when we met him to discuss the film's score. 'Did you say two? Listen again. I generated a sound that was like two accordions playing together. There was only one. I played the melody using my ring and little fingers, and the chords using the other three to give it a jazz effect.'

R.D. Burman also used Carnatic instruments like the mridangam (played by Ramu), veena and the nadaswaram to fit the situations in the film. The Carnatic feel was exemplified by Manna Dey's immaculate rendition of '*Ek chatur naar*' and '*Sooni re sajaria*'.

The song '*Mere bhole balam*' was conceived on the shooting floor. The credit for this enormously energetic song laced with frolic and frivolity goes entirely to Kishore Kumar who spun a story along a traditional Baul tune. His creative inputs, and Pancham's apposite arrangement using instruments like the Bengal dotara, were woven snugly into the fabric of the song.

This movie was an avalanche of talent. Though Jyoti Swaroop

is credited as the director of the film, for all practical purposes, it was directed by Mahmood. Grapevine has it that Kishore had floored so many with his make-up that both Mahmood and Sunil Dutt were caught unguarded and hurried on to design their get-ups and fancy headgear for the film. The synergy of so many creative souls bent on outclassing each other made *Padosan* a cult film.

Teesri Manzil might have been explained away as beginner's luck by cynics but *Padosan* reinstated that Rahul Dev Burman was here to stay.

5

If *Padosan* was pure entertainment, *Abhilasha* (1968) was a hope killed. Made by editor Amit Bose, it was a sincere effort and had nicely carved-out details. Unfortunately, it was a commercial washout and took Pancham's most underrated compositions of the 1960s down with it.

Abhilasha was a first in many aspects. This was the first film where singer–guitarist Bhupendra collaborated with Pancham. Manohari Singh describes the chemistry between the troika (Basu, Manohari and Maruti), Bhupendra and Pancham as 'amazing'. In his opinion, Bhupendra's entry completed the team. A connoisseur of Indian semi-classical music, Bhupendra debuted as a singer–actor in Chetan Anand's *Haqeeqat* (1964) and followed it up as a singer–actor in Chetan Anand's *Akhri Khat* (1965), both bit roles at best. He also released an album of ghazals in the 1960s, when the non-film ghazal was far from being a fad. A Hawaiian guitarist, he was initiated into learning the Spanish guitar by Bhanu Gupta, and became one of the few who patented the bluesy style of guitaring in India. After *Abhilasha*, there was no looking back and Bhupendra became a permanent member of Pancham's team till the early 1980s.

'*Yaaron hamara kya*' sung by Manna Dey, Bhupendra and Maruti Rao is probably the first song in which Pancham worked around the calypso, giving it a Goan feel. Loosely based on the style of songs fashioned by Harry Belafonte, this number was a mix of happy, often mad, emotions. It seemed more appropriate for a gala party scene in a Raj Kapoor film. Picturized on Agha, Polson and Mohan Choti, the song commanded relatively low recall at that time.

'*Ek jaanib sham-e-mehfil*' was the first duet Pancham composed for Manna Dey and Mohammad Rafi who sang the song in the soft, misty and butter-smooth voice he reserved for SD, Madan Mohan and Chitragupta. The ebullient '*Pyar hua hai jabse*', Pancham's first Kishore–Lata duet, was wasted on Nanda trying to find Sanjay Khan amongst a cavalry of men wearing Zorro masks. Pancham also brought in the male–female tandem song in the film with '*Wadiyan mera daaman*'. Sung separately by Lata Mangeshkar and Mohammad Rafi, the tune gradually climbs in the antara while the electric guitar strums in a choking style. The tune of the mukhra was remodelled and used in the antara in the Raga Nand-based Bengali song '*Jete dao amaye deko na*', which Pancham composed for Asha Bhonsle.

'*Munne mere aa*', the only song featured on Meena Kumari, was traditional in its extensive use of the leather, the hammered dulcimer and the flute. However, Pancham broke away from tradition in his choice of playback singer for the song. It was customary for composers to use Lata Mangeshkar for the motherly songs and Asha Bhonsle for songs suggesting coyer sentiments. It is probable that any other composer during that time (with the exception of O.P. Nayyar who never worked with Lata, and Ravi who extensively composed for Asha) might not have had the nerve to consider Asha for a song echoing the spirit of the wannabe mother. Pancham successfully repeated the experiment in later years.

6

Autumn Leaves and Ruby Ray

For years, the annual Durga Puja in West Bengal has been the platform to release new music albums, or 'pujor gaan', by eminent singers, composers and budding artists. In the mid-1960s, people would eagerly await new albums by Hemanta Mukhopadhyay, Manna Dey, Sandhya Mukhopadhyay, Satinath Mukhopadhyay, Shyamal Mitra and composers Salil Chowdhury, Nachiketa Ghosh, Sudhin Dasgupta, among others, during the autumn.

The pujor gaan collection, given its consistent demand year after year among a captive audience, was something every artist wanted to be a part of. Pujor gaan often ended up with higher commercial gains than its cinematic counterpart, and far outlived cinema songs in its recall value.

Pre-puja 1965, public attention was focused elsewhere as the country gathered itself in the immediate aftermath of a war with Pakistan. India's statement on 6 September that its troops would capture Lahore in an hour resonated 2,000 kms away in Bengal.

The war with Pakistan, however, abated. A ceasefire was called three weeks ahead of Durga Puja, and soldiers rushed back to their families, leading to the reinstatement of the puja spirit. Musically, the puja of 1965 aroused the curiosity of people when news got around that Rahul Dev Burman was making his debut as a composer of puja songs. This was a chance happening. RD was too rebellious a name for the common Bengali, whose musical taste was somewhat limited to music that was sombre and solemn.

It turned out that Bengali lyricist Pulak Banerjee was keen to produce a few songs with SD. Although he agreed initially, SD passed the ball to his son, stating that he would only sing songs penned by his wife Meera that year. An unwilling Pancham expressed his discomfort in composing Bengali songs. Nevertheless, assured of Lata Mangeshkar's voice for the songs, Pancham agreed. He travelled to Calcutta and offered a selection of eight tunes to Pulak Banerjee who selected two: *'Amar malati lata'*, which was later recorded in Hindi twice, as the title songs of *Deewaar* (1975) and *Hamare Tumhare* (1979) by Manna Dey and Kishore Kumar respectively; and *'Ami boli tomaye'*, recorded in Hindi as *'Deewana karke chhodoge'* in *Mere Jeevan Saathi* (1972).

S.D. Burman did not compose at all during the pujas in 1965. In fact, he did not record to Meera Dev Burman's lyrics until 1968! Was the reason proffered to Pulak Banerjee, then, an excuse, a ruse to introduce his son to Bengali music as an alternative means of establishing himself in the face of the lean patch that he was going through? Or was SD simply not well enough to sing? The fact that he had no releases in 1966 does support the latter theory. Maybe it was a bit of both.

Pancham's debut on the Bengali music scene was similar to

the one in Hindi – applauded in patches, but lukewarm overall. His performance was further diluted by the insinuation that S.D. Burman must have had a hand in the compositions. But, despite his detractors, Pancham's songs had earned him a foothold in Bengali music.

His next round of Bengali compositions began in 1967 with *'Ek din pakhi ure'* (*'Tum bin jaaon kahan'* from *Pyar Ka Mausam*, 1969), written by lyricist and director Mukul Dutta whose biography of Kishore Kumar was also named *Ek Din Pakhi Ure*. He followed it up with hits like *'Akash keno daake'* (*'Yeh shaam mastani'* from *Kati Patang*, 1970), *'Jete dao amaye deko na'* (*'Jaane do mujhe jane do'* from the non-film album *Dil Padosi Hai*, 1987) and *'Jabo ki jabo na'* (*'Ab jo mile hain toh'* from *Caravan*, 1971) which he created, according to Bhanu Gupta, in a matter of minutes when he heard Bhupendra casually strumming A-minor and A-minor 9th chords on open strings.

A similar chord pattern was evident in Pancham's first released and probably best-known Bengali solo, *'Mone pore Ruby Ray'*. (Though this was his first released Bengali song, Pancham's first recorded song was a duet with Kishore Kumar which he sang for his father in Guru Dutt's *Gouri*, but the film, like *Raaz*, was shelved.) Scenarist Sachin Bhowmick had lost his heart to a certain lady who, unfortunately, spurned his affections. Her name was Chhobi Ray, and she was immortalized as Ruby Ray in the song which Pancham coerced Bhowmick to write. Loosely based on Raga Kirwani / Basant Mukhari, the switch between minor and minor 9th chords gives the song a very Western feel. The song also talks about hot, sultry Calcutta afternoons using a raga that is supposed to be sung late at night. However, the impact is one of contrast, not discord. The Hindi version, *'Meri bheegi bheegi si'* (*Anamika*, 1973), was full of loss and longing, and the arrangement completely unlike the original.

During its time, *'Ruby Ray'* struggled for acceptance.

Birajmohan Das recalls: 'A common friend, Kamal Chattopadhyay, who wrote poetry in Bengali, wanted Pancham to set his poems into music. Pancham was non-committal. And composed songs like *"Mone pore Ruby Ray"* for lyricist Sachin Bhowmick instead ... songs that were generically branded as chenchamechi (cacophony) in our time.'

For good measure, *'Ruby Ray'* was criticized as a reflection of the degenerate westernization of music, something that was blasphemously un-Indian. Time and again, Pancham was accused of anglicizing Indian music. Even SD had had to shut the doors on prissy know-alls when he composed trendy songs during the early and mid-1950s. Using the piano like a harmonium and combining it with beats on dholaks was an accepted norm and the critical worth increased manifold if the composer stated that the tune was based on some raga. Today, *'Mone pore Ruby Ray'* is regarded a benchmark track.

The other side of the album contained the cult song *'Phire esho Anuradha'*, which sounded like another dedication, to a lady addressed as Anuradha. In an interview with the authors, Sachin Bhowmick puts an end to all speculation and asserts that he used the name Anuradha since that was the name of his first full-fledged script written for director Hrishikesh Mukherjee (who made it into a National Award-winning film in 1960). Pancham later recast this tune as *'Sajan kahan jaungi main'* in the film *Jaise Ko Taisa* (1973). The Anuradha chapter was closed in 1986 with the Pancham–Asha duet *'Phire elaam dure giye'*, a sequel to *'Phire Esho'*, creating the mood of a reunion of sorts.

Related to the second round of Pancham's Bengali compositions, one must perhaps mention Kishore Kumar's first stage show in Kolkata in the winter of 1967, because it gives an insight into the changing equations in the world of Hindi film music. Kishore Kumar was reportedly awed by the crowd that had gathered at Rabindra Sarobar Stadium near Dhakuria Lake to hear him. Mohammad Rafi had already raised public expectations with the rendition of *'Aaja aaja main hoon pyaar tera'*. Bystanders recall that the instant Kishore began humming the starting notes of *'Ek din pakhi ure'*, the crowd went into raptures. The spontaneous applause restored his confidence and a while later the audience settled down in a silence that illustrated the public's respect for the song and the artist.

The incident that wintry evening was destined to be repeated a year later. Kishore and Rafi would take centre stage again. Once again, there would be a mammoth audience that would applaud. And make a critical choice between the two of them.

2

Perhaps more by design than coincidence, the period from 1965 to 1969 saw Pancham compose for only two movies each year. After the failure of *Baharon Ke Sapne*, Nasir Husain got ready to start his next venture, *Pyar Ka Mausam* (1969), an out-and-out musical with a lost-and-found theme that the producer–director jokingly claimed to have patented.

Songs, the foundation of the film, were obviously prioritized, and Husain spent long hours arranging the script with his now in-house composer Rahul Dev Burman. The title song of the film, the Lata–Rafi duet *'Ni sultana re pyar ka mausam aaya'*, was Pancham's first foray into the folk music that one heard in the hills of north India. In this number, as in the Rafi solo of the film, *'Che khush nazare'*, Pancham brought his favourite two-paced stylization. In the former, he used a mix of duggi tarang, santoor and the clicking of fingers and his own voice in the piece that trails off as *'O Rama . . .'*; in the latter, he toyed with a long prelude not quite related to the main song. Both these numbers are bright and animated, in sync with the youthful mirth of the principal characters, their folksy flavour echoing the hills in the midst of which the film is set.

'*Aap se miliye*', a melody based on popular Marathi folk, was presented as a dance item in Lucknawi, Arabic and Spanish settings. The use of the sax and strings in the third interlude resulted in a tune that would resurface nine years later as '*Raju chal Raju*' in Pramod Chakraborty's *Azaad* (1978).

The pathos of '*Na ja o mere humdum*' brought to mind O.P. Nayyar's '*Jaiye aap kahan jayenge*' (*Mere Sanam*, 1965). But while Nayyar's number is studded with string notes and Nayyarian foxtrot, Pancham composed the song with church bells, acoustic guitar, triangles and chimes with leather-covered mallets that produce a mellow sound.

Kishore Kumar had only one song in *Pyar Ka Mausam* – and one that was not picturized on the hero. To top it all, only the first stanza made it to the final version of the film! Despite that, and in spite of Rafi's energetic rendition of '*Che khush nazare*' and '*Ni sultana re*', Kishore Kumar's incomplete, single-track '*Tum bin jaoon kahan*', using the tune that was originally '*Ek din pakhi ure*', became the high point of this film.

Mohammad Rafi might have been right to feel that history had dealt unfairly with him by chronicling the purported Kishore vs Rafi 'duel' as the highlight of this film. '*Tum bin jaoon kahan*' was used five times in the film. Initially, all five instances were supposed to be in Rafi's voice, till Pancham and his musicians coaxed Nasir Husain into giving the version to be picturized on the hero's father, Bharat Bhushan, to Kishore Kumar.

The rich baritone and emotional intensity of Kishore's voice wove magic like nothing else into the film. Rafi's version, for all its silken elegance, paled in comparison, even though it was featured on the hero, Shashi Kapoor, who went around in the film in a blazer, tie and fluffy cap (which was funny, since the rest of the cast dressed differently). Apart from the standard version available on tape, a slower version sung by Kishore is also used in the film.

Pancham's compositions in the film entailed extensive use of instruments like the mandolin and the guitar. More known for his skill with wind instruments, Manohari Singh played the mandolin in the preludes of both the Kishore and Rafi versions of *'Tum bin jaoon kahan'* to great acclaim.

The last name that featured in the star cast of *Pyar Ka Mausam* was Pancham's. Another comic role, this time as secretary to the imposter who called himself Jhatpat Singh, played by Rajendra Nath. Pancham's dialogues were restricted to 'very true', his only response to anything his boss said. Pancham called it quits as an actor with *Pyar Ka Mausam*, only to play himself in a cameo in a Bengali film, *Gayak* in 1987.

3

Having seen Rajesh Khanna's performance in *Baharon Ke Sapne*, producer–director Shakti Samanta decided to offer him his next film after *An Evening in Paris* (1967), *Subah Pyar Ki*. The name was inspired from the last line of the mukhra of the incandescently romantic song from *An Evening in Paris*: *'Raat ke humsafar, thak ke ghar ko chale, jhoomti aa rahi, hai subah pyar ki'*. The film went through several hiccups before it finally saw the light of day.

For one, actor–director Aparna Sen turned down the role of the leading lady in favour of *Vishwas* (1969) opposite Jeetendra. Shakti Samanta's next choice was Sharmila Tagore. Distributors were reportedly unhappy with the *An Evening in Paris* bikini girl donning widowhood even before the audience went to get their interval popcorn, as well as with Samanta's decision to cast rookie Rajesh Khanna in two roles, one of which was opposite Farida Jalal, a certified 'saheli' to heroines.

Samanta, who could not hire Shankar–Jaikishan to score the music of the film because of budgetary constraints, asked S.D. Burman, who demanded more remuneration than before. The producer–director offered one hundred thousand rupees. SD, who was expecting eighty thousand, jumped at the offer and promised a spectacular score for the film.

Despite the tumultuous start, the leaky ship *Subah Pyar Ki*, renamed *Aradhana* (1969), came to be adored and turned into a luxury liner which, along with its songs, cruised for months.

The film gave Hindi cinema its first superstar: Rajesh Khanna. *Aradhana* bagged the awards for best film, best actress (Sharmila Tagore) and best male playback singer (Kishore Kumar for '*Roop tera mastana*') at the Filmfare Awards. S.D. Burman's rendition of the title song, '*Safal hogi teri aradhana*', won him the National Award for best male playback singer.

The pleasant Indianization of Mitchell Leisen's film *To Each His Own* (1946) aside, it was *Aradhana's* music that was an instant hit with the public. From the eroticism of '*Roop tera mastana*' (made even more so by Kersi Lord's staccato accordion), to the gay, swinging, boisterous abandon of '*Mere sapno ki rani*' and the romance of '*Kora kagaz tha*', it was Kishore's voice all the way. Coming immediately after *Pyar Ka Mausam*, the success of *Aradhana* catapulted Kishore miles ahead of his peers. Interestingly, Shakti Samanta had initially rejected the tune of '*Kora kagaz tha*', only to use it later, reportedly after Pancham played the song on the harmonium saying that it was a different composition.

During the press party of *Aradhana*, critics and the media alike showered SD with applause while Pancham stood

According to Javed Akhtar, Kishore was the voice of the city slicker, while Rafi was the voice of the small-towner. Could the shift in audience preferences from Rafi to Kishore have something to do with the fact that the early 1970s saw rapid urbanization?

on the sidelines, away from the limelight, even though he'd been the one pulling the strings during recordings. Bhanu Gupta who played the rhythm recounts:

> We were recording 'Mere sapno ki rani' and SD was hooked to a particular rhythm which I had played during the rehearsal. During the actual recording of the song, the guitarist hired to play the rhythm could not reproduce the typical locomotive beat that SD wanted; so he opined that we cancel the recording. By that time the shooting crew was to move to Darjeeling and a delay could lead to huge financial losses. I was playing the harmonica in the song. Pancham sensed the urgency, asked me to bring my guitar from the car and play the rhythm I had played previously, while he himself played an impromptu piece on the harmonica which segued into the strings section to become the starting point for Kishore Kumar's vocals. He kept the prelude short, though not within four bars as mandated by SD, but crisp enough to not supersede the main melody that was to follow. You can see the result.

It is agreed by musicians that Pancham's presence is felt in *Aradhana*, including the resonant humming which was used as a leitmotif in the film. Many years later, singer S.P. Balasubrahmanyam, an expert at analysing music, emphasized that the orchestration and stylization was typical of Pancham.

Badal Bhattacharya says, 'It is usually said by stage performers today that S.D. Burman had composed a very traditional tune for *"Roop tera mastana"*, and that it was Kishore Kumar who sang the Bengali nursery rhyme *"Kalke jabo shoshurbari / ahlade khai goragori"* to him, which inspired SD to modify the tune. In reality, it was Pancham's brainchild and he had provoked Kishore Kumar to walk up to SD and influence him to modify the original folksy tune.'

In the dubbed Bengali version of *Aradhana* released in 1976, Shakti Samanta probably spilled the beans, as the publicity material contained the names of both father and son as composers of the film.

The chemistry between father and son was interesting in its contrast. SD was a minimalist who emphasized on conservative parameters like limiting the number of musicians, cutting down on the use of new instruments, and restricting preludes and interludes within eight bars. Pancham, on the other hand, would always experiment with beats and diverse instruments. The combination of minimalism and exuberance often gave rise to interesting results. While the tune for *'Kora kagaz tha'* and the prelude of *'Mere sapno ki rani'* were Pancham's contribution, it was SD who dictated the number of musicians who would play in each recording. According to Shakti Samanta, Pancham had asked for twelve musicians during the recording of *'Safal hogi teri aradhana'*, the title track of the film, while SD had mandated only eleven. The extra musician had to be paid off and relieved prior to the recording on SD's insistence.

These exercises in putting his resources to good use held Pancham in good stead throughout his career. He became proficient in generating sounds that were sharp, clear and devoid of clutter, in spite of using an orchestra where there would be more than one musician for a particular instrument. He was one of the few mainstream composers who never used 'outstanding musicians', industry jargon for musicians who

Inspired by the shooting technique used by Leni Riefenstahl in the magnum opus *Olympia* glorifying the Berlin Olympics in 1936, the shoot of *'Roop tera mastana'* was the first instance in Hindi films where the camera continuously moved on a track. The song was shot in a single shot and was part of the study material in FTII.

were made to play standing outside the recording studios due to lack of space. This earned him both the respect and the envy of fellow composers and of the new breed that followed in the 1990s.

According to Bhanu Gupta, Pancham's style of arrangement as a composer was distinct from the one that he followed while assisting his father. Like a proud son, he wanted to be original; but not without contributing towards building the Burman brand.

Till 1969, Pancham had had three big hits. He had developed a style of music based on blues, bossa nova, folk, Indian classical music and jazz, and was considered a composer with a keen musical ear who could be trusted to bring out detail and variety in the songs he composed. He had forged crucial alliances with leading film producers like Nasir Husain and had found an ally in Kishore Kumar.

Dipankar Chattopadhyay was privy to a recording that was conducted around 1966–67. He recounts how Pancham had grown in stature since the time he had left Calcutta: 'I was in Bombay at Pancham's residence. After savouring a peg of fine gin with Pancham and Rita, I went to his recording. This was the late 1960s and it was a song where there was a large violin ensemble with four or five rows of fiddlers. I cannot recall the song, but I think it was Kishore singing. During the take, Pancham, with whom I was in the recording room, pointed: "The violin of the musician second from left on the last row is not in tune," and proceeded to communicate the same to the assistant, to my utter amazement.'

Pancham's core team too was in place. Basu, Manohari, Maruti, Kersi, Devichand Chauhan, Amrutrao, Bhupendra, Homi Mullan, Bhanu Gupta – they had all tasted success together, and had grown to like Pancham as a person for the respect he gave them as individuals and to their talents. 'People first, strategy later,' say corporate management gurus in the new millennium. Half a century ago, Pancham seemed to have discovered this bit of corporate wisdom and put it to good use.

By this time, he had entered the camp of film-makers from the south too, with a hit in the form of *Waris* (1969). The pivotal song *'Lehra ke aaya hai jhonka bahar ka'*, a tune he had created during the making of Guru Dutt's *Raaz*, with its distinctive Arabic flavour, was a hit with the masses. Decades later, in a show in the UAE, Pancham played the song he had created in his salad days on his harmonica to the delight of the audience.

Amit Kumar recalls another statement by Jaikishan about Pancham, 'Ye jo ladka aayega, aake sabki chutti karne wala hai. Ye guni hai. Iska music maine suna hai. Ye aake sabko change kar dega. Isko underestimate mat karo,' (This boy will outshine everyone. I've heard his music. He has it in him. He will change music as we know it. Do not underestimate him).

The ladka was spreading his wings, willing to soar. To fly like an unbridled kite. Before long, he would do that ... in a film ironically named *Kati Patang*.

Book Two

MOON IN LIBRA

A square block of marble, upon which is the regalia of sceptre and crown.

It denotes a person of ambitious nature: desiring to be held in esteem, and possessed of such force and firmness of character that he will triumph over rivals and opponents. In whatever station of life he may be, the native will evince the characteristics of command, and will sway the destinies of others.

7

Dawning of the 1970s

On 20 July 1969, Neil Armstrong fulfilled John F. Kennedy's dream of taking a small step on the moon. Closer home on Earth, America's Big Three car makers motored along assertively. Golda Meir was appointed the prime minister of Israel, the third woman ever to hold such a high office. Music found its great escape from commerce in the form of Woodstock – live music was never the same again. Led Zeppelin introduced the world to heavy metal and hard rock with the release of the album *Led Zeppelin I*. Boeing 747 took flight. The first ATM machine was installed in Rockville, New York. The Beatles gave their last public performance.

It was the evening of the 1960s dawning into the 1970s.

The decade when Syd Barrett was synonymous with LSD, and bubblegum pop was very much part of the urban music lovers' record collection. Music media, like music itself, was changing. Vinyl replaced shellac, 12-inch diameter 33 1/3-rpm Long Play records edged out 78-rpm ones. The Grundig- or

Garrard-make spool player was an import to be envied and, budget permitting, bought and displayed prominently in Indian homes.

In Hindi films, colour was in and black-and-white was out. Most masala Hindi films found red-blooded, middle-aged heroes painting the word 'love' in various hues and bashing the villainous characters blue. The Hindi film heroine was transformed from the salwar–kameez- or sari-clad, quiet, diligent woman of the late 1950s to one sporting wide hairbands, flower-patterned short kurtis and thigh-hugging, bright-coloured slacks, the quintessential college girl with a chirpy, loud voice and a solitary notebook clasped to her chest.

It was also the time of the long-haired, jean-wearing hippie generation, sporting Lennon glasses and guitars.

Closets were being opened and bold questions being asked. The modern gay-rights movement started at Stonewall, New York. *Midnight Cowboy* – premiered on 25 May 1969 – became the first X-rated film to receive the Academy Award for best film, in 1970.

In the same year, Mrinal Sen's *Bhuvan Shome* (1969), the debut venture of the newly formed Film Finance Corporation (FFC), won the National Award for best film in India. The film, along with Basu Chatterjee's debut venture *Sara Akash* (1969), was the first in a class of cinema that would run parallel to the standard song-and-dance routines and dhishum–dhishum fare of mainstream Hindi movies. The Dadasaheb Phalke Award, the highest honour for an Indian film personality, was instituted and Devika Rani became its first recipient.

All India Radio introduced the Yuvavani channel, airtime devoted to the youth. 'This was the seventies, when the youth of India bonded with the rest of the world. It was impolite to ask someone, "Where are you from?" The answer obviously was "I'm global." Yet, it provided for one-on-one bonding,' says singer Susmit Bose, a member of the hippie generation. 'We

spoke German, Italian, Indian, but we bonded through music.'
The power of youth was easing into high gear.

2

Change had begun lapping the shores of Bombay too. The end
of the 1960s brought into prominence the composing duos
Laxmikant–Pyarelal and Kalyanji–Anandji. Anil Biswas retired
from cinema with Motilal's *Chhoti Chhoti Batein* (1966) (though
he later contemplated coming out of retirement to compose for
a Basu Bhattacharya film in the 1980s which got shelved). His
skilled handling of the media and glib perception management
notwithstanding, Naushad too was fading, as was
C. Ramachandra. O.P. Nayyar had, it seemed, given all that he
had to offer. His self-imposed distance from Lata and Kishore
resulted in the composer receiving fewer offers.

Shankar never really recovered from Jaikishan's passing in
1971; and although he carried the Shankar–Jaikishan banner
alone, he found lesser success in his ventures. 'Shankar sahab
had become a shade incoherent, tending to shoot his mouth off.
This got him into trouble with his strongest sponsor, Raj
Kapoor, when he got into an argument with Randhir in *Kal Aaj
Aur Kal* [1971],' recalls Nandu Chavathe, a violinist for many
leading composers.

Among the composers who worked selectively, Roshan, too,
fell silent in 1967, leaving behind a legacy of classics. His
qawwalis were the most authentic to ever feature in Hindi
cinema. His wife Ira Nagrath completed the music of his last
film, *Anokhi Raat* (1969). Salil Chowdhury, who had returned to
Bombay around that time to work on a few prestigious
assignments, composed the background music for the film.
Jaidev and Khayyam's classical brilliance put them on a deserved
pedestal, but they were denied access to the playing field that

was popular film music. Chitragupta catered to smaller films and film-makers. Ravi, despite cornering a chunk of his assignments via B.R. Films, was marginalized in this phase.

The only composers from the old school still in the running were Madan Mohan and S.D. Burman. Madan Mohan's association with Lata Mangeshkar brought him unlimited credit and one successful album after another. Although he composed widely for Asha and Rafi as well, the mystic magic of the Madan Mohan–Lata combine was destined to be a topic of musical research even decades after. S.D. Burman, recharged by the success of *Aradhana*, composed Pramod Chakraborty's *Naya Zamana* (1970) and Samir Ganguli's *Sharmilee* (1971) to acclaim.

3

Crime was the forte of the American writer Cornell Woolrich and his work found takers in well-known film directors worldwide. Alfred Hitchcock's *Rear Window* (1954) and Francois Truffaut's *Mississippi Mermaid* (1969) were based on Woolrich's short story 'It Had to Be Murder' and the novel *Waltz into Darkness*, respectively.

In 1950, Woolrich's story *I Married a Dead Man* was made into the film *No Man of Her Own*, starring Barbara Stanwyck as the protagonist who fakes her identity to gain social acceptance and in the process becomes the object of blackmail. Popular Hindi writer Gulshan Nanda based the plot of his novel *Kati Patang* on Woolrich's story. In the words of R.D. Burman, the film of the same name became the most important milestone of his career.

Aradhana had made one star (Rajesh Khanna), resurrected another (Kishore Kumar) and ignited a relationship between the two. *Kati Patang* made both of them, and the composer, superstars. Hindi film music was being redefined by the Rajesh–

Kishore–RD combine that spelt musical genius hitherto rarely heard. And never since. *Kati Patang* was quite like a dramatic successor to *Aradhana.*

The storylines of both were set in the Himalayan range. In *Aradhana*, Sharmila Tagore played a widow in the second half; while in *Kati Patang*, Asha Parekh donned the robes of a widow almost from reel one. Neither of them was officially married to the hero at any point in both movies!

However, some things provided variety. In *Aradhana*, Kishore Kumar used his vocals to create the echo effect in the songs, specially the song '*Kora kagaz tha yeh man mera*'. In *Kati Patang*, Kersi Lord used the Roland echo machine, having the generic name 'echolite', to generate the feel of an echo throughout the songs and the background music. Interestingly, while Samanta had expressed dissatisfaction with the tune of '*Kora kagaz tha*' in *Aradhana*, in *Kati Patang*, he accepted the new piece of technology (the echo machine) quite grudgingly since he felt that it was only going to create a lot of noise. Both the albums, however, turned out to be mega hits.

The main difference was in the use of voices. *Kati Patang* did not have any song by Mohammad Rafi. *Aradhana* had two duets. Kishore Kumar had taken over as the voice of Rajesh Khanna, with three landmark solos – '*Pyar diwana hota hai*', '*Yeh shaam mastani*' and '*Yeh jo mohabbat hai*'.

The tune of '*Pyar diwana hota hai*' had been used with little success for the Asha Bhonsle song '*Gun gun gun gunje amar*' in the Bengali film *Rajkumari* (1970). In contrast to the Bengali version which, though being in 16-beat format, has a waltz-like cadence, '*Pyar diwana*', with piano notes in the prelude, interludes and refrains, has a more matter-of-fact feel. In one of the interludes, pianist Mike Machado's samba-based two-octave can be heard. This was recorded at Film Centre, the only studio that had a grand piano in those days.

'*Yeh shaam mastani*' was redone from the 1968 Pancham–
Kishore Puja number '*Akash keno dake*'. Many Kishore Kumar
fans consider this *the* quintessential Kishore–Rajesh song. It
establishes a bond between the lead characters as they walk in
the park amidst the green meadows, the waterfall of the Kumayun
Mountains and the autumn evening sky.

'*Yeh jo mohabbat hai*' broke new ground as the first-ever
'broken-hearted-man-seeks-solace-in-booze' melody composed
by Pancham. Unlike its filmi predecessors, the hero neither
sports a stubble, nor does he have dark circles under his
eyes; Rajesh Khanna sways from one table to another in a bar
sporting a rather cool
evening jacket. The hero
seems to 'celebrate' an
important part of growing
up – being ditched in love
for the first time – and
instead of dragged-out
emotional notes, '*Yeh jo
mohabbat hai*' is a waltzing
rhythm with lively acoustic

Satyajit Ray, usually dispassionate
about Hindi film music, used '*Yeh
jo mohabbat hai*' as a reference in
his story *Sonar Kella* (The Golden
Fortress), which was later made into
a film by the same name in 1974.

guitar notes further embellished with the deep sound of the
cello and the violin harmonies.

According to Shakti Samanta, the last of the male solos, '*Jis
gali mein tera ghar*', was also composed for Kishore Kumar, but
was finally recorded by Mukesh (probably the only song he
sang for Shakti Samanta) since Kishore was abroad. The echolite,
the vibraphone and the transicord play major roles in the song,
primarily to generate the sound of the oars moving through
water. The song was shot in a studio but superimposed on the
Naini Lake backdrop amidst a flurry of multicoloured sailboats.
V. Gopi Krishna, Samanta's favoured cinematographer in the
1960s, vividly captured the fog that characterizes the lake. The
number is used once more in the film, during the climactic
sequence at the Ranikhet Golf Course.

Pancham had said in an interview (published in the Bengali magazine *Alokepath* in September 1993) that he had wanted to use Talat Mahmood for a song but Rajesh Khanna did not agree. The track in question may have been '*Jis gali mein*' as the lyrics and the mood are similar to the songs in Talat's repertoire.

Lata Mangeshkar had only one song in the film: '*Na koi umang hai*'. Barring an uncharacteristic aberration in the last line, '*Yehi mera . . .*', where her voice deviates from the tune for a split second (which may have been a recording error), the song is like a carry-over from the *Baharon Ke Sapne* period. Composed in a manner which might resemble the structure of Raga Nat Bhairav, the song is nevertheless very stylized and Western in form, and ably conveys the leading lady's anguish.

S.D. Burman had warned his son early in his career: 'Whatever you compose sounds like a Madan Mohan or a Roshan melody. You need to have a style of your own.' Perhaps this was what prompted Pancham to mould even the most conventional thoughts into melodies which were innately unconventional. It is this nonconformity that helped RD carve a style that was distinguishably his – reflected best in the song '*Mera naam hai Shabnam*' sung by Asha Bhonsle who was well on her way to be the load-bearing cog in his musical wheel.

'*Mera naam hai Shabnam*', a cabaret sequence picturized on Bindu, is a composition devoid of any base metre; it is a series of phrases intoned in a cadence. The song is characterized by the jazz-like use of brass interspersed with Pancham's huffing and Asha's taunting laughter, threatening to unmask the impostor. 'I had never done a cabaret before. I had practised for 5–6 days. Pancham was not there during rehearsal. But when he saw the output, he was all praise for the way I had timed the lip sync at each point,' remembers Bindu.

Both '*Na koi umang hai*' and '*Mera naam hai Shabnam*' feature in Pancham's list of all-time favourites.

The background music of *Kati Patang* was high on melody, and alternately featured refrains of *'Yeh shaam mastani'*, *'Na koi umang hai'* and another tune which was later remodelled into the third line of *'Bahon mein chale aao'* from the film *Anamika* (1973).

'Kati Patang had Pancham combining genres with great dedication and intelligence. He roped in diverse forms like the samba, paso doble, calypso, jazz, and Indian classical and gave the mix a very chic flavour. I had great fun arranging the songs. I revere it especially as I had to whistle throughout the film,' says Manohari with a chuckle.

Why did Pancham refer to *Kati Patang* as the turning point in his career? There could be more than one reason. Here was a film where the producer–director of *Aradhana*, despite its roaring success, had taken a major decision in bringing in the younger Burman. And if *Aradhana* was the lift-off for Kaka, the music of *Kati Patang* put him in stratospheric orbit; his mere presence on the screen was creating mass hysteria. In *Kati Patang*, all elements of cinema locked into place with a sweet click, with results that were very different from the beating that the music by the same composer had taken a little earlier.

Rajkumari, Pancham's first Bengali film which released a few months before *Kati Patang*, was a commercial disaster. Though the film had fascinating music and an interesting background score with a blend of Indian classical and jazz, one of the reasons for the film's failure was attributed to the Uttam–Kishore mismatch. Kishore too admitted that he had sung without understanding the finer points of Uttam Kumar's voice. *Rajkumari* had a weak script too, and an even weaker choreography, which made the song sequences appear sketchy. Pancham did not compose for Bengali films for almost a decade after this.

The commercial success of *Kati Patang* inspired Samanta to

sign Pancham for another film which, in later years, was considered Pancham's best work of all time.

But before that arrived *The Train* (1970), which had Rajesh Khanna as Inspector Shyam Kumar, chasing suspects involved in serial crimes in Igatpuri on a train on the Bombay–Nagpur route. When he was not pursuing his lady love, that is. The film flagged off a lifelong friendship between Pancham and film-maker Ramesh Behl. RD achieved some important 'firsts' with the film – his first duet with Asha Bhonsle; a background score that had voices for a change, with Usha Iyer (later Usha Uthup) joining Pancham; and the introduction of the electric bass guitar in Hindi film music.

The title music of the film was later modified and used in *Trimurti* (1974).

The music of *The Train*, albeit bright, did not quite belong to the 1970s. Apart from '*O meri jaan maine kaha*', the remaining songs were a throwback to the previous decade. Lata Mangeshkar's exceptional solo '*Kis liye maine pyar kiya*' had much in common with the feel of '*Aaja piya*' from *Baharon Ke Sapne*. Somehow, *The Train* did not find its way into the list of Rajesh Khanna's hits. Perhaps because it had no songs by Kishore Kumar.

4

In Bengal, hinger kochuri is a favourite late-afternoon accompaniment to ginger tea. It is also the name of Bibhutibhushan Bandopadhyay's short story about a schoolboy who befriends a prostitute named Kusum. The tale is narrated by the child.

Arabinda Mukherjee, writer, film director and younger brother of Dr Balai Chand Mukherjee, or Banaphool as he was popularly known, based the script of his film *Nishipadma* (1970) – a poignant story of the platonic romance between Ananta Babu and Pushpa, a prostitute – on 'Hinger Kochuri'. Uttam Kumar and Sabitri Chatterjee were cast in the lead roles. The music by Nachiketa Ghosh earned singer Manna Dey his second National Award for the song '*Ja khushi ora bole baluk*'.

Shakti Samanta enlisted the services of Arabinda Mukherjee and had the script translated into Hindi. The film was named *Amar Prem*, and the hero's name changed to Anand Babu, to make it more neutral-sounding to an all-India audience (maybe even to cash in on Kaka's screen name in *Anand*). The story was set in Calcutta of the early 1950s, where one hears sex workers debating the relative merits of Ashok Kumar in *Sangram* (1950) over Dev Anand in *Baazi* (1951). It is widely believed that Rajesh Khanna watched *Nishipadma* more than twenty times to capture the intensity that Uttam Kumar had brought to the role of Ananta Babu.

Commenting on Pancham's work routine during *Amar Prem*, Shakti Samanta remarked, 'He would be in his music room from nine to nine.' For a person who supposedly displayed a very low level of patience in any sphere, including composing, this metamorphosis was remarkable.

In an interview, Pancham said that he had heard his father sing a song – '*Bela boye jaye*' – which stayed in his mind during the composition of '*Raina beeti jaye*'. Apparently, when he heard the Lata Mangeshkar solo, Madan Mohan called SD and congratulated him. Dada Burman clarified that it was his son's composition and not his, but Madan Mohan was reluctant to believe him.

The song is a mix of two ragas – Todi in the mukhra and Khamaj in the antara. Unlike SD's disinclination to mix ragas, Pancham let his listeners savour the seamless merging of notes. The number is on minor scale, uses consecutive sevenths, and has the minor–major shift, all characteristic of Pancham's penchant for experimentation. Like '*Na koi umang hai*', this song too is unconventional in the way it is structured, though it follows the rudiments of Indian classical music. The seldom-used Iranian santoor (played in the song by Pandit Shiv Kumar Sharma) along with the esraj and the flute (played by Pandit Hari Prasad Chaurasia) were used to create the sublime effect, according to Kersi Lord.

Singer Arati Mukherjee recalls a chat with Pandit Mallikarjun Mansur during a classical music conference in Dharwar, northern Karnataka. During the conversation, to her surprise, she found him humming '*Raina beeti jaye*'. On seeing her surprised expression, he remarked on how beautifully SD's son had glided the notes upon each other in the song. Coming from a classical vocalist of repute, this is possibly the greatest testament to Pancham's understanding of classical music during that time.

As is usual with Pancham, though Todi is an early-morning raga and Khamaj a late-night one, he used these ragas to set a song that was to be picturized in the evening. 'This song had a bandish of the mood rather than the time of the day,' analysed Gulzar on the radio show *Meri Sangeet Yatra* (1993). The tune is apt for the situation: Pushpa singing in her chamber for her newest admirer who, on the verge of leaving, stops on hearing her, turns around and staggers up the stairs. He discovers his only other solace in this world in his drunken stupor.

Khamaj greatly influenced Pancham's compositions for *Amar Prem*. Two more songs from the film, '*Bada natkhat hai re*' and '*Kuch toh log kahenge*', are based on the same raga, yet, all three are distinct. Lata Mangeshkar's '*Bada natkhat hai re*' captured the playfulness associated with the naughty Krishna and his relationship with Yashoda. In the film, the tainted woman enjoys a few fleeting moments of motherhood that she knows she is not destined for.

Kishore Kumar did an exceptional job in conveying the angst

of the lonely businessman seeking comfort in the music and care of Pushpa. His soulful vocals in *'Chingari koi bhadke'*, *'Kuch toh log kahenge'* and *'Yeh kya hua'* set these songs apart as some of the finest of the RD–Kishore combine.

For a generation of music lovers, *'Chingari koi bhadke'* was the archetypal ballad that laments the loss everyone faces. Pushpa, banished from her husband's home, refused entry into her parental home, lands up in a prostitute's house in the big city. Her body and talent are up for sale every evening when the lamps are lit. But for all the messages conveyed, the song remains a purveyor of the deepest and most passionate romance. The song sequence, with dusk setting in and the lead pair enjoying a boat ride on the Ganga under the Howrah Bridge, is an escape from the confines of the separate worlds they inhabit. Samanta filmed the entire song in a studio and projected the same on the backdrop of the softly lit Calcutta skyline as seen from the banks of its twin city, Howrah.

Carnatic classical singer, veena player and music analyst Prince Rama Varma adds about the arrangement: 'Rahul Dev Burman, who always experimented with new sounds, opens the song with a minor chord strummed on a guitar, which gives the rhythmic pulse as much as it does the melody. This hauntingly beautiful chord is repeated throughout the song and keeps increasing in its hypnotic quality as the song progresses and as we hear it again and again. Kishore-da sings "*Chingari koi bhadke* ..." and leaves it hanging in the air, when the divine flute takes it up and plays a sublime little passage, generously utilizing the Teevra Madhyam. I don't think there would be many Bhairavi songs which use the startling Teevra Madhyam, either in the orchestration or in the singing, as much as "*Chingari*" does. From the "*Usey*" in "*Saawan usey bujhaaye*" the sombre waves of Teevra Madhyam start, creating a mood like very few other songs do. Violins play in the background right from the time the singing starts. Generally speaking, the screech of the violins, especially in the higher octave, is second only to the screech of female voices in Indian film music from the late 1940s onwards. In *"Chingari"*, though, the sound of the violins is mercifully muted, though they are there for sure.'

The minor chord, which grows on you as mentioned by Rama Varma, was part of Pancham's wizardry. Bhanu Gupta has talked about it in many forums: 'On my way to winding up one evening, I played the F-sharp minor chord with an open third string. This produced a strange sound and people laughed. But Pancham insisted that I play the chord once more, and he made me play it incorrectly. What appeared as discord to me and to people all around us was music to Pancham. See how brilliantly he used the faulty chord in the song *"Chingari"*. Surely a genius.'

As the tune roughly follows the structure of Raga Bhairavi, it also boils down to using an early-morning raga for a song featured in the evening. And Pancham builds the feeling of the evening smartly by fusing the Teevra Ma – a note representative of evening – into the song.

As Rama Varma has elucidated, the arrangement of *'Chingari'* is one of a kind. The song starts with a very unconventional guitaring, followed by the soulful flute intro by Pandit Hari Prasad Chaurasia. The resso, the maracas and the kabashe provide the percussion base. The occasional use of the qanun (an Arabic zither instrument) by Sumant Raj, the poignant tar shehnai obligato by Dakshina Mohan Tagore, and the subdued violin ensemble by Basu Chakravarty's section, all add to Kishore Kumar's voice to create a song of undefinable dimensions.

'Chingari koi bhadke' could well qualify to be among the best songs of all time. It has a wide appeal, from the connoisseur to the common man. In an episode of *Vishesh Jaimala* on All India Radio, singer and composer Hemant Kumar admitted that this was his favourite composition. Pandit Ajoy Chakrabarty marvels

at the cadence of the tune and the mood it creates. Shakti
Samanta earmarked this song as his best during an informal
discussion at the Tolly Club in Calcutta. On a visit to the
Sangeet Research Academy in Calcutta in 2002 to meet Pandit
Ulhas Kashalkar, classical music aficionado Archisman Mozumder
recalled hearing a voice singing *Chingari koi bhadke* from one
of the bungalows in the compound. His inquisitiveness led him
to Pandit A.T. Kanan's bungalow. On inquiring why a classical
expert like him was singing a light song, Pandit Kanan opined
bluntly: 'One who does not love Kishore Kumar and cannot
adore a wonderful song like this is mad.'

Needless to say, this was one of Kishore Kumar's favourites
too – perhaps more than *Kuch toh log kahenge*, which is still
growing in stature, and is conceivably more celebrated today
than when it was released. *Kuch toh* is a philosophical statement
that incisively and accurately defines the hazy contours of
morality. Pandit Ajoy Chakrabarty played it during one of his
shows, illustrating how efficiently the raga framework was used
in the genesis of a song that qualified as light music, creating
such a monumental impact. While discussing the melodic pattern
of *Kuch toh log kahenge* where Khamaj gently dissolves into the
notes of Raga Kalavati, documentary film-maker Brahmanand
Singh remarked, 'It is the chalan of the tune which makes it
unique.'

This statement probably summarizes it all. It would be a
shame to pin down *Kuch toh log kahenge* as just a raga-based
composition. It is much more than that. The song is a chapter
from the lives of people brought up in the early 1970s. For a
generation that constantly pushed the envelope in the way they
conducted relationships, the song was a sort of mantra.

Three solos from the same film endorsed by three doyens of
Hindustani classical music is a significant tribute to R.D.
Burman's brilliance.

The last of the Kishore numbers, '*Yeh kya hua*' mocks sorrow. It is like a denouement in a trilogy of the three Kishore solos: '*Chingari koi bhadke*' mourns the loss, '*Kuch toh log kahenge*' says 'let them be' and '*Ye kya hua*' conveys 'Don't worry, be happy'.

The mood of the original Bengali song, '*Ae ki holo*' sung by Kishore Kumar in *Rajkumari*, was one of resignation, of hopelessness. The Hindi counterpart has a positive chime; life must, after all, go on. It is an endeavour to smile away the grief of loss.

The background score of *Amar Prem*, with small musical pieces on various Indian classical instruments, is also a treat. From the full bellows of the harmonium to a slow 'gat' (composition) on the sarod, *Amar Prem* has it all. The title track '*Doli mein bithai ke kahar*' was the only song Dada Burman ever sang for his son, though Dada himself composed it despite it being a Pancham album, confirms Manohari Singh.

5

It was to be a busy year for Pancham, and one that amply demonstrated his hold over both Indian and Western music. *Buddha Mil Gaya* (1971), a thriller where fun took precedence over the heinous murders that were part of the film's story, was Pancham's first step into the cosy family world of Hrishikesh Mukherjee, though work on *Phir Kab Milogi* (renamed from *Bandagi*) which released in 1974, had started way back in 1966. Mukherjee would turn out to be the director for whom Pancham would do the highest number of films – eleven.

Highly respected for his directorial and editing skills, Mukherjee started his career as a sitarist for All India Radio before joining Bimal Roy as an assistant in 1951. His sharp ear helped him extract the best from his composers as a director and producer, but he seldom interfered in the compositions.

The theme song of *Buddha Mil Gaya* was '*Aayo kahan se*

Ghanshyaam', sung by Manna Dey and featured on veteran actor
Om Prakash, with Archana Gupta giving him company at the
fag end. This number runs like a motif through the film and is
heard every time a murder is discovered by the two young and
penniless photographers played by Navin Nischal (he was not
Nischol yet) and Deven Verma. The tune was based on a
traditional classical bandish *'Kaun gali gayo Shyam'*. The song
was in Raga Khamaj – Pancham's latest obsession, it seemed.
The tune of this song was played in the background during Om
Prakash's first appearance in *Amar Prem*, to rather comical
effect, as well as during a wedding ceremony sequence in the
film *Rajkumari.*

The other songs from *Buddha Mil Gaya* that became immensely
popular included *'Raat kali ek khwaab mein aayi'*, a soft Kishore
Kumar solo that the maestro breezes through, while a trademark
acoustic guitar riff in the prelude takes the listener back to *'Rula
ke gaya sapna mera' (Jewel Thief)*. *'Bhali bhali si ek soorat'*, the
Kishore–Asha duet, is vibrant, impish, and reminiscent of
the calypso style. Pancham also used the main melody as an
interlude in his Bengali composition *'Cholechhi eka kon ajanaye'*,
sung by Kishore Kumar. The Lata Mangeshkar solo, *'Jiya na
lage mora'* – taut, devoid of any superfluities, yet lovingly
passionate – was yet another Raga Khamaj composition.

6

Caravan was a musical journey through the lands of Hindustani
folk, the blues, jazz and East European rhapsody. It was the
story of an heiress running for her life and finding refuge in a
gypsy camp, which gave the composer just the excuse he needed
to conjure up the folksy *'Goriya kahan tera des re'* and *'Chadhti
jawani meri chaal mastani'*, the unbridled energy of which reflected
the spirit of the gypsy tribe.

In startling contrast to the folk influence of these two numbers, '*Piya tu ab toh aaja*' became the quintessential Pancham–Asha duet with its urban cabaret theme. Based on the hexatonic blues scale, this song was like a scream against traditionalism. It was a no-holds-barred expression of sultry, carnal longing. The number starts off on a slow metre with the tenor sax, Charanjit Singh's bass guitar and Burjor Lord's vibraphone, while piano keys convey the sound of a clock striking twelve. It picks up pace abruptly, and the metre of the song – with keyboards by Kersi Lord and George Fernandes's trumpet – has no resemblance to the intro: a signature element in quite a few Pancham compositions.

By Asha Bhonsle's own admission, '*Daiya yeh main kahan aa phasi*' – one of the less popular tracks of *Caravan*, featured in a scene where the heroine's tormentors come searching for her while a nautanki is on – is one of the most difficult songs she has ever sung. She had also complained jokingly to Pancham that he always reserved the toughest for her, something that dancer Sitara Devi echoed to Asha Bhonsle as well.

It was while Pancham stood beside director Nasir Husain, watching the shot construction for the song – hens flying around, a man tumbling off a chair, people scampering about – that he suddenly found the idea for the arrangement. This was a greenfield project for Pancham, and one can hear claps, boot thumping, etc., contributing to the jamming, a sound that he would reproduce in *Satte Pe Satta* (1982), Raj N. Sippy's version of Stanley Donen's film *Seven Brides for Seven Brothers* (1954).

Surprisingly, the movie had only one song by Kishore Kumar, '*Hum toh hai rahi dil ke*' – the first time that Kishore lent his voice to Jeetendra. An air horn and cycle bells were used in the interlude as the hero made his way down the road in his gaudily painted lorry, 'Toofan Mail'.

Asha Bhonsle had another solo, *'Ab jo mile hain toh'*, the Hindi version of *'Jabo ki jabo na'*. The innovative chord structure and bossa nova apart, the highlight of the number was Asha singing for two actresses in succession, the vamp and the heroine, and in the process modulating her voice to express the different roles. Little wonder that this song has often matched *'Piya tu ab toh aaja'* in popularity, at least with musicians, and was quoted by Pancham as one of his favourites.

While her little sister was shining in her new professional partnership with RD, Lata Mangeshkar added a couple of feathers to her tiara with *'Dilbar dil se pyare'*, a song that Pancham would normally have reserved for Asha. The intro to this sultry gypsy-ish song had a Pancham special – he created a new sound by striking wood on the brass lining of the timpani. He also made liberal use of the rabab in the song. This composition later featured in Aditya Bhattacharya's *Raakh* (1990), and the tune was re-engineered and used in the Tamil film *Badshah* (1995) starring Rajinikanth and Nagma.

Lata's duet with Mohammad Rafi, *'Kitna pyara wada hai'* – the refrain of which would later become the tune for the line *'Jaane tu ya jaane na'* in the song *'Tera mujhse hai pehle ka nata koi'*, from the film *Aa Gale Lag Jaa* (1973) – was one of the sweetest melodies of its time. The manner in which the tune goes high in the antara and the skill with which Lata and Rafi injected the right quantum of feeling to the song made it an exquisite number. Nasir did try to reproduce a similar sequence in *Hum Kisise Kum Naheen* (1977) half a decade later with the Asha–Kishore duet *'Humko to yara teri yari'*, which was racier and sounded more matter-of-fact and less romantic in contrast. The difference in the texture of the two songs may have been deliberate. In *Hum Kisise Kum Naheen*, Rishi was not in love with Kaajal Kiran; she was a mere conduit for a more serious business.

Following the not-so-successful *Baharon Ke Sapne* and *Pyar*

Ka Mausam, insiders had reportedly tried to dissuade Nasir from using Pancham for his forthcoming film. Nasir felt otherwise, and this time, in spite of a script whose beginning is remarkably similar to *Teesri Manzil* and a title music that bore a faint semblance to Maurice Jarre's opening track in *Lawrence of Arabia, Caravan* rocked.

Pancham, in an interview to the magazine *Showtime,* in July 1992, said: 'Nasir Husain had to only narrate the screenplay for me to get charged. I used to get the sort of vibrations that made me compose songs immediately. That's how he inspired me to compose songs for *Caravan* – extempore – when actually I was in no mood to compose.'

In the same year as *Caravan,* director Rajendra Bhatia produced and directed *Paraya Dhan* (1971), setting the story in the Kulu Valley in Himachal Pradesh. The locale was perfect for Pancham to wave his wand and the film had, among others, the saccharine-sweet Lata–Kishore duet *'Tu pyar tu preet'* and the Apache-style *'Aaj unse pehli mulaqaat hogi'* solo by Kishore Kumar. Pancham had previously used the tune as a background score for the boy-meets-girl situation in *Pyar Ka Mausam* and had also repeated the tune in the background of *Caravan. 'Holi re holi',* Pancham's second 'holi' composition after *'Aaj na chhodenge' (Kati Patang)* was dyed with variegated rhythms.

7

Pancham, his fans lament, often gave away his best tunes to films which were commercially disastrous. S.S. Balan's *Lakhon Mein Ek* (1971) was one of many such.

The film, a remake of the Tamil movie *Edir Neechal* starring comedian Nagesh, marked the return of the Mahmood–RD combination after a gap of three years. Never mind the juvenility of the film, it had two of Pancham's best compositions: *'Chanda o chanda'*, a lullaby sung as a solo by Lata Mangeshkar and as a duet where Lata joins Kishore Kumar, perhaps a far cry from the actual structure of a lullaby, but haunting nevertheless; and *'Jogi o jogi'*, another Kishore–Lata duet, a mix of swing, R&B, and jazz. This song had to be played at a higher speed while being picturized as it mandated that the final song would be presented in slow motion on the screen as a dream sequence – possibly the first technical innovation of its kind in Indian cinema and music. According to Mahmood, actress Radha Saluja ran up a fever in her anxiety to synchronize the lip movement for the song.

This film also saw Pancham using a medley as he had done successfully in *Waris* (1969). And like in the medley in *Waris*, where he used songs from *Junglee, Brahmachari* and *An Evening in Paris*, among others, here too he employed songs composed by other music directors. Unlike most composers who would stick to their own compositions in an attempt to further publicize them, Pancham had no qualms in using songs by other composers as part of his medley.

Lakhon Mein Ek is rumoured to have marked the official separation of son and father in the music room. Apparently, RD was recording with Basu Chakravarty and Manohari Singh in Madras, but SD wanted the duo back for his recording for Vijay Anand's *Tere Mere Sapne* (1972). When interviewed for this book, Manohari Singh commented that the resultant delay of one shift made stickler-for-time SD furious enough to shift to a different set of assistants and arrangers – Arun Podwal, Anil Mohile and Gagan Chauhan. However, Basu Chakravarty, Manohari Singh and Bhupendra continued playing for him.

Pancham had more music to boast about in 1971, with *Mela* – Prakash Mehra's retelling of Nitin Bose's *Ganga Jumna* (1961) – in which the scintillating music was kept essentially rural to match the surroundings. S.M. Sagar's *Adhikar* (1971) is now remembered for the Kishore–Asha duet '*Koi mane ya na mane*' and the Rafi–Asha duet '*Rekha o Rekha*', both of which were received well by music lovers. *Hungama* (1971) and *Pyar Ki Kahani* (1971) had mediocre music by Pancham's standards. Films like *Paraya Dhan*, *Pyar Ki Kahani* and *Adhikar* started out with the disadvantage of relatively unknown male leads: Rakesh Roshan, Amitabh Bachchan (pre-*Zanjeer*) and Deb Mukherjee, respectively.

Hulchul (1971) saw Zeenat Aman and Kabir Bedi make their Hindi film debuts. Directed by O.P. Ralhan, the film is about a simpleton who accidentally overhears a murder plan. Many suspects and surreptitious investigations later, the film ends with guffaws of laughter in a courtroom. The film had no songs, a novelty for its time, just a catchy title track with vocals by Bhupendra (uncredited) and Asha Bhonsle that was played at different pitches throughout the movie. *Hulchul* had a sequence that was seven minutes and forty-five seconds long, showcasing dance forms from across the world, and Pancham coloured it with instrumental music, lots of chorus and the occasional scatting.

A major characteristic demonstrated by Pancham in the beginning of the 1970s was splitting the orchestra to allow each section its space through crisp solo pieces, yet retaining control of the overall progression. He was also experimenting with differential metering within the same track – slow in the intro and fast in the mukhra or a shift in rhythm patterns even within the mukhra. Before Pancham, background sound in films (apart from Salil Chowdhury and Shankar–Jaikishan's films) was almost an extension of the music used in plays, led by the sitar, the dholak and the tabla, and the occasional piano, vibraphone and percussions. The string section used to be a chorus of violins. Brass and guitar were mere back-ups. The other extreme in orchestration was blatant copying of Western melodies and too much clutter. However, Pancham moderated, blended, mixed and patented. He was on fire. Unstoppable.

8

Inexpensive Grass, Free Love

Writer–reporter Patrick Marnham's *Road to Katmandu* traces the author's journey from Turkey to Nepal as the landscape morphs from the beautiful European valleys to barren mountains, treading the Indus plains all the way up to the hilly temple town. Along the jaunty path are seen weirdly dressed men and women, some ambling in dissolving and reassembling clusters, some riding vehicles, and others on horseback. The provisions of these backpacking youngsters included very little outside of their ever-bulging quota of pot. And their guitars.

Marnham's wasn't a one-off journey. It is a detailed study into the route followed, in the 1960s and the 1970s, by a generation of Americans known as hippies. The trail (later branded the Hippie Trail) would start from Delhi airport and would wind its way through Barauni (Bihar) to the Promised Land of Kathmandu. After a satisfying break (in more ways than known), the hippies would drift to destinations like Goa and Varanasi and Delhi, avoiding Calcutta and Bombay for reasons only they knew. They treaded the same path that Maharishi Mahesh Yogi and a Ravi Shankar-inspired Beatles had walked, recalls Susmit Bose, a singer and former hippie.

Being a virtually toll-free market for ganja, Kathmandu was the obvious hippie haven. The hippies' cavalier lifestyle and outlandish appearance jarred against the tranquillity of the terrain, yet interestingly blended into it. The expanse of the Himalayas not only accepted the contrast but also embraced these troubled children.

One such child was timid Jasbir (an unusual name for a girl of non-Sikh parentage). Spooked by images of domestic violence and her parents' impending divorce, hers was a classic case study of a child deprived of stability and self-confidence.

Dev Anand, in his autobiography *Romancing with Life*, reminisces about meeting an Indian girl named Jasbir/Janice in the Bakery, Kathmandu, an (in)famous hippie den. The girl had travelled the hippie trail all the way from Montreal to Kathmandu in search of peace in the mystic East, seeking solace in marijuana, hashish, LSD and the companionship of like-minded parvenus.

It was a story for a potentially great film.

Dev Anand brought Jasbir's story to the celluloid screen in *Hare Rama Hare Krishna* (1971). It would give India its first pin-up icon. Zeenat Aman, having made her debut in O.P. Ralhan's *Hulchul*, would become a star, courtesy the songs in the film – '*Dum maro dum*' and '*I love you*'.

Singer Usha Uthup remembers: 'The Navketan unit, including Dev Anand and R.D. Burman, had come to listen to me singing at the Oberoi, Delhi, in 1969. After the show, Dev Anand asked whether I would like to sing in his forthcoming film *Hare Rama Hare Krishna*. I was all of twenty-one and naturally excited. The song "*Dum maro dum*" was conceived and we went into major

rehearsals. It was to be [sung] as a duet between me and Lata
Mangeshkar, with me singing for the bad girl and Lata-ji for
the good girl.'

Surprisingly then, '*Dum maro dum*' ended up as an Asha
Bhonsle solo.

'Pancham expressed regret, but with the trademark quote,
"*Yaar, kuch kartein hain*", added that he had another song in
mind for me,' Usha carries on.

Pancham kept his promise to Usha with '*I love you*' which was
designed as a duet with Asha Bhonsle singing for Zeenat and
Usha Uthup for another girl in the gang.

How would '*Dum maro dum*' have sounded with Lata
Mangeshkar's trifle shrill voice and Usha Uthup's canyonish
contrast? Post the decision to turn it into an Asha solo,
Pancham probably had to colour the song differently as the
voices of Lata and Asha are very different. An Asha Bhonsle
track like '*Dum maro dum*' had to have a blend of sultriness and
wildness. Recorded in a number of versions and used in bits and
pieces in the film, the song became the anthem of the hippie
generation with its psychedelic view of life and anti-establishment
convictions.

In the song, through the smoky haze, one makes out silhouettes
of youngsters in a swagger ... and the only sober man in the
den has his mouth pursed and head disapprovingly cocked to
one side.

It is interesting that despite the song's volcanic popularity,
Dev Anand kept just one stanza in the film when it was first
used in the film. '*Dum maro dum*' is followed immediately after
by the Kishore solo '*Dekho o deewano*'. 'Using both the stanzas
might have diluted the brother's entry as the second one was
repetitive,' says he. The Long Play record, however, carries both
the stanzas and has classified the two songs as discrete tracks.

How was the song constructed? In a discussion on television

between Pancham and lyricist Anand Bakshi, the duo casually remarked that it just happened. It was not a surprise that music came so easily to Pancham. Yet, his inability to articulate in public on the 'hows' and the 'whats' of this spontaneity was his drawback because being able to trumpet one's achievement is vital for success in every business.

The song had a very catchy prelude on the lead guitar, played, once again, using the minor chords by Bhupendra. The guitar riffs, the wah pedal, Charanjit Singh's transicord and the back-up vocals were the foreplay to the wild act that followed. Ramesh Iyer adds: 'This song saw Pancham use elements of soul rhythm for the first time in his career and quite possibly in Hindi film music.'

'I love you', the Asha–Usha duet, was like an 'extra cheese' version of 'Dum maro dum'. Asha held her own with the treble, and Usha resonated an octave lower. Front-ended with an outdoor picturization presenting downtown Kathmandu by night, Pancham allows Usha Uthup to take over the extended tailpiece of the track as it picks up speed and shifts a note higher to 'We go a l'il faster man'. 'I love you' was, in chronicled memory, the first-ever bilingual song in Hindi cinema.

The contrast in styles between Usha and Asha shattered the Indian paradigm that female singers had to have a sharp and shrill voice. With singers like Khursheed Bano migrating to Pakistan during the partition, the idea of women singing light music with a baritone was inconceivable in post-independence India. Till Usha Uthup dared to change the norm. She introduced not only the Western bass but also the correct intonation of English words without the fake accent. For all their talent, the first family of female singers in India were lacking in that particular department. To hear 'I love you' blaring over loudspeakers in metros and small towns close on the heels of 'Dum maro dum' was a part of growing up in the 1970s.

Lata Mangeshkar as the voice of the good girl in the first flush of womanhood was accompanied by Kishore Kumar in the delectable '*Kanchi re Kanchi re*'. '*O re ghunghroo kaa bole re*', a Lata solo, was shot with half the population of Bhaktapur gathered around to watch Mumtaz as she danced to the tune for three days, the duration of the shooting. Apart from the tabla and mridangam, a new percussion sound was heard in the song for the first time in Hindi film music. Until then, it used to be the duggi, but with these two songs, Ranjit Gazmer and his madal joined RD's coterie. Pancham aptly named the Darjeeling boy Kancha, and he still loves to be addressed that way. Ranjit 'Kancha' Gazmer gave the composer a new sound that he used in many compositions that followed. Kancha too is an independent music director, having scored music for over a hundred Nepali films.

The recorded version of '*Kanchi re Kanchi*' starts with Kishore Kumar humming. However, Dev Anand preferred to film it otherwise and the song appeared in the film without the humming. Pancham later said that this was one of the tunes that came to him in his sleep, almost in a dream.

The song '*Phoolon ka taron ka*' was Pancham's first duet with Lata Mangeshkar. He lent his voice to Kishore Sahu, an actor and director, albeit only for two lines, while Lata brilliantly modulated her own to sound like a ten-year-old boy, Master Satyajit. A brother–sister reunion makes for a very unusual climax. But here it was with the adult version of '*Phoolon ka taron ka*' sung by Kishore Kumar, with Bhupendra and Charanjit Singh on twelve-string guitars, and profound lyrics by Anand Bakshi: '*Jeevan ke dukhon se yun darte nahin hain/ Aise bach ke sach se guzarte nahin hain/ Sukh ki hai chah toh, dukh bhi sehna hai*'.

Though Pancham would at times get irritated by Bakshi trying to impose his tunes on Pancham's, he also complimented Anand Bakshi as a super lyricist in one of his interviews.

The job of composing for *Hare Rama Hare Krishna* came to Pancham after the theme failed to appeal to his father. According to Dev Anand, 'Dada Burman did not like the theme of hippies and brother–sister relationships. Pancham was given the opportunity and he grabbed it. He completed the tunes of this film in two weeks flat. With this film, Pancham's career really took off.'

Apparently, Dev Anand had first offered Jasbir's role to Zaheeda, his heroine in the film *Gambler* (1971), but she turned him down. Her decision won her more public gratitude than any popularity she might have gained had she accepted the offer. Zeenat Aman, Miss Asia Pacific International 1970, revolutionized the image of the female lead from the ample-hipped, delicate lady to the svelte, slim and coolly urban woman who was bold enough to walk the ramp in thigh-length haute couture. She became the first-ever reigning fashion queen to sashay into Bombay filmdom and changed how the Hindi film heroine would be perceived for all times to come.

As far as the music was concerned, the Navketan baton had passed safely from father to son.

2

Generation gaps have always existed in society, but the noisy clutter of joint families had somehow helped bridge them over the years. However, the West, with its bra burning, its call for more power to the youth, flower power and the Beatles, brought out the hidden fractures in Indian society as well. Having someone to watch and imitate can have a huge impact on a generation, and that is what youngsters in India found in the hippies and Woodstockers. A new-found aggressive disdain for authority, coupled with the idealism of youth, resulted in some radical student and youth movements in the political arena; the haze of the ganja smoke sought to hide the disillusionment that came in the wake of idealism. With so much happening, the usually insular world of Hindi cinema, though steering clear of any ideological moorings, found it hard not to reflect the angst of the young, in the choice of clothes, in the kind of music they preferred and in their choice of partners.

Hare Rama Hare Krishna and *Jawani Diwani* were two such films. They were stories of the frustration of youth wanting to be heard. While *Hare Rama Hare Krishna* depicted youth seeking refuge in drugs, *Jawani Diwani*, a more light-hearted and popcorn-ish look at the same situation, advocated head-on confrontation. Pancham's music captured the difference. It was aptly intense in the former and feather-light and peppy in the latter. The songs of *Jawani Diwani* were easy on the lips, easy to move with. The film had copious helpings of slapstick comedy, college campus practical jokes, canteen cacophony and classroom paper-planes. The music, likewise, included gibberish lyrics, Tarzan screams, falsetto notes, tumba beats, shakers, rhythms – elements that Pancham introduced into Hindi film music, sparing not a thought for tradition.

In the Asha–Kishore duet '*Nahin nahin abhi nahin*', for example, Pancham used the structure of Brazilian blues. This is more apparent in the notes of the Bengali Puja version sung by Asha Bhonsle, '*Chokhe chokhe kotha bolo*'. What set the song apart at the time was the major scale shift in the third stanza and the application of deep bass lines.

The use of the bass guitar in films like *Hare Rama Hare Krishna* and *Jawani Diwani* caught the fancy of a young undergrad student. 'Someday, I need to play for this guy,' thought the boy, then pursuing electronics engineering at Sardar Patel College, Bombay. 'Tuning in to Radio Ceylon, I could toggle between the brothers Hameed Sayani and Ameen Sayani by shifting the radio knob by one millimetre as the two shortwaves were barely twenty-five metres apart. Pancham's music surprised me. I couldn't help marvelling at how bass guitar had found its way into Hindi music,' he recollects. This youngster could have landed meaty corporate jobs on passing out in 1975, but he chose a different path.

He was Ramesh N. Iyer.

'Pre-Pancham we only saw double bass being used. "Boss" [as Iyer refers to Pancham] made a big difference with electric bass guitar,' says he, at his residence in Kandivali, Mumbai. Agrees Amit Kumar: 'Pancham used the electric bass guitar for the first time, shifting from double bass. It was fresh and still is today.'

The most celebrated hit from *Jawani Diwani* was '*Jaan-e-jaan dhoondta phir raha*', a minor chord-based composition with soul-style strumming and a rapid bongo beat. The strength of the number lay in its harmony, which, unlike most harmonies in Hindi film songs, was not left to the chorus, but was performed by the lead singers Kishore Kumar and Asha Bhonsle. Normally, the harmony in Hindi film songs was used for colouring at critical points, but here, the harmony was almost like a parallel tune. Furthermore, the change of octave, with Asha Bhonsle pulling off an Usha Uthup, imparted to the song a flavour very different from what Pancham had composed before. It was neither folk, nor rock 'n' roll, nor Latino; it was an Indian melody wrapped in a very Western shell. Pancham also used the echolite for the English flute echoes in the song.

'*Samne yeh kaun aaya*' found RD clubbing genres – marrying a calypso–Latino tune with a rhythm on a pedal matka. This rather unconventional instrument, played by Vijay Indorkar, was reused later, notably in the songs '*Arre kaise mitti ke maadho*' (*Imaan*, 1974) and '*Muttu kudi kawadi hada*' (*Do Phool*, 1974).

An introductory background piece used in a discotheque, just before '*Samne yeh kaun aaya*', saw a medley of musical flavours – continental, jazz, Indian, Latino, etc. The base instrument holding the melody together was the transicord. With a constant echo factor, the sound has a tranquil tone that tempts the listener to linger. It is almost a visible sound, a resonance that creates images in the mind's eye.

Jawani Diwani cemented a lifelong friendship between Pancham, Ramesh Behl and Randhir Kapoor. 'Pancham and I had a common friend in Ramesh Behl,' says Randhir Kapoor. 'All of us were in love at that time,' Madhu (Bubbles) Behl, Randhir's aunt, reminisces. 'Ramesh and I were newly-weds. Daboo [Randhir] and Babita were just married after wriggling out of parental pressures; Jaya was deep into her courtship with Amit [Amitabh Bachchan]. Pancham too had left his tough marriage behind and was single again.'

RD's best music came when he was in great spirits. He admitted that he needed to be in a good mood, even for composing songs that conveyed the saddest thoughts. The prevailing sense of freedom would then, undoubtedly, have inspired him to create music of such class!

Jawani Diwani may well have been a wedding gift for Behl's new bride Madhu. '"This song will live even after me," my husband has prophesied about *"Jaan-e-jaan"*,' she recalls.

3

Dil Diwana (1974), Ramesh Behl's next film, predictably had Randhir in the lead and music by Pancham. Once again, RD brought in the harmony, but with a difference in the song '*Ja re ja bewafa*'. The defining feature of the harmony was the use of the mukhra as the harmony for the antara and vice versa. Pancham may have been inspired by Salil Chowdhury's technique. Pancham knew many of Chowdhury's songs by heart, even though he maintained his own distinct style at all times.

Another Asha–Kishore duet '*Kisise dosti kar lo*', replete with flamenco-style guitaring and castanet beats in the intro, has a teasing essence to it, portrayed on the screen by a cocky, self-assured hero romancing actress Komal. The mood is carried on in the third Asha–Kishore duet *'Mujhko mohabbat mein dhoka toh na doge'*, picturized on an audaciously two-timing Randhir. This contrasted with the broken-hearted Kishore solo *'Sun Nita'*, which has the spirit of another Kishore solo *'Ye dard bhara afsana'* from *Shreeman Funtoosh* scored by L-P.

Despite the peppy musical score, *Dil Diwana* fared badly at the box office. Neither did it have a proper storyline, nor any direction. Also, with *Jawani Diwani*, Ramesh Behl had raised the audience's expectations, and *Dil Diwana* simply failed to match the zaniness of its predecessor.

4

The phrase *'Hee haa khichi khichi'* holds little meaning; even less so when it happens to be a greeting between two persons.

Pancham and Mahmood exchanged this rather unconventional pleasantry a number of times in the early 1970s while they worked together on two projects – Apsi Irani's directorial venture *Garam Masala* (1972) and N.C. Sippy's *Bombay to Goa*.

It is hard to say if the audiences were convinced by a lanky Amitabh Bachchan as an all-in-one fight master called Robert Taylor who wears a patch on his left eye in the movie *Garam Masala*. The heroine of the film, who is also Amitabh's student in it, is called Garam Masala. In a role similar to the one in *Chhote Nawab*, Mahmood plays a prince with a low IQ, only to be rescued by the leading lady, Aruna Irani.

Three songs from the film, showcasing some of the best composed by Pancham for Asha Bhonsle, featured on three different actresses – Hema Malini, Aruna Irani and Bindu – went without critical or popular acclaim at the time.

'*Haye re na maro*', a gypsy, blues-style number with a lot of passing notes, is supposed to represent pain, but is done in an exotic rather than maudlin manner, full of verve and panache, representative of the tenacity of gypsies. The second of the solos, '*Raja bana mera chhaila kaisa*', is an interesting concoction of a series of notes coupled with a lilting beat. The mukhra dramatically ends in Teevra Ma, almost a climactic move, generating a feeling of anxiousness during the shift-over.

The final song, '*Tum jaison ko*', is a reworked version of the chase music of *Jewel Thief.* The tune is also used in the title of *Garam Masala*, with Pancham warbling his way through with the sound of gunshots and hammer-hitting-stone thrown in for good effect. The tune starts with major notes and then 'caves' down into the blues. This song makes guitarists Ramesh Iyer and Soumitra Chatterjee's eyes light up. 'This is blues. This is Pancham making magic with blues.'

Someday, this number – with its brass mix, intoxicating rhythm, rousing tune and inspired rendition by Asha – may be cited as the coming together of Pancham's Western music-inspired ideas. In the 1970s, Hindi popular music hardly found a place in people's drawing rooms, thereby denying it the opportunity to be evaluated. Apart from being Pancham's ode to the blues, this song with the flood of brass, percussion and jazz was Pancham's tribute to his inspiration, Henry Mancini.

All the three songs in *Garam Masala* are used in dance sequences and are fast paced, but at the same time, they exude a composure that is indicative of the grasp Pancham had acquired over composing foot-tapping numbers without sounding 'noisy'.

In the 1970s, normally, the music of a film reached the audience only if the producer managed to get the film past the gates and into the theatres. A big banner and a famous lead pair were critical to enticing the audience, and *Garam Masala*, like some other Pancham films, failed here. The lead pair of Mahmood and Aruna Irani wasn't about to sell in a hurry. Had Apsi Irani thrown in a couple of songs by a strong male singer like Kishore Kumar, the film might have fared better.

But then, Kishore had to go abroad around that time, making the film fraternity wait for him to return and complete the schedules. Before embarking on his trip, he completed the recording of just one track, that too on being persuaded by Madan Mohan.

5

All through the 1960s, up till the early 1970s, Mahmood was considered Hindi filmdom's counterpart to ace Tamil comedian Nagesh, and starred in many remakes of successful Tamil films – the quixotic wannabe moviemaker in *Pyar Kiye Jaa*, the triple-combo in *Humjoli*, the lonely star in *Main Sundar Hoon*, the hapless errand boy in *Laakhon Mein Ek* . . .

And then there was *Bombay to Goa*. With Mahmood and his brother Anwar Ali in the lead, this was designed to be just like the Tamil original – *Madras to Pondicherry* – hilarious, action-packed and full of non-stop, clean fun. Like *Garam Masala*, this film too had Aruna Irani as the heroine. And Amitabh Bachchan, the long-legged karate instructor of *Garam Masala*, was the hero. Incidentally, Mahmood had first offered the role to Rajiv Gandhi, son of the then prime minister of India, Indira Gandhi. Rajiv refused. Here, one is tempted to say that cinema's loss was politics' gain, but the fact remains that Rajiv's decision influenced the course of Hindi films too. This was probably Amitabh Bachchan's only solo hit in the first four years of his career and probably helped him stay afloat till *Zanjeer* (1973) turned the tide.

However, more than the hero and the heroine, it is the array of hilarious cameos that made the film such fun to watch. A girl fleeing her captors, a corpulent family who need to gag their son's mouth at all times to prevent him from devouring anything that resembles food, a sleepwalker, a sanyasin with locks of hair that are tougher than metal, a purse-snatcher who is tied to the bumper of a bus as punishment – it was a picnic all through the drive down the coast. On one of its innumerable unscheduled halts, Kishore Kumar (playing himself) boards the MP Travels bus (name probably derived from Mahmood Productions) because his car has broken down on the highway. As can be expected, he gets all the passengers to jive with him to his 'new' song, another one of Pancham's characteristic songlets, *'Bombay Goa, Bom-Bombay Goa'*.

Bombay to Goa had popular songs like Kishore Kumar's peppy number *'Dekha na hai re'*, a favourite with the remix brigade these days, which was also the second Kishore Kumar solo that Pancham composed for Amitabh Bachchan after *'Roop yeh tera jisne banaya'* for S.S. Balan's *Sanjog* (1972). Singer Amit Kumar, then nineteen years old, was present at the recording and Mahmood introduced the words *'Dole dole dole'* to mark his presence. 'Dole' was Mahmood's nickname for Amit. Shooting this high-energy number was rather tricky for Amitabh as he was expected to prance in and out of the bus, swing from poles and jump onto the roof. Nevertheless, the energy of the song has made it the default song on any long drive. The song *'Tum meri zindagi mein'*, Pancham's second attempt at Indianizing the theme from Chaplin's *Limelight,* was not featured in the film.

The deft screenplay tided over some of the obvious constraints such as having too many faces in a frame and multiple characters in a crammed bus, as well as the difficulty in orchestrating several subplots. The fact that the bus driver and conductor were named Rajesh and Khanna respectively, spoke volumes about the popularity of Rajesh Khanna at the time.

The music of the opening sequence in the film was a brass-based track with a bossa nova rhythm pattern.

Bombay to Goa was important for both Pancham and Amitabh Bachchan for one special reason – a scene which was shot in the restaurant of Caesar Palace Hotel. This hotel was significant in Pancham's personal and professional life.

Recalls Sachin Bhowmick, 'In the late 1960s, I think just after *Aradhana*, when we were at a party, Rita, Pancham's wife, abruptly left on her own in a car. Shakti Samanta asked me to follow her to see if she was okay. I saw (that) she had safely parked her car at the house. When I entered the house, she saw me and started crying. The reason cited was that people at the party were praising S.D. Burman and were commenting how Meera was like a backbone to SD. That had provoked jealousy in her. She started drinking again. When Pancham reached home, he found that Rita had broken his parents' photograph. Pancham got wild at this and left (home).'

This incident forced Pancham to move out of Sur Mandir and check into Room 304 of Caesar Palace Hotel where he lived for the next two years. Some of his best compositions bloomed in this suite which can be said to stand as a testament to his shattered personal life.

'Rita stayed at Sur Mandir till the divorce came through in 1973,' recalls Samir Chowdhury, younger brother of Salil Chowdhury.

'Rita insisted on a large sum of money for the divorce. At the behest of Meera Boudi, overnight, the 15th Cross house was sold as a distress sale by getting Pancham to sign up for the sale. Rita asked for three lakhs in black. Pancham had one lakh and Asha-ji pitched in with two lakhs. And the divorce was through with mutual consent,' reveals Sachin Bhowmick.

For a nightclub sequence in the film, shot at the restaurant of Caesar Palace, Pancham and Mahmood roped in Usha Iyer to sing live. Usha belted out her favourites, which included *'Listen to the pouring rain'*, *'Temptation'*, *'Fever'* and *'It's all right with me'*, in quick succession. The popular Goan song *'I married a female wrestler'* was Pancham's selection. To avoid infringing upon copyright, Usha took liberty with the lyrics and added her own, changing the subject from 'love' to 'hate' in *Fever* and modifying 'charming face' to 'lovely face' in *'It's all right with me'*.

The numbers were remodelled on rhythm patterns familiar to those who have followed Pancham's music. *'Listen to the falling rain'*, a Jose Feliciano original, was given a bossa nova rhythm. *'Temptation'* (original music score by Nacio Herb Brown and lyrics by Arthur Freed, sung first by Bing Crosby in the film *Going Hollywood* in 1933, and popularized by Perry Como) had a soul-style rhythm guitar backbone. *'I married a female wrestler'* had pronounced bongo beats and in *'Fever'* (original by Little Willie John, popularized by Peggy Lee in the late 1950s) the bass guitar played notes on the blues' scale.

The nightclub sequence climaxed in a fight between Amitabh Bachchan and Shatrughan Sinha. The angle of Jal Mistry's camera as it focused on Amitabh's long legs made him look taller than his 188-cm frame. It is now part of Bombay filmdom folklore that it was this fight sequence that led him to the role of Vijay in Prakash Mehra's *Zanjeer*, the film that made him the Angry Young Man of Indian cinema.

Pancham found inspiration in Usha Uthup's version of *'Temptation'* for two compositions which followed soon after. One is the Kishore Kumar solo *'Jaan-e-jaana jao kal phir aana'* for Prakash Mehra's *Samadhi* (1972), where the twin guitar accompaniment created the mood for the road song. The other was for a not-so-popular Asha Bhonsle solo *'Main haseen hun'* picturized on Neetu Singh in the film *Rickshawala* (1973), where the mood of the song changes from chirpy to pensive as the transience of youth unfolds on the stage.

Pancham had plans to do a rock album with Usha titled *Pancham and Usha*. But, fate, as always, had other plans. The album was never recorded.

6

Samadhi marked the beginning of Pancham's second innings with Dharmendra, almost seven years after he had composed for *Chandan Ka Palna*. The film also found Pancham working with director Prakash Mehra for the second time.

Despite the sepulchral title, the film's music pulsated with vigour. Pancham turned the Asha–Lata pair inside out, giving Asha the soulful '*Jab tak rahe tan mein jiya*' and Lata the raunchier '*Bangle ke peeche*' with its interesting beats

Dharmendra was also the leading man for RD's first diamond jubilee hit, *Yaadon Ki Baaraat*. It had a run of over 100 weeks in Madras.

created by using sticks on leather, with the central rhythm maintained by Devichand Chauhan. Thirty years later, this Pancham–Lata classic was released as a remix '*Kaanta laga*' but without the duggi, tabla and other percussions. Needless to say, it provided a skimpily dressed Shefali Zariwala her five minutes of fame and set the cash registers ringing for the audio company.

Samadhi had another experimental song '*Maine dekha hai ek sapna*' where the notes, in the Dha-Ni-Dha-Pa-Dha formation, change in quick succession. This formation is also used in the antara of the song, with the scale shifted by two notes. 'O *yaara yaara*', an Asha Bhonsle solo, stuck close to the tradition of gypsy songs with a very distinct Arabic tune and exposition – another genre in which Pancham was honing his skills. The

1970s saw him compose quite a few such numbers inspired by
the Arabian style of music.

Pancham and Prakash Mehra teamed up again for *Khalifa* (1976). 'Anand Bakshi
sahab was originally supposed to write the lyrics for *Khalifa*. But then Daboo,
who had worked with Prakash Mehra in *Haath Ki Safaai*, recommended me,'
recounted lyricist Gulshan Bawra to us in what was to be one of his last
interviews before his death in August 2009. 'Pancham wasn't quite convinced
till I wrote to the metre of one of his compositions, "*Dekh ke tujh ko dil ne
kaha*", for the film. And we hit it off.'

Pancham and Dharmendra worked in three films in 1972, all
major hits, of which *Seeta Aur Geeta* set the box office rocking.
Strength of a Woman is what the film could well have been
named. The heroine bests a greedy, mean woman while the men
play cheerleaders on the fringes. Ramesh Sippy called it *Seeta
Aur Geeta* (1972). Loosely based on *The Prince and the Pauper* –
with scriptwriters Salim–Javed cleverly reworking the Dilip
Kumar hit *Ram Aur Shyam* (1968) – it reinforced Sippy's
credentials as an entertainer after his debut success in *Andaaz*
(1971). The risk he took by using Pancham in *Seeta Aur Geeta*
despite Shankar–Jaikishan's success in *Andaaz* paid off well. The
film had bubbly performances by Hema Malini in a double role,
Dharmendra playing a smart aleck Bambaiya acrobat and Sanjeev
Kumar as the responsible doctor.

The kokiro, a wind instrument – one of the more uncommon
ones that Pancham used earlier in 'Gulabi aankhen' in *The
Train* – was heard in the Asha–Kishore duet 'Hawa ke saath
saath'. Pancham experimented with Manna Dey as the voice of
Dharmendra in songs such as 'Zindagi hai khel' where he is
performing tricks on the street and 'Abhi toh haath mein' where
the hero walks down Marine Drive in a drunken daze while
balancing a bottle on his palm.

Ramesh Sippy, Prakash Mehra, Hrishikesh Mukherjee, Shakti Samanta, Dharmendra, Rajesh Khanna, Mahmood – in the early 1970s, Pancham had the good sense to stay close to well-known actors and producer–director combinations. To this list, he added Raj Khosla when the latter signed him on for *Do Chor* (1972). It wasn't clear at the time where Pancham fitted in: the two had never worked together before, and the film didn't sound much like a musical.

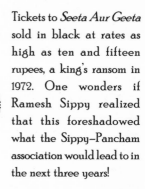

Tickets to *Seeta Aur Geeta* sold in black at rates as high as ten and fifteen rupees, a king's ransom in 1972. One wonders if Ramesh Sippy realized that this foreshadowed what the Sippy–Pancham association would lead to in the next three years!

Do Chor, directed by Padmanabh, Raj Khosla's assistant, had five jovial songs out of which four were big hits. Leading the brigade were the Kishore–Lata duets, '*Kali palak teri gori*', a song which embodied S.D. Burman's style of melody, and the very Pancham-ish '*Chahe raho duur, chahe raho paas*'. Padmanabh and Pancham collaborated again, in 1974, for Atma Ram's production *Imaan*.

7

The year 1972 was a landmark in Pancham's career – eighteen films, of which fifteen had 'hit' music. A staggering 80 per cent success rate. He would repeat this success story the following year too.

Rakhi Aur Hathkadi, Savera, Dil Ka Raja, Parchhaiyan, Rani Mera Naam and *Gomti Ke Kinare* were all otherwise nondescript films released in 1972 that were illumined by Pancham's compositions.

S.M. Sagar's *Rakhi Aur Hathkadi* had two Kishore–Asha duets which were the only highlights in an otherwise bland film which had Asha Parekh in a double role, one as the Bharatiya nari forced into prostitution and the other in her usual avatar, the tomboy. '*Achchi nahin sanam dillagi*', very loosely inspired by '*C'est la vie*' by Emerson, Lake and Palmer, was framed like a lovers' quarrel by lyricist Majrooh Sultanpuri. A series of structured notes on the guitar gave the song a structured but fragile feel.

'*Tum toh kya ho jee*' had its origins in the Puja number '*Ekti katha ami je sudhu jaani*' sung by Asha Bhonsle. This chirpy number – again in the question–answer mould – was staged as a feature in a college cultural function. The Asha Bhonsle solo '*Jiye tumhaaro laalanaa*' was based on the S.D. Burman number '*Aami soite pari na bola*'. The same tune became Rahul's last duet with Lata Mangeshkar: '*Kya bura hai kya bhala*' in Gulzar's *Libaas*, a film

Rakhi Aur Hathkadi was Pancham's second film in which Asha Bhonsle sang all the songs, seven in this case. Released a few months earlier, *Garam Masala* was the first, with five songs sung by Asha.

that was never officially released in India though it was shown in some foreign film festivals in 1991.

Sawan Kumar Tak's *Gomti Ke Kinare* saw the third of the Khan Brothers, Sameer (after Feroz and Sanjay), romancing Mumtaz. Marred by a theatrical screenplay and ordinary performances by the lead pair, the emotional saga drowned on the banks of the Gomti, and took Pancham's music with it.

In his interviews over the years, Pancham has often spoken about being addicted to the music of Quincy Jones, an Afro–American who, like our own Vanraj Bhatia, studied music under Nadia Boulanger in Paris. And in *Gomti Ke Kinare*, he composed '*Aao, aao jaan-e-jahan*' based on Jones's title track '*Old Turkey Buzzard*' in *McKenna's Gold* (1969). Pancham at times used one or two lines from songs which inspired him and built his compositions around the same. In this case, Pancham used one line and transformed a song of the Wild West into a penthouse party melody.

Structurally, this song does not have a defined mukhra or antara. A single tune is used in three separate stanzas, backed by a harmony. However, the line *'Aao jaan-e-jahan, dil ne dhoonda tumhe kahan kahan'* is used as the signature tune and works as the mukhra in the conventional sense. Interestingly, the song begins with an antara and segues into the mukhra. The harmony structure is almost like *'Ja re ja bewafa'* in *Dil Diwana* with the antara coming in during the signature tune and the signature tune being used during the antara. Here, Pancham used a chorus to sustain the feel of the party, while Asha Bhonsle and Kishore Kumar's voices were used to keep the guests grooving.

Gomti Ke Kinare was actress Meena Kumari's last film. Released in late 1972, this film did not elicit the response, box office or critical, that the more celebrated, official swansong *Pakeezah* did.

Gomti Ke Kinare had a mujra *'Aaj toh meri hasi udayi'* sung by Lata Mangeshkar. Featured on Meena Kumari, who plays a nautch girl, the song was a mix of a dulcet mukhra, and an antara where the notes of the first line were in avarohana mode, a novelty in film songs. When Meena Kumari passed away in March 1972, crowds flocked to pay tribute to her, not at the nursing home where she died penniless, but in cinema halls where *Pakeezah* was running since it was widely, but incorrectly, believed to be her last film. Thus the audiences lost out on a beautiful song too, the last one to be lip-synced to by Meena Kumari, which could have matched the likes of *'Chalte chalte'* and *'Mausam hai aashiqana'* in popularity.

8

Meanwhile, the Rajesh Khanna juggernaut rolled on with three Kaka–Pancham films in 1972 – *Apna Desh, Shehzada* and *Mere Jeevan Saathi.*

Producer Surinder Kapoor, actor Anil Kapoor's father, may have been right if he ever felt that *Shehzada* – which was dedicated to actress Geeta Bali – did not have exceptional music. For some reason, Pancham sounded more like some of his contemporary composers in this film. Other than the title music, parts of the background music and the two Kishore–Lata duets '*Na jaiyo*' and '*Rimjhim rimjhim dekho*', the film lacked Pancham's trademark sounds. The demands on RD to create a rural Punjabi soundtrack may have cut into his creative space.

Actor M.G. Ramachandran (MGR) was a brilliant strategist. He rode a propaganda vehicle and had begun capturing the electorate long before his political foes even realized what he was doing. And the public thought they were merely being entertained. They were, in reality, facilitating MGR's ascension to the chief ministerial chair. *Nam Naadu* (1969) was one such MGR 'rally' that drew thousands to the theatres. The engrossing storyline was remade as *Apna Desh* in Hindi by Jambulingam, but with dollops of melodrama. Still, it is one of Rajesh Khanna's super-hit movies.

In *Apna Desh*, Pancham the singer recorded his first song for the superstar with Asha Bhonsle. '*Duniya mein logon ko*' is known for Pancham's grunting bass and almost-impossible-to-replicate flawless breath control. Scoffed at by purists during its time and lauded by the youth of the era, this classic, with its soaring energy, has now become a cult hit and remains a party favourite.

The songs '*Kajra lagake*' and '*Sun champa sun tara*', with their dholak-based rhythm, found Pancham replicating the Laxmikant–Pyarelal style, and doing so successfully too. Pancham and

Maruti Rao often changed tack and composed as their friends Laxmikant and Pyarelal would. It was fun, and often well reciprocated by the duo, who sporadically joined Pancham during his musical sittings. The 'competition' between RD and Laxmikant–Pyarelal fed the media's starved imagination. In truth, however, the duo and Pancham had great admiration for each other and even contributed to each other's success at times. If Pyarelal Sharma helped Pancham arrange music in 'Matwali ankhon wale', Pancham allowed all his key musicians to play for L-P's 'Aa jaane ja' (Inteqam, 1969) when Pyare bhai was awestruck with Pancham's 'Aja aja'.

Kishore Kumar's solo 'Rona kabhi nahi rona' was a sombre song set to a racy rhythm that defied the tradition of sad songs which usually waddled painfully through a sea of tears. Salil Chowdhury once said in an interview that he loved to experiment and never wanted to be branded a conformist. Citing the Bengali song 'Nishidin nishidin' – 'Nis din nis din', in the Hindi version used in Annadata (1972) – he said that though the song conveyed a sad emotion, he had deliberately used a fast-paced tune. That is precisely what RD did with 'Rona kabhi nahi rona'.

In the spunky Asha Bhonsle solo 'Aja o mere raja', part inspired by the Japanese song 'Blue light Yokohama', Pancham used blues notes on the transicord in the interlude – a loop he had almost patented.

Apna Desh would end up as one of Rajesh Khanna's last box office successes. Kaka could have learnt a lesson or two from MGR on how to glide across careers using the first one as a stepping stone. But that was not to be, and the spectacular downward spiral of Khanna's career was just around the corner. Interestingly enough, the film that heralded his 'fall' remains one of Hindi cinema's finest musical achievements, a feather in the caps of both R.D. Burman and Kishore Kumar.

9

Starlit Nights

'Many girls married my photograph and some reportedly committed suicide when I got married ... Some college girls took turns to pour ice water on my forehead in a photograph when they heard that I had fever.'

Women waited for him at crossings to kiss the windowpane of his car; some of them wrote to him in blood. No star had been blessed with such frenzied adoration and love. There had been none like Rajesh Khanna.

His hits flooded the box office. He was the quintessential romantic hero – the do-gooder with generous helpings of poetic love, heartache, longing, beach-side philosophies – turning women all over the country into jelly by his mere appearance. Distributors lined up with cash advances well ahead of release even as tourist buses counted his bungalow as an unofficial halt due to popular demand.

Kaka had hit upon a style that worked and he did the sensible thing by continuing with the formula. It helped that he was working with the crème de la crème of Hindi films, be it directors like Hrishikesh Mukherjee, Raj Khosla and Shakti Samanta, or writers like Gulzar and Salim–Javed, or a clutch of composers who were at their creative best at that time. In fact, what stands out about Rajesh Khanna's reign at the top was the quality of music his films had. Some of Hindi cinema's most enduring numbers have been shot on Rajesh Khanna, and almost all belong to this phase, beginning with *Aradhana*.

With each new venture, each of Rajesh Khanna's three main composers, all in the prime of their musical careers, kept raising the bar. Pancham was miles ahead of the pack for sure, but Laxmikant–Pyarelal and Kalyanji–Anandji were peaking too. With *Sachaa Jhutha* (1970), *Safar* (1970) and *Maryada* (1971), Kalyanji–Anandji recorded some of Kishore's best songs, as did Laxmikant–Pyarelal with *Haathi Mere Saathi* (1971), *Dushman* (1972), *Mehboob Ki Mehndi* (1971), and *Daag* (1973). All were in the mood for innovating.

But Rajesh Khanna wasn't. And that is where he lost his way. Three years and a dozen or so monstrous hits later, the spell began to wear off. It did not help to choose films that had nothing to offer except good music. Khanna had begun to believe that he could carry an entire film on his lone shoulders, which made him sign films with weak plots, without reading the screenplay or verifying the directors' track record. He should have taken a step back and chosen projects thoughtfully; he was a star who could afford to be selective. When they came without the padding of a good script, the audience began to tire of the standard Khanna mannerisms. 'I hope they will still have some love to spare for me for afterwards when I need it,' he said once, at the height of his career. Futile longing. His misfortune multiplied when his flight rammed into a cliff called the 'Angry Young Man'.

It was Ravikant Nagaich's *Mere Jeevan Saathi* that exposed

the potholes developing on the road on which Kaka was running
his dream run. Despite having signed up a talented cast, and
being blessed with a superb musical score, Nagaich's screenplay
was poor. His weak control was evident from the way Rajesh
Khanna was allowed to overwhelm the film. True, the history
of Indian cinema does chronicle icons whose movies were a one-
man affair, like Rajinikanth and Dr Rajkumar, but they chose
their films cautiously, whereas Rajesh Khanna did not.

As was customary, the songs of *Mere Jeevan Saathi* – the title
track, five Kishore solos, a Kishore–Lata duet and an Asha
Bhonsle solo – were released a few months prior to the release
of the film. For most films, this made for a successful teaser
campaign – the songs were pronounced hits or flops consistent
with the film's performance at the box office. *Mere Jeevan Saathi*
came with the promise of a blockbuster and went back bust. But
in a major departure from the norm, its music broke free from
the shipwreck, surfaced and soared. Thirty-five years on, there
are very few R.D. Burman, Rajesh Khanna or Kishore Kumar
compilations that do not carry at least one song from the film.

Apparently, the first song Pancham composed for the film
was rejected by both producer Harish Shah and Rajesh Khanna.
Disturbed, Pancham came back with an alternative score within
fifteen minutes which became '*O mere dil ke chain*' after Majrooh
Sultanpuri's inputs.

However, in his article 'All for a Song', published in *Filmfare*,
7 September 1973, V. Sridhar writes: 'The tune of "*O mere dil
ke chain*" haunted Rahul Dev Burman so much one night that he
got up at four in the morning, hummed it into his cassette
recorder, went to his music room and wrote the score. The
same evening, Majrooh Sultanpuri supplied the lyrics for it in
a matter of minutes.'

In 2008, at a function to commemorate Pancham's birth
anniversary, Manohari Singh, when asked to play a song which

he considered to be truly representative of Pancham's spirit and style, played '*O mere dil ke chain*' on his alto sax.

What makes it the trademark Pancham song? The song is in the minor scale, has simple notes spread on both sides of the root (the stable note of the melody). The use of the Ga note in lieu of the anticipated Komal Ga in the very first singing note (in this case, humming leading to the song) stands out as the differentiator. The minor chord gives the song a calm feel, while the use of the lone major chord courtesy the Shuddha Ga note in the beginning suggests a strong request rather than humble submission. Keeping it ephemeral, Pancham does not use the note again in the song.

The prelude to the song later became the leitmotif of the film as well as the title track sung by Pancham himself. With words like '*He is a sexy playboy*' escaping the censor's scissors, one wonders what the board in 1972 misheard it as!

The Kishore Kumar solo '*Diwana leke aya hai*' was an offshoot of '*O mere dil ke chain*'. The chasms of grief bridged by optimism in the song made it yet another Kishore–Rajesh classic. A poignant piece of violin refrain played by Uttam Singh in the second interlude evokes the lovers' pain of separation.

And then there was '*Chala jata hun*' with its phenomenal yodelling, the scale-changing duet '*Deewana karke chhodoge*', the unconventional bhajan '*Aao Kanhai mere dham*' and the Asha solo '*Aao na gale lagao na*' in which the evil heiress tries to seduce her sightless prisoner – sheer musical delight.

Kishore Kumar's catch-me-if-you-can manner of singing '*Kitne sapne kitne armaan*' in the sequence where the hero meets the heroine was used to capitalize on the superstar's image, a legacy from his previous films. It was a flawed assumption because every film resets the counter to zero. An actor needs to work hard all over again. There is no carry-over of a previous film's success. The pre-release media hype around *Mere Jeevan Saathi* was presumptuous. Between the songs, the script sagged helplessly.

Ironically, the years that saw Rajesh Khanna's fall from grace were Pancham's best, musically – testimony to the fact that RD's success rarely depended on a bankable composer–hero partnership.

In the months following the success of *Kati Patang*, Pancham, by his own admission (in the magazine *Showtime* in July 1992), was composing for around fifty films, sometimes recording two songs on the same day, and totalling more than thirty songs per month. 'We worked day and night. We did songs, background, the whole lot,' Manohari Singh recalls. 'Today, I wonder how we did it. Life with Pancham was like this during that phase: simply amazing. We had stopped counting. Pancham would never count – some astrologer told him not to count his films. We just went on and on. Ma Saraswati's blessings were upon us.'

2

After *Mere Jeevan Saathi*, it was downhill all the way for Rajesh Khanna, his fall gathering momentum with almost every alternate film. Temporary relief came with Hrishikesh Mukherjee's *Namak Haraam* (1973). Director Hrishikesh Mukherjee and writer Gulzar refashioned Peter Glenville's masterpiece *Becket* (1964), the true story of the friendship between King Henry II and Thomas à Becket – courtier and confidant whom Henry appoints as Archbishop of Canterbury – turning it into a modern-day, urbanized conflict between capitalism and trade unionism, with 'friends' Amitabh Bachchan and Rajesh Khanna finding themselves on opposite sides of the ideological divide. This was the only film after *Anand* in which Rajesh Khanna and Amitabh Bachchan starred together.

Angry young men do not sing. Thus, Pancham's three solos for Kishore Kumar had to be featured on Rajesh Khanna, and the fourth one on Asrani. Despite the sombre story, Gulzar's clever screenplay and Hrishikesh Mukherjee's deft editing created the opportunities for the seamless musical intermissions, be it the labourers' Holi celebrations or an election campaign, a dying poet's last couplet or one friend recording another singing, on a video camera.

'Nadia se dariya' remains unlike any other Holi song in Hindi cinema, doing away with the customary group dancers and the conventional (mis)use of the dholak. 'Main shayar badnaam' ranks among the classiest lyrics by Anand Bakshi. The poet, played by Raza Murad, in the final stanza of his life, hands down a list of unfinished tasks and the intangible inventory of things that one would find in his dwelling, to his friend Somu (Rajesh Khanna) to recite back to him. As the song unfolds, so does the mystery behind the poet's tragedy as his lost love, played by Manju Asrani, walks up to his door for a last glimpse. The poet at least gets the satisfaction of dying in her presence.

Kishore Kumar was on familiar turf. His powerful, full-throated yet controlled and emotionally stirring voice gave the songs an infectious dynamism, making it impossible to believe that anyone else could have sung them to the same effect. Moving from intoxicated comedy to utter tragedy, blending ebullience and sorrow, the songs underline Kishore's incredible versatility.

Namak Haraam was, in tone and sprit, a political statement, similar to Nasir Husain's Baharon Ke Sapne but with none of the melodrama or preachiness of the latter. Mukherjee merely told the tale and did not resort to any last-scene overt didacticism. The resultant neutrality has brought in repeat audiences over the decades as each socio-economic subgroup has drawn different conclusions at different points in time from the film.

Producer Satish Wagle had initially decided to offer *Namak Haraam* to his friend Shankar who had composed for him in *Pyar Hi Pyar* (1969) and *Yaar Mera* (1971), but was advised by his partner Rajaram and other friends to opt for the winning horse – Pancham. Pancham's compositions in *Namak Haraam* were some of the finest among the 115 released in 1973.

Though overshadowed by Amitabh Bachchan's seething act, Rajesh Khanna did offer a sensitive contrast with a heartfelt performance. Battling dwindling box office returns, he needed more *Namak Haraam*s, strong stories, honest screenplays and mature directors who could get the best out of him. The films he ended up signing instead were *Raja Rani* (1973), *Humshakal* (1974) and *Aap Ki Kasam* (1974) – modern-day fairy tales with weak screenplays.

In his article 'Kishore Vs Kishore' published in *Screen* (http://www.screenindia.com/old/oct22/music2.htm), October 1999, film critic Rajiv Vijaykar denounced the music of *Humshakal* (along with some of Pancham's other compositions in 1974 – *Ishk Ishk Ishk, Dil Diwana, Madhosh* and *Trimurti*) as utterly lacklustre, also pronouncing the music of *Raja Rani* as mediocre and repetitive.

We differ. Vijaykar may have done his homework, but Pancham had done his too. One small example would suffice to show the kind of homework Pancham did for creating melodies. For the mukhra of the Kishore Kumar solo *'Rasta dekhey tera'* in *Humshakal,* he used the Ni note as the melody. This was incredibly suited for the sense of longing the situation demanded. Pancham had used the seventh chord to good effect before, but this was one of his first applications of the 'major seventh' (Shuddha Ni) to create empathy for the deprivation a loved one has been subjected to. This chord would find prominent usage in Pancham's songs later too, a case in point being *'Qatrah*

qatrah milti hai' from *Ijaazat* (1988) – again, a craving for the absent.

Popular music criticism in India has struggled to extricate itself from the film–composer–lyricist–singer cycle. The deeper understanding of *what* a note/chord combination/rhythm pattern depicts and *why* it has been used, etc., will comprise the new paradigm for critical appraisals of light music some day. And between now and the new paradigm, our critics will need to study hard to upgrade themselves.

In the Asha–Kishore 'honeymoon' duet *'Hum tum gum sum raat milan ki'*, Pancham uses a fast-paced, two-note start in the mukhra, exemplifying the anxiety the occasion stirs up in the protagonists. The high notes in the antara and the persistent chorus impart a festive flavour to the song; and one finds the sequence, with a dance in a fisherman's cove, fitting for the composition. The Asha solo *'Dekho mujhe dekho'* was a signature blues song, picturized on Tanuja as a woman gone insane, the screaming, near-hysterical laughter representing her unhinged mental state. A remake of Pancham's original Bengali number sung by Asha, *'Elo melo katha'*, this was a throwback to the 1960s' RD with his experimental tunes. Though he used the blues scale in this song, the opening note was the very unconventional Teevra Madhyam. The use of alternative scales, vocal harmonies, the sporadic scats, etc., did catch the average Indian listener – used to conventional major and minor scales – unawares.

Only a set of thoroughly untrained ears could lead somebody to condemn the music of *Humshakal* (or, for that matter, the music of *Ishk Ishk Ishk, Dil Diwana, Madhosh* and *Trimurti*).

If Vijaykar equated quality with popularity, Pancham's own duet with Asha in *Madhosh*, *'Sharabi ankhen gulabi chehra'* was the darling of radio channels and paan shops, and still attracts crowds at hip outlets. Two of Pancham's compositions in *Raja*

Rani – '*Jab andhera hota hai*' and '*Main ek chor tu meri rani*' – were, and still are, immensely popular. The film was incidentally a huge flop. Both songs were fleetingly inspired by the '*Age of Aquarius*' from Galt MacDermot's musical *Hair* that Pancham had seen at the Shaftesbury Theatre in London. There is an interesting tabla tarang in the song '*Jab andhera hota hai*', a rolling pattern played in the style of Ustaad Samta Prasad. When he heard the tune, RD's first tabla guru Brajen Biswas reportedly told him: 'I know how to play the instrument, but you know *where* exactly to play.'

Raja Rani was storywriter Sachin Bhowmick's only directorial venture. He persuaded producer J. Om Prakash, his former colleague at Mohan Sehgal's production house, to shift loyalties from the Laxmikant–Pyarelal camp to RD. Subsequently, when J. Om Prakash made his debut as director with *Aap Ki Kasam*, he opted for Pancham. *Aap Ki Kasam* had a moderate run at the box office, but was noted more for the on-set differences between Rajesh Khanna and Sanjeev Kumar with the latter vowing to never work with Khanna again – a promise he kept. The plot went something like this: boy meets girl, they fall in love, marry and then part because of a misunderstanding. From there on, the script lost its way. Most of Pancham's compositions from the film, from the Raga Behaag-based '*Zindagi ke safar mein*' to the Raga Khamaj-based '*Chori chori chupke chupke*' were huge hits, with the racy, '*Jai jai Shiv Shankar*' hogging most of the air time.

The interlude music in '*Zindagi ke safar mein*' was unique in that it followed the visuals in the film (where the camera covers Rajesh Khanna's journey through time and seasons) to create the sound specific to the changing seasons in the picturization. The song also played cupid in Pancham's life. He said in an interview with the *Times of India*, Bombay, on 29 September 1985, that music had saved his relationship with Asha Bhonsle in the 1980s: 'And it's music that always brings me back to earth ... Terrible fight with Asha ... break off the same evening ... Just then, my song *"Zindagi ke safar mein"* came on *Chaaya Geet* ... We stopped quarrelling, stared at the TV set in a daze, hugged and made up immediately.'

The Lata–Kishore duets *'Karvatein badalte rahe'* and *'Suno, kaho, kaha, suna'* have a strange common link – a fan. Folklore goes that despite the availability of proper gadgetry, pedestal fans were used to create the feel of an echo in *'Karvatein badalte rahe'*.

The second fan story comes from Bhanu Gupta who recalls, 'I was sitting in Pancham's music room on a hot day and somehow the fan was not working properly, making a distracting sound with every cycle. Pancham heard it, and suddenly started composing along with the cyclic sound. *Suno.* One cycle. *Kaho.* Another cycle. And in a matter of minutes, the song *"Suno, kaho, kaha, suna, kuch hua kya"* was born.'

All the three films – *Humshakal, Aap Ki Kasam* and *Raja Rani* – had at least one song where Pancham arranged music using dholaks: *'Kahe ko bulaya'* (*Humshakal*), *'Paas nahin ana'* (*Aap Ki Kasam*) and *'Phir aankh se aansoo barse'* (*Raja Rani*). He did it in style, leading to a superior listening experience of dholak-based compositions opposed to what the audience was used to hearing.

That Rajesh Khanna's fortunes were beyond redemption was amply proved with the tepid response to *Ajnabee* (1974), in which writer Gulshan Nanda tells the story of a couple who separate only to patch up after some action and drama. The film had Shakti Samanta, Rajesh Khanna and R.D. Burman collaborating once more. Pancham's innovations included shaking asbestos sheets to create the sound of thunder, which he used in the introduction of the sensual *'Bheegi bheegi raaton mein'*, and using pre-recorded music for the interludes in *'Hum dono do premi'* since the musicians were on strike. With *'Ek ajnabee haseena se'*, Pancham waltzed away with three all-time hits from the film, while Rajesh Khanna's superstardom entered its last lap.

3

After *Kati Patang*, Pancham found producers outside the Samanta, Husain and Mahmood camps willing to engage his services as a composer. The house of the Nadiadwalas was one such, with Prakash Mehra's *Mela*, produced by A.A. Nadiadwala, being the first of their associations. Nadiadwala followed it up with two films in 1972: *Dil Ka Raja* and *Rampur Ka Lakshman*.

Manmohan Desai was still not the Manmohan Desai that he would become in the late 1970s, when he and Pancham worked together on *Rampur Ka Lakshman*, a standard Desai lost-and-found formula flick with Randhir Kapoor doing a Raj Kapoor à la *Chhalia* to add nostalgic value.

The Lata–Kishore duet *'Gum hai kisi ke pyar mein'* was built on the Pancham formula of using the minor chord with embellishments and has remained the most popular track from the film. Sung in a leisurely intonation, punctuated by words spoken with a lilt, the song depicted two lovers tentatively admitting their feelings for each other. The bhajan *'Kahe apno ke kaam nahi'* by Kishore and Asha, and the zippy Asha solo *'Albela re'* highlighted Asha's versatility. Another rather undervalued number was *'Sanwla rang hai mera'*, an Asha Bhonsle solo which featured great range in the notes. *'Pyar ka samay'* will be remembered as Pancham's first-ever Kishore–Lata–Rafi song.

The next film, and unfortunately the last in which Pancham scored music for Manmohan Desai was A.K. Nadiadwala's *Aa*

Gale Lag Jaa (1973). Although he delivered super hits like *Amar Akbar Anthony* (1977), *Dharam Veer* (1977), *Suhaag* (1979) and *Naseeb* (1981), Man-ji, as Manmohan Desai was affectionately known, always referred to *Aa Gale Lag Jaa*, originally titled *Hum Dono*, as the film closest to his heart.

Leading the quartet of songs in the film was *'Tera mujhse hai pehle'*, inspired by the traditional Texan folk song *'Yellow rose of Texas'*. It had two versions: a solo by Kishore Kumar and a duet between Kishore and Sushma Shrestha (present-day singer Purnima). The song was the backbone of the story. Kersi Lord who was actively involved in the making of this song, says, 'The sound of the guitar that resembles a human voice singing is the one that is unmistakably played by Bhupendra,' saluting Bhupendra's skills. Kersi Lord himself spun magic with his accordion in the song *'Na koi dil mein samaya'*, which is remarkable for fusing different instrumental pieces – violins, electric guitar, accordion, brass and bells – into each other.

The Kishore–Lata duet *'Wada karo'* may have been inspired by Horace Silver's *'Song for my father'*. Though Pancham used the bossa nova, the resemblance of the tune with *'Song for my father'* is very slight. The phrase *'Wada karo nahin'* does not have a metre and the rhythm actually starts after the fourth word *'chodoge'*. The use of brass/wind for the harmony during the mukhra is remarkable. The Kishore Kumar solo *'Aye mere bete'* is an example of how a wild tune like *'Dum maro dum'* could be tamed into a song conveying deep affection. In the mukhra, Pancham uses a note progression similar to that of *'Dum maro dum'*, but packages it so differently that the resemblance is not apparent.

Musically, the heroes of *Aa Gale Lag Jaa* were Pancham and Kishore Kumar. Still, Man-ji, for some reason, never worked with Pancham again, and in subsequent interviews, did not acknowledge Pancham and Kishore's inputs to the film he called

closest to his heart, going to the extent of rubbishing Kishore
as a singer. But then, considering that he went on to make such
trash as *Mard* (1985) and *Coolie* (1983), with their bottom-of-
the-barrel music, Pancham and Kishore can count themselves
lucky.

Considered a poet rather than a lyricist, Sahir Ludhianvi was
the unlikely choice for writing the lyrics for the music of *Aa
Gale Lag Jaa*. Pancham and Ludhianvi were working together
for the first time after *Pyaasa* – which was released fifteen years
ago and in which Pancham was assisting his father – a film
which unfortunately witnessed the last partnership between
Sahir and SD. The next film in which Pancham collaborated
with Sahir followed shortly after. It was called *Joshila* (1973).

4

Film distributor and producer Gulshan Rai began his career in
the film industry as a distributor in the early 1950s. He started his
production company Trimurti Films in 1969 and his maiden
production venture *Johnny Mera Naam* (1970) became a blockbuster.
Rai's next venture *Joshila*, reluctantly directed by Yash Chopra,
repeated the lead pair of Dev Anand and Hema Malini and
brought Pancham and Sahir Ludhianvi together again.

The film failed to replicate the box office magic of *Johnny
Mera Naam* and even its music, by common consent, was rather
a let-down compared to the standards Sahir and Pancham had
set in *Aa Gale Lag Jaa*. If it continues to be relevant to RD's
oeuvre, it is because of one standout number: '*Kiska rasta dekhey,
aye dil aye saudai*'. Sung by Kishore Kumar and picturized inside
a jail with flashback shots of the Kanchenjunga creating a
montage of sorts, the song, with its soul-searching lyrics and
serene tune, was a favourite with both the composer and the
singer. One Mr Chandrahasan, a businessman and a diehard fan

of RD, was party to an interesting conversation between Kishore and Pancham during the recording of '*Mujhko agar ijazat ho*' (*Ishk Ishk Ishk*). Apparently, Pancham had made Kishore record '*Kiska rasta dekhey*' over a dozen times till he was satisfied, and the next day found Kishore promising to compose an equally compelling tune to be recorded in Pancham's voice!

Though largely ignored at the time of its release, *Joshila*'s songs became a grab in later years, mostly with the advent of T-Series when the songs were released in a cassette around the mid-1980s. Pancham forums fiercely debated the relative merits of the songs of the movie, which were mostly about Asha Bhonsle.

The cabaret song '*Kaanp rahi main*', which has Padma Khanna gyrating in a nightclub to support her family, was spectacular in the sense that the mukhra and the antara started with Sa on two separate Saptaks. With his musicians jamming, Pancham was back with the minute-long prelude. The ambience created in '*Sharmana yun*' was of slumber, of seduction; and this was effected by an intonation conducted in whispers. For such overt eroticism, the songs were deceptively slow paced. '*Sona rupa*', the climax track, was like an ethnic instrumental song wedded to the voices of Asha and the chorus, where Pancham stretched Asha's chords to impossible highs. In the other, folksy, '*Dil mein jo baaten hain*', Kancha's madal was employed liberally, and Pancham used his flagship dual metering within the mukhra – one metre each for Kishore's and Asha's lines.

The Kishore–Lata duet '*Kuch bhi kar lo*' with its changing beats, sudden breaks, and occasional vocal harmonization was the quintessential Pancham song – pacy and frolicsome, without sounding loud. The icing on the cake was the solo '*Jo baat isharon mein kahi*', where the flute, sitar and percussion complemented the subtle playfulness that Lata injected into her rendition.

Pancham's enduring contribution to the music of *Joshila*

remains its title music. Based on a canopy of simple note progressions repeated in a cycle of sixteen beats, it has been used liberally by film studios as canned music for the title tracks of many films. These include films for which Pancham composed music, for example, *Deewaar* (logical, as it was again Trimurti films), *Ujala Hi Ujala, Heeralal Pannalal* and *Ganga Meri Ma;* and films which had other composers: *Mahabadmash* (Ravindra Jain), *Laaparwah* (Bappi Lahiri), *Anpadh* (Hemant Bhonsle) and *Yaarana* (Rajesh Roshan), among many others. The first four notes may have been the base for George Fernandes's trumpet notes in the prelude of '*Bachna aye haseeno*' in *Hum Kisise Kum Naheen.*

<h2 style="text-align:center">5</h2>

Two years later, Gulshan Rai and Yash Chopra returned with a 'quiet' film that hardly had any background music, a mere five songs – two of which were left out in the final cut – all irrelevant to the script, and four lines of humour in all. There was just one booming, deep baritone that silenced all critics and left the audience speechless.

'*Keh doon tumhe*' was later used on Aamir Khan in his first adult role in the FTII diploma film *Subah Subah* by Indrajit Singh Bansal in 1983.

Deewaar firmly established Amitabh Bachchan as the Angry Young Man of Indian cinema. Of the songs that made it to the film, only the Asha–Kishore duet '*Keh doon tumhe*' has survived the test of time. '*Maine tujhe manga*', another Asha–Kishore duet, was structured on an offbeat rhythm pattern and was delivered with great panache by Asha, particularly during the glide into the antara from the mukhra. RD's predicament was that *Deewaar*'s powerhouse script had no space for anything save brawn. The two Asha–Kishore duets, despite being as good as they were, were consigned to a parallel track.

Javed Akhtar, of Salim–Javed fame, who designed the script says, 'There was hardly any scope for music in the film. It was meant to be a film about a person who rebels against the establishment.' All of Bachchan's scenes were sombre and serious. An angry young Vijay had nothing to do with the finer elements of life like music (even the booze he gulped rather than savoured). *'Koi mar jaaye'*, the mujra Pancham composed for Asha Bhonsle, was forced upon the film by the financers. It too was designed to support the script without detracting attention from the action. As part of the background score, natural sounds like the horn of a distant ship preparing to drop anchor near Mahalaxmi Docks, and an English song spun in a bossa nova beat in a nightclub in the Oberoi Sheraton (now The Oberoi, Mumbai) were heard. This song, *'I am falling in love with a stranger'*, Pancham's only one as lyricist, segues into a piece of background music and is fascinating for its change of pace when Vijay prepares for a rendezvous with death in the film.

Pancham collaborated with Sahir later in films under B.R. Chopra's baton. The brothers Balwant Raj and Yash moved in different directions when choosing the composers for their films. While Yash drifted from Ravi to Laxmikant–Pyarelal to R.D. Burman to Shiv–Hari, B.R. Chopra migrated from Ravi to Pancham in the mid-1970s.

Speaking of associations, there was another one already in the making.

10

Archimedes' Principle

Sampooran Singh Kalra was born into a Sikh family in undivided Punjab and was forced to migrate to a rented house in old Delhi's Pul Bangash near Subzi Mandi area in the aftermath of the Partition, the experiences of which shaped his formative years and continue to resonate in his writings. Sampooran was pulled out of St Stephen's College after his first term and packed off to Bombay by his father Sardar Makhan Singh so that he might find a long-term career for himself. In Bombay, Sampooran struggled more with his lack of conviction in the jobs he did than with his ability to execute them. These included working in a garage where he was told to supervise the painting of cars. He rebelled against his father, his elder brother with whom he was living in Bombay, and his religion (by dispensing with his hair and beard) in pursuit of what he wanted to do with his life. It would henceforth be heart over mind and tales of human sensitivity over everything else for Gulzar.

Gulzar's simple beginnings in the Bombay film industry happened with the lyrics he wrote under the nom de plume of Gulzar Deenvi for films directed by Pradeep Nayyar (*Choron Ki Baaraat*, 1960; *Diler Haseena*, 1960) and S.M. Abbas (*Shriman Satyawadi*, 1960). His association with the Burmans owes its origin to a fortuitous face-off between S.D. Burman and lyricist Shailendra on the sets of Bimal Roy's *Bandini* (1963). Another lyricist had to be summoned, and Gulzar penned '*Mora gora ang layi le*'. He and the younger Burman hit it off during the sitting sessions of this song.

After close to a decade as a lyricist and scenarist, he crossed an important milestone in 1971 when he turned independent director with *Mere Apne* (1971) and followed that up with *Koshish* (1972). Then came his first film with Pancham – *Parichay* (1972).

There has to be something about bathtubs and showers that brings forth solutions. Gulzar had given Pancham the first two lines of '*Musafir hun yaaron*' to compose. While Archimedes might have had a reason for his principle of buoyancy to surface just where it did, Pancham did not. Yet, it was under the shower that Pancham came up with what would become the first gem in a glittering array.

'I was sitting in Pancham's music room one morning and warming up by strumming chords on my guitar,' Bhanu Gupta recalls. 'Pancham, who was taking a shower, opened the bathroom door, poked his head out and said, "*Bajate thako, themo na* (Keep playing, don't stop)." So I continued playing the chord progression. When Pancham came out, he was humming a tune that fit the chord sequence I was playing. The line was "*Mujhe chalte jana hai*". Later, he went back to the first two lines. So, in effect, Pancham composed the tune for the refrain first and then for the mukhra.'

Gulzar's night out with Pancham in his car, with the latter

keeping beat on the dashboard and singing the full tune of
'*Musafir hun yaaron*' is now part of film folklore. By dawn, the
composition was complete. '*Musafir hun yaaron*' was one of
Pancham's definitive compositions for the road, along with
songs like '*Chala jata hun*' (*Mere Jeevan Saathi*), '*Meri jaan meri
jaan*' (*Do Chor*), '*Jaan-e-jaana jao kal phir aana*' (*Samadhi*) and
'*Aaj unse pehli mulaqaat hogi*' (*Paraya Dhan*).

There seems to be a slight structural resemblance between the starting notes of
the theme tune of Satyajit Ray's film *Pather Panchali* (1955), composed by Ravi
Shankar, and '*Musafir hun yaaron*'. It is a point of conjecture that Pancham
might have heard the dhun being played at the Ali Akbar Khan School and
that the tune might have stayed with him.

Gulzar is one of the troika of film-makers – with Hrishikesh
Mukherjee and Basu Chatterjee – who popularized middle-of-
the-road Hindi cinema, high on entertainment but without the
ostentatious make-believe fluff, while not going the whole
minimalist hog like the New Indian Cinema of the 1970s. Each
film picked up an issue that the common man would be able to
relate to and narrated its story simply, in a language that
resonated with the audience. There were no heroes or villains,
nor were there beggars dying of starvation while the wealthy
drove past in their Rolls Royces; only circumstances – favourable
or adverse.

The source of inspiration behind *Parichay* remains hazy. The
consensus is that writer Mani Barma borrowed the basic outline
of Robert Wise's *The Sound of Music* for the Bengali film *Joy
Jayanti* (1970). This in turn inspired Gulzar's *Parichay*. However,
the film credits well-known Bengali writer Rajkumar Moitra as
the storywriter. The fact that his then fiancée Raakhee gave
him the idea after reading Moitra's story also made news in film
magazines in the early 1970s.

Gulzar has never denied that he was inspired by *The Sound of Music* – his tale of rebellious children tamed by a teacher had far too many similarities to the Hollywood musical. 'Sa Re Ga Ma Pa Dha Ni Sa' is the Hindi equivalent of 'Do Re Mi Fa So La Ti Do' which made '*Sa Re ke Sa Re*' Pancham's answer to '*Doe a deer, a female deer*'. Both songs served as an explanation of the seven basic notes of music. However, to Pancham and Gulzar's credit, the tune, the rhythm and the feel were all very original. The sargam had hitherto been used only in songs based on classical music. '*Sa Re ke Sa Re*' experimented with the sargam in a lighter vein. Using musical notes like Dha-Ni to take a mischievous dig at the colour of the eldest siblings' saree added to the song's appeal. In the interlude, Pancham employs the sound and rhythm of a running train. This was done by making Kersi Lord use a technique called 'bellows shake'. In the film, the song stops midway, almost purposefully, for a few dialogues between Jeetendra and Jaya Bhaduri, and resumes ingeniously at Pa – the *Pancham* note!

Child actor Master Raju (Shrestha) who played the youngest child in the family was used for a specific purpose in the song. Gulzar wanted to insert the sound of the siren that the toddler had picked up during the curfew and blackout regime of the Indo-Pak war in 1971 (around the time that *Parichay* was being made).

Pancham created the effect to a nicety. Kersi Lord narrates: 'Whenever Pancham wanted something new, he used to tell me: "Hey, a song is going to be recorded in six or seven days. I want this type of effect," proceeding to make a "Woooo Woooo" sound. Those days, synthesizers were not controlled by keyboards. I remembered that my friend had a radio repair shop and used to have oscillators which generated a flute-like sound, which is a normal sine wave. Datta Raojekar is a fine musician and music director and an expert in electronic instruments. I told him, "DT, this is what I want. I want four oscillators and I want octave switches and wave form switches so that I can convert sine wave into wave forms like square and rectangular waves." Within a couple of days, he showed me a small box with four knobs which were switches for wave change and switches for octave. These four knobs were connected to an output and the sound of the siren was generated by turning the knobs. If I had had the Moog synthesizer [which came later, in 1973], the tuning would have been perfect.'

Parichay also allowed Bhupendra to resume his career as a mainstream playback singer, this time of semi-classical songs. Based on a mix of various ragas, mainly Yaman and Khamaj, '*Beeti na bitayi raina*' was Pancham's first duet composition based on Indian classical music. Keeping in tune with the period and the tradition, he made elaborate use of the sitar and the tabla. Bhupendra's deep voice was refreshingly different and blended well with Sanjeev Kumar's expression of resignation. This song became one of Pancham's strongest defences against accusations that he was too westernized and incapable of composing songs based on Indian classical ragas. The tender emotions of the song moved even the Angry Young Man to tears when he happened to hear it at RK Studios. It won Lata Mangeshkar the National Award for the best female playback singer. Inexplicably, neither Pancham nor Bhupendra were awarded the same.

Incidentally, Sandhya Mukherjee too won the National Award for *Joy Jayanti*, for the Bengali counterpart of '*Doe a deer*'.

'*Mitwa bole meethe bain*', another Bhupendra solo, picturized on Sanjeev Kumar, was based on a mix of Raga Rageshri and Raga Hemant. Prince Rama Varma feels that the song is closer to Raga Hemant (Raga Bhinna Shadja). Aashish Khan feels that Pancham might have learnt Raga Hemant when he was a

student under Ali Akbar Khan since it is considered to have
been developed by the Allauddin Khan family. Hemant is a
controversial raga: various musical gharanas have chiselled it
under different names and claimed credit for its genesis. The
Vilayat Khan Gharana has supposedly been playing it for
generations, calling it by a different name, Raga Pancham.

Who knows, Pancham may have deliberately used Raga
Pancham for a character playing the role of a musician.

The overall brilliance of the film not withstanding, its last scene was flawed in
announcing the marriage of the lead pair on 9 April, for it falls in the month of
Chaitra, when Hindu marriages do not take place. Gulzar's own wedding (to
Raakhee) was slated for 18 April 1973, in the month of Baisakh.

2

Gulzar worked with Pancham in three more films in quick
succession: as lyricist in *Doosri Seeta* (1974), and as director and
lyricist in *Aandhi* and *Khushboo* (1975).

Directed by Gogi Anand, one of Pancham's closest lifelong
friends, *Doosri Seeta* bombed big time at the box office. With
that, three RD–Gulzar gems went virtually unnoticed. It was
only after the composer's resurrection post-1994 that the
audience could enjoy melodies like the Lata Mangeshkar solo
'Din ja rahe hain ke raaton ke saaye' and the Asha solos *'Tu jahan
mile mujhe'* and *'Aaye re aaye re'*. Many found the use of Nitin
Mukesh for the tandem *'Tu jahan mile mujhe'* surprising and
wondered if Pancham had buckled under pressure from the
financiers, or if he was experimenting with a newcomer who
was working, without much success, as an assistant to director
Hrishikesh Mukherjee.

Khushboo, starring Jeetendra as the Panditmashai, was Gulzar's
first venture into Saratchandra Chatterjee territory. The

Panditmashai angle was just one of the various subplots unfolding within the film, permitting Gulzar the luxury of landscaping a more present-day village and a more orchestral music score than what one would have expected in rural Bengal. This was seen in the Asha Bhonsle solos, '*Bechara dil kya kare*' and '*Ghar jayegi*', which had the right dose of ebullience and grace but posed the risk of being interpreted as modern, given the period setting. The tragic mood of the story was reflected in the use of the sarod in the background, played by Aashish Khan.

The Lata Mangeshkar solo '*Do naino mein aansoo bharen hain*' was recorded in two versions and is, with its mix of the flute, tabla and the extended taan in the antara, an example of how a sad song can be composed without it getting maudlin. The film uses a version where, apart from the vibraphone, there is little instrumental accompaniment with the vocals.

The one song which has stood out for more than three decades is Kishore Kumar's '*O majhi re*'. With its underlying Bhatiyali philosophy, this modern version of Bengali folk music is known as much for Pancham's technical innovations like the use of the reverb and the blowing on a bottle filled with water to simulate the upper C note on the normal octave, as for its compositional and lyrical brilliance.

3

Gulzar started writing the screenplay of *Aandhi* shortly after *Parichay*. He had penned down some thoughts, though the main characters eluded him. While working on the script, he met writer Kamleshwar Prasad Saxena who was writing a story titled 'Aagami Ateet' for producer Mallikarjun Rao. This story had a stark resemblance to A.J. Cronin's *Judas Tree* and would be named *Mausam* (1976).

During the course of the discussion, it was decided that Kamleshwar would write a novel based on the storyline Gulzar

had in mind. The result was the novel *Kaali Aandhi*. Although
some shots of *Aandhi* were based on the story by Kamleshwar,
Gulzar maintains there were differences between the screenplay
and the novel as far as the characters were concerned.

The music of *Aandhi*, considered at par with *Amar Prem*, is
the result of a symbiosis of the best of both Pancham's and
Gulzar's worlds. One needs to go back a few years, when
Gulzar was fascinated by '*Raina beeti jaye*'. He had said in *Meri
Sangeet Yatra*: 'The use of shuddha notes [in '*Raina beeti jaye*']
were representative of the purity of the courtesan.'

Gulzar probably extended this idea to Arati Bose in *Aandhi*,
for the title music which had all the seven shuddha notes woven
in a simple mesh. Though not similar in any way, a parallel
could be drawn to the Indian National Song '*Jana gana mana*'
which is based on Raga Bilawal where only the seven shuddha
notes are used.

With the Kishore–Lata duet '*Is mod se jaate hain*', Pancham
further used the title track, added a Teevra Madhyam, and
delved into the territory of Raga Yaman. Replete with Gulzar-
esque imagery and references, the lyrics baffled Pancham. With
his limited knowledge of poetry and precious little knowledge
of Urdu, he had inquired of Gulzar if 'nasheman' was the name
of a town. Often thought of as excelling only in minor-scale
compositions, Pancham was possibly divinely inspired to create
the song that shattered the notion. The interludes too are
worth a study. While Hariprasad Chaurasia's flute and Zarine
Daruwala's sarod were used to impart a dominating tone,
Jairam Acharya's sitar and a violin ensemble gave the melody a
touch of frailty. '*Is mod se jaate hain*', like '*Beeti na bitayi raina*',
is one of the best major-scale songs in Hindi film music.

In '*Tere bina zindagi se koi*', Suchitra Sen and Sanjeev Kumar
revive the memories of their love in Golconda Fort twelve years
after their separation. Emotions are mellower, and so is the

tune. Pancham almost surreptitiously introduces the minor scale even while tackling shuddha notes. The mood is delicate, and Pancham uses Acharya's sitar to create a sentimental prelude to the duet. The beginning of this Lata–Kishore duet is reminiscent of Pancham's composition in Raga Nand, '*Jeete dao amaye deko na*'; hence the shuddha notes, but the similarity ends there. The elderly couple does not sing; and the song, playing in the background, acts as a medium to convey their thoughts so delicately expressed as '*Tere bina zindagi se koi shikwa toh nahi/ Tere bina zindagi bhi lekin zindagi toh nahin*'. Initially created by Pancham as a Puja song in the form of '*Jete jete pothe holo deri*', Gulzar took to the tune and penned the lyrics which fit in snugly. Despite this, the song has a made-to-order feel as far as the theme of *Aandhi* is concerned.

The monumental success of the song can be gauged by the response it gets even today. The number of views on YouTube is around 3.5 million, definitely the highest for any Hindi film song considered 'retro', and probably the highest among all Hindi film songs.

Sandwiched between '*Is mod se jaate hain*' and '*Tere bina zindagi se*' is Kishore–Lata's '*Tum aa gaye ho*', where Pancham steps back into the familiar terrain of flat notes and minor scale.

Aandhi came into national prominence when it was banned during the Emergency in 1975. The character of Aarti Devi, portrayed by Suchitra Sen, purportedly resembled Indira Gandhi, a conjecture fuelled by a film magazine capturing a film poster of *Aandhi* with the tagline: 'See your Prime Minister on Screen'. In fact, far from being anti-Indira Gandhi, *Aandhi* showed the protagonist as a courageous, diligent political figure struggling to keep unscrupulous power brokers at bay. However, a couple of scenes had to be re-shot, including the one in which Aarti Devi points to a wall photograph of Indira Gandhi and tells her father: 'Yeh meri ideal hai.'

The film, when re-released after the Emergency, Indira Gandhi no longer in power, continued to pull crowds. Kishore Kumar's songs which had been banned on public media by Sanjay Gandhi suddenly found unprecedented attention, and could be heard everywhere.

4

What Soumitra Chatterjee was to Satyajit Ray, Max Von Sydow to Ingmar Bergman, and Toshiro Mifune to Akira Kurosawa, Sanjeev Kumar was to Gulzar, acting in six of the twelve feature films Gulzar directed till 1985, the year the actor passed away. RD composed the music for four of these films. In the 1970s, the three almost seemed like a package deal. Not surprising, therefore, that Gulzar dedicated the published screenplay of *Aandhi* to the 'Anchorplayers of my films – R.D. Burman and Sanjeev Kumar'. Each represented three distinct aspects of film-making, and worked with a remarkable synergy.

As Gulzar remembers, Sanjeev Kumar had a very relaxed disposition towards most things in life. For example, he was always the last one to deboard an aircraft, waiting till all other passengers had done so. This rubbed off on his on-screen persona as well. Sanjeev's maturity as an artist, the innate calm that he carried in and out of the studio despite his troubled personal life, was reflected in a number of RD compositions picturized on the actor.

Two almost back-to-back Pancham–Sanjeev films were Raghunath Jhallani's *Anamika* (1973) and Shakti Samanta's

> Gulzar, for one, never interpreted the character of Aarti Devi to represent Mrs Gandhi. When Kamleshwar was asked about this, he is supposed to have answered: 'Indira Gandhi? I thought my character had a semblance to Nandini Satpathy, the politician and writer from Orissa.'

Charitraheen (1974). The films were like two sides of a coin – in the former the heroine leaves the hero, while it is the other way round in the latter. '*Meri bheegi bheegi si*' (redone from Pancham's first Bengali solo '*Mone pore Ruby Ray*') in *Anamika* was composure and pain personified. On the other hand, '*Dil se dil milne ka*', an enchanting Kishore–Lata duet in *Charitraheen*, reverberated with the rhythm of the earth.

   Charitraheen had an archetypal Pancham–Asha Bhonsle solo, '*Teri meri meri teri*', featured as an item number with the heroine Sharmila Tagore joining the dancing girls for a stanza. The number had a typical metallic sound effect with Asha's voice caressing more than one octave and the one-off staccato in a falsetto (Asha's short, abrupt '*He he he*' rendered in a voice an octave higher than the rest of the song) adding an element of intrigue to the hero's anguish. Pancham reminded everyone again that sad songs need not be slow.

   The coyness that Jaya Bhaduri had patented in films like *Guddi* was seen once again in *Anamika*, in its sweet and dreamy romantic numbers. Quantitatively, Asha Bhonsle got a bigger share with the bhajan '*Jaoon toh kahan jaoon*', the girl-full-of-beans '*Logo na maro isey*', and the cabaret, '*Aaj ki raat*' (which had Bhupendra's guitar riffs on the minor chord, a touch of blues with a surprise passing note, Komal Dha, used as the backbone) done in immaculate style.

'*Aaj ki raat*', redone by the Kronos Quartet in 2005, was nominated for the Grammy Awards too.

   And yet, Lata had the icing on the cake. 'You have given some of your best numbers to Didi,' Asha Bhonsle 'complained' in jest to RD in the radio programme *Meri Sangeet Yatra*. Though it was a joke, she may have had a point. '*Bahon mein chale aao*' was a Lata single malt on the rocks. It achieved the right blend between Majrooh's impish lyrics, Lata's velvety rendition, the blithe spirit of Jaya Bhaduri and Sanjeev Kumar's unpreparedness for the impromptu midnight romance – the perfect nightcap. The arrangement too was minimal, with the acoustic and the bass guitars accompanying Lata's voice as it whispered in the night.

5

The calm and collectedness of Sanjeev Kumar's on-screen personas in *Anamika* and *Charitraheen* needed a break; there were other facets to this remarkable actor that needed to be tapped. And he opted to do this with the confused neighbourhood 'thulla' who wears a pyjama underneath his constable's uniform and hesitates to undress in a prostitute's presence in her bedroom.

Manoranjan (1974) was Shammi Kapoor's directorial debut. It may not have been great entertainment, but the film did score a point over Billy Wilder's version of the same play, *Irma la Douce* (1963), courtesy its music. A common misconception is that Shammi plagiarized *Manoranjan* from Billy Wilder's film. As a matter of fact, both Billy Wilder and Shammi saw the original play on the West End.

'Both Billy Wilder and I had watched the play in London in 1960 and both of us were inspired by it,' Shammi Kapoor recounts. 'And both of us came out and decided that we would make a movie on the play. Billy made *Irma la Douce* (the movie) and I made *Manoranjan*. The movie was not a success as it was ahead of its time. Heroines as prostitutes were not accepted those days. But I enjoyed making the movie. The entire cast had great fun during the moviemaking process. But adding to my woes was the fact that *Irma la Douce*, which had been banned for ten years, was released just before *Manoranjan*.'

Sanjeev Kumar played the Jack Lemmon equivalent in this

film. Zeenat Aman replaced Mumtaz, the original choice who
had demanded a huge fee, as the female lead. *Manoranjan* had
some remarkable melodies like *'Goyake chunanche'* and *'Aaya hun
main tujhko le jaunga'*. The second song was inspired from the
Latino number *'After sunrise'* by Sergio Mendes. It was funk,
bossa nova and jazz rolled into one, with the distinctive presence
of Arabic music.

'"*Aaya hun main tujhko le jaunga*" was totally Pancham's
wizardry. It was an unusual composition. "*Goyake chunanche*"
was a theme that Abrar Alvi and I had worked on. "Goyake"
and "chunanche" are two different words. My favourite song
from that movie is "*Dulhan maike chali*", which was picturized
entirely inside a police bus. "*Chori chori solah shingar karungi*"
was another of my favourites. I choreographed the sequence as
the dance director's wife was pregnant at that time and he was
not available. I enjoyed *Manoranjan*,' Shammi Kapoor says
about the film and its music.

'*Dulhan maike chali*' carried in its interludes the moog
synthesizer interventions similar to what one heard later in the
intro of *'Ye ladka haye Allah'* (*Hum Kisise Kum Naheen*). The
prelude of *'Chori chori solah shingar'* was similar to that of *'Roop
tera mastana'* (*Aradhana*), with the transicord and vibraphone
playing a major role in the former as opposed to the piano
accordion in the latter. Asha's vocals coupled with Zeenat's
sensuousness made for delicious urban erotica not seen before in
Hindi films.

Shammi Kapoor's next and last directorial venture was a
modern-day *Aladdin* story named *Bundalbaaz* (1976). The
composer was Pancham again. In spite of sweet melodies like
'Nagma Hamara' and *'Bemausam bahaar ke din kaise aaye'*, the
frolicksome *'Ruk meri jaan'* was the only song in the film which
became popular.

6

Following the success of *Andaaz, Haathi Mere Saathi* and *Seeta Aur Geeta*, screenplay and dialogue writers Salim–Javed had started inching towards becoming the proverbial 'king makers'.

In the early 1970s, they sold a story to Prakash Mehra which became *Zanjeer*. Around the same time, the duo convinced director Nasir Husain to buy another one of their stories. After completing the film, Nasir Husain remarked that Salim–Javed had successfully sold the same story to both Prakash Mehra and him!

'It was too late when I realized that Salim–Javed had palmed off the same basic plot to me and Prakash Mehra. But our characters and treatment were completely different, and so both *Zanjeer* and my film were major hits in the same year!' Husain said in an interview published after his death in the *Screen* dated 22 March 2002.

Nasir had initially thought of Amitabh Bachchan for the lead role in his film, only to be deterred by others in the film fraternity. In walked Dharmendra who had, along with Raj Kumar and Dev Anand, rejected Amitabh's role in *Zanjeer*.

Unlike Nasir's last film, *Caravan*, where he had launched his brother's career as a producer, this film shifted from the rural dusty roads to Bombay, the city of dreams. The music too changed from the folk-based rhythms of *Caravan* to the Western beats that Pancham is celebrated for. In fact, it is the music that laid the foundations of *Yaadon Ki Baaraat* (1973).

Kaushik Bhaumik, film and art historian and an important member of Osian's Connoisseurs of Art, Mumbai, in a lecture titled 'Why Ajit had to die a spectacular death in *Yaadon Ki Baaraat*', delivered at Jadavpur University, Kolkata, said, 'With *Yaadon Ki Baaraat*, a new kind of cinema is born that makes it really the first "masala" classic as well as the first "Bollywood" film. The filmic space becomes fragmented to allow for the depiction of multiple storylines within a single film as well as convey a sense of social chaos through images of fast action and violence. It seems that India is falling apart and heroes of films are running desperately for their lives as everything falls apart. Sex becomes a whirlpool into which fatigued nerves are threatened with disappearance. With *Yaadon Ki Baaraat*, we see a very direct depiction of this world of greed and violence. The camera moves closer to the body and the zooms take over. The violence becomes more visceral, "realistic" and brutal. Also, the decor of films becomes gaudy and kitschy to project a world of greed. The world is on the move as well as being broken apart by violence, and nothing of value can be created in a world in hurry and a world that is being attacked by the greedy all the time.

'Rahul Dev Burman's score for *Yaadon Ki Baaraat* is a breakthrough in his music and Hindi film music as he turns to jazz and funk, the use of percussion and horns to create a soundscape that matches the frenetic, violent, fragmented logic of a film like this. The music becomes embedded in the action in intimate ways that was not possible earlier. The darkness of night scenes, Dharmendra running, the funky percussion score to accompany the suspense are all seamlessly part of one "scene". One can see the scoreline for Amitabh Bachchan films a couple of years down the line here – chases, fights, flights, etc. This is the music of a social revolution on the streets; everybody is rising up to the anxieties of a frenetic urban life. The immediacy of the music for the image is a ploy to draw the audience into the action more directly than ever before, and to also tell them that this is what is happening to them. The difference between the space inside the cinema hall and outside is erased. People are physically placed in the street; the music seeks to create the excitement of the street directly in the score,' sums up Bhaumik.

Without a doubt, the violence was loud and stark, the likes of which Hindi cinema had not seen so far. The shrieks of the hero's parents as they are murdered, the shower of bullets disfiguring a man's face badly enough for the police to be deceived that they had found their target (albeit dead) ... *Yaadon Ki Baaraat*, like *Zanjeer*, protracted the wrongdoer's evil run over fifteen years, allowing the audience's hatred for the bad man to marinate over three hours before they could celebrate his fall. His decimation too had to be amidst deafening staccato machinegun battle on the tarmac of a private airstrip. 'Teri maut toh aa rahi hai, woh dekh kutte,' screams the hero loudly in a victory message, moments before the tormentor is crushed under a screeching goods train.

With *Yaadon Ki Baaraat*, Pancham's music became more physical. The audience could associate its own freewheeling emotions with the beat. It is in this film that Bhupendra's twelve-string guitar – purchased at a music shop near the Strand, Bombay, at the persuasion of fellow guitarist Sunil Kaushik – finds one of its finest uses in Hindi films.

In the prelude of *'Chura liya'* (a tune inspired by *'If it's Tuesday, it must be Belgium'* from the 1969 film of the same name), along with the clinking of glasses, it is the twelve-string guitar strumming the notes of minor add ninth (or suspended on the fifth note from the root) chord that sets the ball rolling. The amalgamation of the guitar riffs and the saxophone pieces complements Asha Bhonsle's voice in particular, and makes the song a winner where the elements gel to generate a sound that is hip, sweet, smooth and very city-slick.

Any story on the music of *Yaadon Ki Baaraat* generally starts and ends with *'Chura liya'* as if it was *the* song in the film. Nothing can be farther from the truth. It is also rather ironic that a film with such a violent core plot should have a soft melody like *'Chura liya'* as its masthead. But that was what the multi-track storyline of *Yaadon Ki Baaraat* was all about – all

the subplots were strung together in a screenplay that would
have done a Rajasthani puppeteer proud.

The film had an arsenal of songs that fit the sequences
perfectly. The title song, sung by Lata Mangeshkar, Padmini
Kolhapure and Shivangi Kolhapure, embodies the spirit of the
nuclear families that were just about coming into existence. A
young Aamir Khan plays the youngest son who later grows up
to become Tariq. The same song unites the three lost brothers
after fifteen years. After the song was finalized, Nasir Husain
asked his chauffer to get a bottle of scotch for the team of
musicians to celebrate on the spot.

Fifteen filmi years later, it was time for motorbikes and flares,
with Tariq growing up to become Monty, a winsome singer and
guitarist at a happening nightclub in which youngsters celebrate
their graduation to the sound of electronic music. Cabaret was
now passé; the hero and the heroine did not mind joining the
band full swing in a medley of *'Aap ke kamre mein'*, *'Dil mil gaye'*
and *'Dum maro dum'*.

Pancham has been accused of borrowing the tune of *'Aap ke
kamre mein'* from the title music of *Sujata* (1959). It is agreed by
most Burman fans that S.D. Burman hardly had a vital role in
the arrangement of his songs or in the creation of background
music. As a sitting member in S.D. Burman's team, it is
probable that Pancham had a say in the background score, even
though Jaidev was the official assistant in *Sujata*. Besides, the
tune used as the title track in *Sujata* was itself inspired from
Rabindranath Tagore's melody, namely *'Kothao amar hariye
jabar nei mana'*.

The medley *'Aap ke kamre mein'* introduced to Hindi cinema
a concept commonly used in Hollywood musicals: songs woven
into dialogues, making them an important component of the
screenplay. The song actually walks listeners through a turning
point in the story as two of the three brothers miss being

reunited by a whisker. Pancham uses a snapshot of '*Dum maro dum*' with the rich girl Zeenat Aman sans her giant goggles and chanting beads.

The 'music-being-the-vehicle-for-the-story' idea that Kaushik Bhaumik speaks of is represented in the club number '*Lekar hum diwana dil*'. This wasn't a medley, but the song was tightly packed with events happening throughout the number. One brother is performing with his band at a club where his elder brother (Vijay Arora) works as a waiter. Elsewhere, a loyal henchman is garrotted as a reward for his loyalty; his piercing death scream synchronizes with the beginning of the track. Echoing twangs of the electric guitar, percussion and guitar riff are followed by an abrupt 'air pocket' fadeout, bringing the song to a grinding halt as if a power outage has happened. A halting start again, a picking up of speed, a typical hoot by Pancham, and the song finally gets into the groove – sax, brass, electric guitar, side percussion, wah pedal, female chorus, Asha Bhonsle, rhythm guitar, drum rolls and Kishore Kumar. Talk about musical impact!

Ranjit 'Kancha' Gazmer and Homi Mullan played the madal and the duggi in '*Lekar hum diwana dil*'. On the day of the recording, Kancha was delayed on his way to the studio and the recording was over by the time he reached. But Pancham said, 'Is gaane mein toh RD ka touch hona chahiye (This song should have the RD touch).' Kancha's madal was inserted after both the interludes, just before the antara starts, at the point when Dharmendra, the eldest sibling, glides from the roof of one highrise to the other on his mission to steal an expensive artefact.

The musical conceptualization of *Yaadon Ki Baaraat* was understandably similar to *Teesri Manzil*. Both films begin with murder and the story is propelled by revenge. But in *Yaadon Ki Baaraat*, it is a man seeking revenge whereas in *Teesri Manzil* the one on the avenging path is a woman who is shocked by the terrible discovery that the man she has fallen in love with seems to be the one who killed her sister. The real culprit in *Teesri Manzil*, his cover blown, prefers suicide to arrest despite the hero urging him otherwise. The film subtly suggests forgiving the criminal, considering the circumstances. Given this and the storyline's relative woman centricity, *Teesri Manzil*'s music, despite its Western influences, was a shade softer. *Yaadon Ki Baaraat* allowed no such clemency. Its script went about handing out punishments in cold blood. Its music was sharper, more electronic.

The other Asha–Kishore duet, '*O meri soni, meri tamanna*', in contrast to '*Lekar hum*' and '*Aap ke kamre mein*', had a velvety soft hue about it, showing a contrite Vijay Arora placating Zeenat for having lied to her. This song finds the irrepressible mime artist Kishore Kumar doing a Vijay Arora by mimicking his voice to a nicety, especially while pronouncing the name 'Soni'. The kiss-and-make-up essence of this song was underlined in Sujoy Ghosh's *Jhankar Beats* (2003) – whose story, probably in a first in Hindi cinema, was inspired by RD's music – in a domestic quarrel scene between husband and wife.

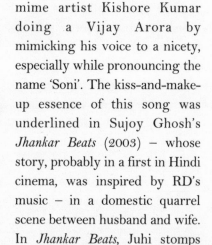

Over the decades, Kishore Kumar has imitated the voices of his colleagues. Examples are Asit Sen and Ashok Kumar (both in *Bhoot Bangla*), Dilip Kumar (in *Chalti Ka Naam Gaadi*) and S.D. Burman (in *Chhupa Rustam* and *Chalti Ka Naam Gaadi*). His most incredible mime was that of Pran in *Half Ticket*.

In *Jhankar Beats*, Juhi stomps off into the kitchen just the way Zeenat struts off across the valley in *Yaadon Ki Baaraat*. In *Yaadon Ki Baaraat* the song had that memorable sound of stone falling down the sheer cliff face; a sound conjured up by Cawas Lord playing the bongo with his nails instead of his fingers. In *Jhankar Beats* it was the kettle slipping from Juhi's fingers and Sanjay Suri catching it just in time.

Thirty years on, the Pancham legacy lives.

If *Yaadon Ki Baaraat* placed Pancham at the top of the heap among his contemporaries, it made a difference to the careers of many of its actors as well. It made Vijay Arora a star for a while, launched Tariq, gave a new dimension to Dharmendra's image and rescued Neetu Singh from *Rickshawala*. The only lead who failed to grab any attention was Jayshree Khosla, who appeared under her pseudonym Anamika. The film left its cast with happy memories of success – their yaadon ki baaraat.

11

The Swan Song

With every film-maker and actor trying his luck with the new formula on the block, the angry-young-man bandwagon was. brimming full. Amitabh Bachchan personifying the same in *Zanjeer* (1973) made the formula a fad; then it was Dharmendra's turn to begin settling into his clenched-fisted 'kutte-kaminey' avatar. Next in line was an unlikely leading man. Rishi Kapoor. Welcome to the 1970s.

For Rishi, *Zehreela Insaan* (1974) was as big a gamble as any. Given the herd mentality so typical of Bombay cinema, after the phenomenal success of *Bobby* (1973), one would have expected Rishi to continue being part of similar teenage love stories. But, though he would subsequently fall prey to the lover-boy image, immediately after *Bobby*, he showed remarkable courage in trying to do something entirely different. As the newest Kapoor on the scene, and one who would make quite a following for himself over the next decade, he was in a position to choose any composer he wished, and by voting for Pancham in some of his

SUDIPTA CHANDA

Father S.D. Burman

Mother Meera Dev Burman, a well-known lyricist who wrote a number of hit Bengali songs composed and sung by S.D. Burman

MILI BHATTACHARYA

HOMI MULLAN

Father and son: It took a lot for Pancham to emerge from the shadow of his father; as Sachin has narrated, Pancham made his father proud when people began referring to Sachin as RD's father after the release of *Hare Rama Hare Krishna*

RD, Mili Bhattacharya, Rita Patel (RD's first wife) and Badal Bhattacharya at Mili and Badal's wedding

MILI BHATTACHARYA

Sachin Bhowmick with his wife Bansari, S.D. Burman, Sharmila Tagore and Meera Dev Burman

SACHIN BHOWMICK

RD with Asha Bhonsle, one of Hindi film music's most enduring composer–singer partnerships

VISHWAS NERURKAR

AMITAVA CHAKRABORTY

From right to left: Basu Chakravarty, Pancham, unidentified, S.D. Burman, Majrooh Sultanpuri, Mohammad Rafi, Maruti Rao and Manohari Singh during the making of *Teen Deviyan* in which Pancham assisted his father on the music

VISHWAS NERURKAR

Together they created magic: *standing left to right*, Chandrakant, sound recordist Deepan Chatterjee, Maruti Rao, Louis Banks, Manohari Singh, Pancham, Ulhas Bapat, D.M. Tagore, Basu Chakravarty; *seated left to right*, Raju, Ranjit Gazmer, Devi Chakrabarty, Santosh, Devichand Chauhan, Homi Mullan, Suresh Bhoi, Binoy Singh and Aman

KUSHAL GOPALKA AND HOMI MULLAN

After the master: *standing left to right*, Homi Mullan, Amrutrao, Kersi Lord, Bhanu Gupta; *seated left to right*, Ranjan Sirkar (a friend), Manohari Singh, Ramesh Iyer and Ranjit Gazmer

At a recording session: *left to right,* Maruti Rao, Bhanu Gupta, Basu Chakravarty, Manohari Singh and R.D. Burman

Drumming it up: Kersi Lord with R.D. Burman

Going over the notes: R.D. Burman with Kishore Kumar and Manohari Singh

Maruti Rao, Pancham and Badal Bhattacharya

In the studios: Manohari Singh (*standing*) with Pancham

On stage with Bhupinder (*extreme left*), Maruti Rao and Manohari Singh

RD was a vibrant on-stage performer and his live performances used to be quite a craze; here, he is seen with Neetu Singh and the composer duo Kalyanji–Anandji (*top*), and with Asha Bhonsle (*middle* and *bottom*)

VISHWAS NERURKAR

VISHWAS NERURKAR

VISHWAS NERURKAR

Pancham composed one of his most memorable songs, 'Bade achche lagte hain', in Balika Badhu; here, he is seen with its producer Shakti Samanta (*extreme right*), director Tarun Majumdar (*second from right*) and well-known Bengali star Sandhya Roy (*second from left*)

Sharing a lighter moment with Lata Mangeshkar and Kishore Kumar, who, along with Asha Bhonsle, were the mainstays of Pancham's compositions

With Usha Mangeshkar and Kishore Kumar

With Kishore Kumar, whose death in 1987 shattered Pancham, leading him to say that with the singer's death, he had lost his voice

With Asha Bhonsle and Rajesh Khanna; Pancham composed some of his most memorable melodies for the star

The maestro with his two muses, Kishore Kumar and Asha Bhonsle

With Asha Bhonsle and lyricist Gulshan Bawra, who wrote the popular songs of films like *Kasme Vaade* and *Satte Pe Satta*, among others

With Laxmikant of the composer duo Laxmikant–Pyarelal; though they were competitors right through the 1970s, they shared a close relationship, with Pancham playing the mouth organ for them in *Dosti*, while they arranged the music for *Chhote Nawab*

With screenplay writer Sachin Bhowmick, during the making of the hit Bengali song '*Mone pore Ruby Ray*', which was Bhowmick's ode to a lady he had lost his heart to

From left to right: Anand Bakshi, Lata, Pancham and Vijay Anand; while Bakshi wrote some of Pancham's cult songs like '*Dum maro dum*' and '*Chingari koi bhadke*', Vijay Anand directed Pancham's first success as composer, *Teesri Manzil*

VISHWAS NERURKAR

MILI BHATTACHARYA

One for the album: with Guru Dutt (*lying down*) and Geeta Dutt

Jiving to '*Dum maro dum*'? Asha, Bhanu Gupta, Anand Bakshi and Pancham

MILI BHATTACHARYA

With lyricist Majrooh Sultanpuri (*middle*) and director–producer Nasir Husain (*right*); the combination created magic with *Yaadon Ki Baaraat* and *Hum Kisise Kum Naheen*

Jaya Bhaduri (*seated left*), producer Gogi Anand (*standing*) and Madhu Behl, Ramesh Behl's wife (*seated right*), at Pancham's Saraswati Puja celebrations

With Dr Mukesh Hariawala, who performed the bypass surgery on Pancham in 1989

Pancham was never academically inclined and thus it was not surprising that he failed twice at his school, Ballygunge Government High School (*top*), after which he was forced to shift to Tirthapati Institution (*middle*)

Pancham's car

Rajat Gupta

Sketch by Subhasis Poddar

Ali Akbar Khan (*top*), at whose school in Calcutta Pancham learnt to play the sarod; Samta Prasad (*bottom*), who was also one of the two tabla players in the celebrated chase scene involving Hema Malini and her tonga in *Sholay*

Mentors

SKETCH BY SUBHASIS PODDAR

AASHISH KHAN AND SAURAV

The blind tabla player Brajen Biswas (*top*);
Aashish Khan (*bottom*), son of Ali Akbar Khan

BRAHMANAND SIINGH

BRAHMANAND SIINGH

biggest successes, he showed that he was willing to give a free hand to the composer rather than prescribe musical ideas to him.

Zehreela Insaan was based on a novel by Sahitya Akademi Award winner T.R. Subba Rao, and was remade from its Kannada version *Nagara Haavu* by the same director, S.R. Puttana Kanagal. It had Rishi essaying his version of the angry young man. Shot at a location near Bangalore, the only news this film made was actress Moushumi Chatterjee's much-publicized showdown with producer Virendra Sinha. Moushumi, who was pregnant at that time with her daughter Payal, claimed that Sinha was not considerate about her physical condition and was unfairly demanding. 'I will never work with him again.' She could not have even if she had wanted to. Sinha as a film-maker did not last very long.

As for Rishi, the drooping moustache did not prove adequate to change his *Bobby* image and for him to be accepted as the college ruffian that he portrayed. In the film, he is a rebel with a golden heart, misunderstood by all except the two women in his life and a teacher who stands as the repository of virtues.

The film's music was the only bright spark in an otherwise dreary screenplay. The bubbly Asha Bhonsle solo '*Yeh silsila, pyar ka chala*', with its locomotive-like rhythm, had an ensemble consisting of the acoustic guitar, the santoor, the conga and the transicord. Composed on a major scale, it exudes a feeling of happiness. The Lata Mangeshkar solo '*Suno kahani*' recounts the hideous tale of Moushumi forced into prostitution by her husband; the mood is more reflective and narrative than maudlin. The first two lines begin without any metre since the song depicts the heroine's numbness rather than the agony that preceded it. Keeping with the norm in sentimental numbers, minor chords rule, but the shift to major chords in the penultimate line of the mukhra '*Phir aandhi aayi, daali tuti*' and in the antara accentuates the consciousness of grief.

Pancham adapted the tune for the title song '*Saanp se badhke*' from a Mikis Theodorakis composition for the background score of *Zorba the Greek* (1964). In contrast to his normally innovative recrafting, this song seems to be a direct lift and Shailendra Singh, in his first solo for Pancham, sounds tuneless and brittle.

Shailendra Singh's duet with Asha Bhonsle, '*Mere dil se ye nain*', with its folksy flavour, was more like what one expected Pancham to extract from a newcomer. The singers were supposed to skip a beat in the second line of the mukhra, a requirement Singh initially had problems with, but eventually mastered to Pancham's satisfaction.

As Asha Bhonsle has pointed out often, even as late as in an interview on 23 May 2009 in the *Ananda Bazar Patrika*, Kolkata, Pancham's man management was exemplary. He knew exactly how to get the best out of his singers and musicians without putting them under undue stress. 'Pancham-da had a unique style of extracting work from singers and musicians,' singer Shurjo Bhattacharya says, based on his keen observation of RD. 'In appearance and style, he was regal; you could see that he was simply made of a different material compared to everyone around him, but he never let this surface in his work. He was funny with Kishore Kumar, serious with Manna Dey, and very warm and friendly with Lata Mangeshkar. In fact, I have often seen him talk with Lata-ji in Bengali and discuss family matters.'

Today, *Zehreela Insaan* is remembered most for Kishore Kumar's solo '*O hansini*'. Legend has it that it was initially supposed to be sung by Shailendra Singh who had become the voice of Rishi Kapoor after *Bobby*, but the recording was postponed by a few weeks, due to a musicians' strike, and the song was passed on to Kishore Kumar. Rishi Kapoor recalls, '"*O hansini*" was probably the first song that Pancham recorded for me. I was very insistent that Shailendra sings the song. Maybe

Pancham's ego or whatever, but he wanted Kishore to sing it.
At that point I was not sure how the song would sound; but I
later realized that it was a marvellous song. It was recorded
down south. It has a very soothing effect. The song *"Mere dil
se"* is also among my personal favourites.'

'*O hansini*' is an exemplary Pancham prototype, with the
ephemeral use of the major note in a song based on the minor
scale, giving it a sweet yet sorrowful flavour. Like many of
Pancham's songs, '*Ab jo mile hain*' and '*Chura liya*' among others,
it starts on the minor ninth chord. The dream-like quality of
the song is captured in the picturization with Moushumi's
swan-like approach, dressed in angelic white, breezing past
Rishi Kapoor like an illusion. Majrooh's lyrics, with a
predominance of consonants but ending in vowels – '*Kahan ud
chali, mere armaano ke, pankh laga ke, kahan ud chali*' – leave
behind an echoing, drawn-out feeling, enhanced by Kishore
Kumar's serene yet powerful execution. The sequence suffers
due to inept camerawork, with Moushumi's pregnancy suddenly
showing all over her face; perhaps due to a significant gap in the
shooting schedules of this film. A website dedicated to Indian
tunes inspired from the West claims that Pancham based the
tune of the first line of the song on Michel Legrand's original
Oscar-winning score for the film *Summer of '42*, which was
released in the US in April 1971, and in Asia in August 1971.
Incidentally, Pancham had used the mukhra of '*O hansini*' as
part of the background score in *Kati Patang* in 1970. It does not
mandate extraordinary intelligence to infer that a piece of music
composed in 1970 could not have been inspired by a score
released in 1971.

What the website missed out was that Pancham was, in all
probability, impressed by the song '*Snow frolic*' composed by
Francis Lai for *Love Story* (1970, directed by Arthur Hiller), and
was inspired by the progression of the same to write the piece
of background music just preceding '*O hansini*'.

2

The following year, Rishi Kapoor was back as the rich young
Punjabi boy with unruly locks, 'chikna' looks, a peculiar 'skidding'
laughter, excelling in areas ranging from college hockey to
sneaking up to girls' hostels and getting caught by the warden.

The melancholy brought about by *Zehreela Insaan* was
smoothed over with the playful saga of Ravi Tandon's *Khel Khel
Mein* (1975). With this film, Kishore Kumar established himself
as Rishi Kapoor's principal voice. Shailendra Singh sang only
one song, '*Humne tumko dekha*'. Pancham himself lent his voice
to Rakesh Roshan for '*Sapna mera toot gaya*', a duet with Asha
Bhonsle. It is one of the very few songs he sang in his *own*
voice – without the guttural inflection one normally associates
with him – which had thinned considerably due to a bout of
tonsillitis he had suffered from as a child. It is evident that
Pancham used the strains of Ennio Morricone's piece '*Story of
a soldier*' from *The Good, the Bad and the Ugly* (1966), but the
inspiration was limited to a single line, and Pancham's song was
radically different. Asha Bhonsle's near-hysterical dialogue
intonation and demented laughter that taper off into a sob at
the end of the track add to the sense of loss that runs through
the song, and are something no other singer in the industry
could have replicated.

Bhanu Gupta and Ramesh Iyer say that Pancham would grill
the director, trying to understand the song sequence in as much
detail as possible. The results are there to see. According to
Rishi Kapoor, 'The image transition from *Zehreela Insaan* to
Khel Khel Mein had happened and the music facilitated the
transformation.'

'*Ek main aur ek tu*' has a college boy and his girlfriend
sneaking out for a midnight romance. The intermittent use of
the recorder and the guitar sets the mood for the night. At
various points in the song one hears only a solitary instrument

at play. In the transition from mukhra back to antara, we hear the hush-hush sound followed by just the percussion. Both Asha and Kishore alternated their tonal volumes from high to a sudden low, consistent with the sequence.

In sharp contrast, in the song '*Aaye lo pyar ke din*', shot in full daylight, the pair cavort, roll, fall, tumble down snowy slopes, full-throated, without bothering about being seen or heard. It's a dream, after all.

'*Khullam khulla*' saw Pancham pitching in with innovative sounds like gargling and even recreating the sound of a man taking a leak after downing a lot of liquor.

'Pancham had this great capacity to take suggestions on everything. The gimmicks in "*Khullam khulla*" owed themselves to a lot of people giving ideas,' remembers Rishi. 'At that point, I was the youngest hero working for RD. So I had the best of his peppy music, *Khel Khel Mein, Hum Kisise Kum Naheen*. Music which was basically youthful. Pancham, by and large, has given me great, great music,' he sums up.

The *Khel Khel Mein* combination of Rishi Kapoor, Neetu Singh and Rakesh Roshan returned four years later with another romcom called *Jhoota Kahin Ka* (1979), in which director Ravi Tandon paid homage to the song '*Greased lightning*' (*Grease*, 1978) with Pancham's version of a garage song based on the blues scale, '*Dil mein jo mere sama gayi*'. Pancham recreated the outdoorsy romantic sound of '*Ek main aur ek tu*' with '*Barah baje ki suiyon jaise*', and the big band sound of '*Sapna mera toot gaya*' with '*Jeevan ke har mod pe*'.

Pancham's relationship with Rishi Kapoor continued right through the 1970s, even in a production from Devar films in the south. A venture that saw Rishi in his maiden double role, *Raja* (1976) had rhythmic numbers, including '*Jee chahe*' and '*Kal yahan aayi thi woh*', which turned out to be among the most searched for numbers a decade later. The film, however, was a mega flop, and did nothing either for Pancham's reputation or for the songs themselves, which caught on among Pancham aficionados only in the age of the Internet.

Raj Kapoor was the only member of the Kapoor family who had not worked with Pancham, although the latter had a high regard for the showman's directorial abilities and was keen on teaming with him. His brothers Shashi and Shammi had already endorsed RD in their actor and director avatars, and the careers of his sons Rishi and Randhir resounded with Pancham's compositions.

'I remember when I was a nobody, Raj Kapoor had come to Calcutta for the premiere of *Jaagte Raho*, where he introduced Salil Chowdhury,' Pancham admitted, in *Showtime*, July 1992, referring to an instance when Raj Kapoor graciously introduced Salil Chowdhury to the press and audience. 'I told myself, "How I wish one day Raj Kapoor would introduce me like that." My dream came true when, years later, he called me on stage during the premiere of *Dharam Karam* [1975].'

'Jaikishan was no more. Since my youth, I was a great fan of Shammi and Jaikishan. I had a fascination for Jaikishan. But then he was no more and I had got into the R.D. Burman mould. *Rickshawala* had very good music too. Pancham gave tremendous music in *Dharam Karam*,' says Randhir Kapoor, the director of the film, whose support for Pancham opened the doors of the R.K. family for the composer.

Interestingly enough, Pancham made *Dharam Karam*'s music sound like Shankar–Jaikishan's. He catered to the style patronized by Raj Kapoor and rolled out the same six years later in R.K. Films' *Biwi O Biwi* (1981). In *Dharam Karam*, an eighty-piece orchestra with the piano accordion leading the way created the ambience Raj Kapoor wanted for the song '*Ek din bik jayega*'. Albeit a shade loud, this became one of Pancham's biggest hits during that time. The suspended fourth chord was used delectably in the Mukesh–Kishore–Asha song *'Tere humsafar geet hain tere'*.

According to Pancham, Raj Kapoor had wanted to use him for *Prem Rog* (1982) again, but changed his mind and declared that he wanted newcomers, only to finally opt for Laxmikant–Pyarelal. But Pancham's awe for Raj remained throughout his life. Continuing in the same interview, (*Showtime*, July 1992), Pancham expressed his admiration for the precision with which some of the stalwarts he composed for described their song situations: '. . . people like Raj Kapoor, Nasir Husain and Dev Anand make you sing extempore.'

Of course, Randhir Kapoor remembers Pancham fondly. Like many other people we have interviewed for this book, he also vouches for Pancham's remarkable ability to find inspiration in his surroundings. Sounds from any source, the whirr of a ceiling fan (*'Suno, kaho'*), a faulty note (*'Chingari koi bhadke'*), a foot scraping against paper – could spark music in his mind. 'He would land up at 10.30 p.m. at my Malabar Hills residence from Tardeo Studios excitedly wanting to play his new tunes to me over a drink,' says Randhir, recounting his friend's spontaneity and exuberance.

3

This spontaneity was the hallmark of Pancham's scores for two of Dev Anand's films, *Heera Panna* (1973) and *Ishk Ishk Ishk* (1974) – films where Pancham composed without preparation, almost on the spur of the moment, to produce results that are revered even today.

'When Dev Anand came to me for *Heera Panna*, I was in a bad mood and I told him so,' Pancham recalled in an interview in *Showtime*, 1992, when discussing the film. 'He said fine, and we got talking; and by the end of the meeting, I had composed all the songs of *Heera Panna*.'

A lilting tune, the bossa nova, the click of the camera shutter
and a westernized Raga Khamaj formed the base of the four
songs in *Heera Panna* (surprisingly few for a Navketan movie).
The title track *'Panna ki tamanna'*, a Lata–Kishore duet, was one
that Dev Anand approved the moment Pancham played it from
his pre-recorded spools. *'Bahut duur mujhe chale jana hai'*, with
its ominous feel of impending separation, was appropriately
composed for the scene just before Raakhee dies in a plane
crash, the bossa nova lending the song its special cadence. A sad
version of the number, hummed by Bhupendra, was used only
in the film, and did not find a place in the vinyl and cassettes
of the film.

The picturization of *'Main tasveer utarta hun'*, the only Kishore
solo in the film, had Zeenat Aman swinging in a hammock in
a multicoloured bikini – underlining her pre-eminence as the
favourite poster girl of the early 1970s. Dev Anand, as usual,
looked more like a fashion statement himself than the fashion
photographer that he played. *'Ek paheli hai tu'*, the Kishore–
Asha 'duet' where Asha only hums, was another of Pancham's
improvisations on the Raga Khamaj framework.

Despite the expansive rocks that lent the film the ambience
of a Western (the film was shot near Tumkur on NH-4, the
Madras–Bangalore highway) and the well-knit songs (a Navketan
tradition), *Heera Panna* was a moderate success. For a story
built around a burglary theme, it moved very slowly in some
parts and too quickly in others, resulting in an uneven screenplay.
Zeenat Aman's swing wasn't enough to pull the film through.

Heera Panna's title track, a guitar riff gradually segueing into
the tune of *'Panna ki tamanna'*, is a perennial favourite with fans.
'Panna ki tamanna' was also one of the first film tracks to be
adopted in a TV ad, for a leading shaving product.

Ishk Ishk Ishk, which followed *Heera Panna*, was Dev's biggest
flop in the 1970s. The film, a tribute to the director's trekking

days, looked more like an exquisite visual documentary on the Himalayan range near places like Pokhra, Shyangboche and Thyangboche in Nepal. A film needs the backbone of a strong storyline; this one was just a pretty picture postcard.

What Dev did manage in this film, apart from getting Pancham to compose a truly different score, was to gather an ensemble of actors starting out on their careers, all of whom went on to become major players on the national and international cinema scene: Shabana Azmi, Kabir Bedi and Shekhar Kapur. This was Shabana Azmi's second film and she was yet to become the torch-bearer of the New Indian Cinema.

According to actress Padmini Kapila, Shabana's role in *Ishk Ishk Ishk* was initially meant for her, but circumstances forced Dev to sign Shabana Azmi. Apparently, the name of Shabana's character, Pammi, was derived from Padmini's nickname. Zarina Wahab, Padmini Kolhapure, and Dev's nephew Shekhar Kapur made their debut with this movie.

The music of the film was a shift from Pancham's prevalent style – the orchestra was smaller, percussion less predominant, the acoustic guitar was used instead of the electric, and Pancham showed a marked, yet uncharacteristic, preference for traditional instruments. The piano accordion added a colonial feel to the songs and dance sequences; snippets of Irish folk and Spanish matador music were also used. The harmonica and acoustic guitar went well with the Himalayan setting, and the yodelling fitted right in. There was also a central motif, the note progression Sa Re Ga Ma Re Ni Sa (C D E F D B C), which was used for four of the songs in the film: '*Tim tim chamka*', '*Achche bachche nahi rote hain*', '*Wallah kya nazar hai*' and '*Bheegi bheegi ankhen*'. The rhythm pattern of '*Chal saathi chal*', a trekking number, would be used by Pancham again, for '*Ye ladka hai Allah*' in *Hum Kisise Kum Naheen*.

Pancham did face flak from the media for *Ishk Ishk Ishk*. He responded many years later: 'Often, of course, I meet people who hold me responsible for having started a lot of noise in Hindi film music. They mention films like *Hare Rama Hare Krishna* and *Ishk Ishk Ishk*. But I loved doing those songs.'

The film's Himalayan failure at the box office impacted its music, which got buried in the avalanche. However, like a lot of other RD compositions, the music of *I3* (as *Ishk Ishk Ishk* is known) is something of a cult on web forums today.

4

In the 1970s, Hindi film producers and directors were shifting camps randomly. The worst hit was Shankar, who found many of the Shankar–Jaikishan flag bearers leaving him after Jaikishan's demise. O.P. Nayyar too was suffering from a crisis of confidence and the loss of inspiration following his alleged 'break-up' with Asha Bhonsle on 6 August 1972. Never a versatile composer and totally at sea with the 'beat' generation, Naushad no longer commanded a following. The decade saw composers Laxmikant–Pyarelal making the most of it, securing the support of Raj Kapoor and the commercially successful, albeit stifled by his partiality for melodrama, director Manoj Kumar. Pancham was an obvious aspirant to some of the seats vacated by S-J and OP. Not that the patronage of directors like Bhappie Sonie, Deven Verma, S. Mukherjee or O.P. Ralhan really helped his career graph, but it definitely gave another dimension to his music.

Sonie, who had run into major differences of opinion with the Sippys while directing *Brahmachari* (1968) for them, made films like *Jaanwar* (1965) and *Jawan Mohabbat* (1971) which were light, melodramatic, and revolved mostly around the charisma of Shammi Kapoor. The music too followed the same pattern, and a song from the house of Bhappie Sonie was no different

from a song from the house of the Mukherjees if the hero was
Shammi Kapoor and the composers Shankar–Jaikishan.

Pancham's compositions for Bhappie Sonie's *Jheel Ke Us
Paar* (1973) – where Sonie collaborated with writer Gulshan
Nanda following Nanda's success with stories like *Kati Patang,
Sharmilee* and *Naya Zamana* – carried considerable ballast. It
was different in style and definitely high on sophistication.

The class was apparent in the Kishore Kumar solo *'Kya nazare
kya sitare'*, the key song in the film. It was probably composed
during the same time as *'Rasta dekhey tera'* from *Humshakal*,
given the prominent use of the Ni (major seventh) note in the
termination of the first line of the mukhra. However, the second
line ends in Sa, the first note of the octave, and gives a feel of
completion, as opposed to the craving for sleep in *'Rasta dekhe
tera'*. A much-underrated number, *'Kya nazare'* is a technically
challenging song for any singer as it mandates hitting very
straight notes; there is little freedom to work around the tune
like in classic rock and roll or the blues.

The Mangeshkar sisters, Asha and Lata, were again placed in
competition with the solos *'Haye bichua das gayo re'* and *'Do
ghoont mujhe bhi pila de sharabi'*. Both were cheeky melodies,
featured on the two lead female characters: one on a mission of
seduction and the other trying to avoid being seduced. These
numbers remain retro-night favourites in pubs and stage shows
even now. In Calcutta, a night-long fare of Hindi songs during
Puja time or a Ganesh visarjan in Pune is incomplete without
'Do ghoont'.

The song also marked the entry of musician Tony Vaz, who
was, in the opinion of most musicians, one of the most vital cogs
in the R.D. Burman wheel. The bass guitar would change
forever in the hands of this shy and eccentric artiste.

The Lata solo *'Babul tere bagian di main bulbul'*, although
reminiscent of her solo *'O babul pyare'* three years earlier for

composers Kalyanji–Anandji in *Johnny Mera Naam*, was different since it was a lullaby. As a lullaby, '*Babul tere*' was inappropriate as it is set at a high pitch, hardly conducive for sleep. But as a stand-alone poignant number, its intensity in portraying a father–daughter relationship is reminiscent of Pancham's more celebrated '*Beeti na bitayi raina*'. More vocal than the former, but certainly not soggy to the point of melodrama.

Bhappie Sonie's name went down as one more film-maker who switched his loyalties to Pancham. The professional relationship continued for the next ten years, till *Bade Dil Wala* (1983).

A self-confessed fan and friend of Jaikishan, comedian and film-maker Deven Verma had used S-J for his hit *Yakeen* (1969), which he produced, and for *Nadaan* (1971), his directorial debut which flopped. With Jaikishan no more, Verma knocked on Pancham's door for his second attempt at direction in *Bada Kabutar* (1973). While the film turned out to be a cold turkey, Pancham's infectious composition '*Haye re haye re*' with its jugglery of beats was like a sedan showroom in the midst of a desert.

Pancham's second film with O.P. Ralhan (after the songless *Hulchul*) was *Bandhe Haath* (1973), the last of Amitabh Bachchan's failures on the way to success (his next film was *Zanjeer*). Stuck with a lousy screenplay, *Bandhe Haath* failed to evoke the tension it tried to depict. Apart from '*O majhi jayen kahan*', quite imperceptibly inspired from '*Mammy blue*' – a sad song composed by Hubert Giraud and Phil Trim and rendered by a number of singers like Roger Whitaker and Julio Iglesias – the other songs were hardly noticed. Three decades later, the song was lauded by Gulzar as an inimitable casting of Bhatiyali folk in a Western mould. Pancham's range of genres, much wider compared to any composer in his peer group, can be gauged from even a non-starrer like *Bandhe Haath*, which had at least

three more songs, each with a different mood and structure.
The title song 'Kya jano main hun kaun' features the hero at the
locus of a confrontation, unable to come to terms with his
denial. Pancham used this as an opportunity to remodel a happy
song 'Tobu bole keno' from the Bengali film Rajkumari into a
song of thoughtful sadness. Wedded admirably to Majrooh
Sultanpuri's lyrics, the tune gradually rises to a crescendo with
the lines 'Dekho, yeh mere bandhe haath'. While the Bengali
original exudes zestful enthusiasm with a hint of pain, the Hindi
version gives vent to the emotions suppressed within the
pusillanimous hero. Perhaps, in order to infuse the desired
emotion into the song, Pancham altered the very sequence of
the original, interchanging the mukhra and the antara.

Lata Mangeshkar's 'Tuney chheen liya' was in contrast to the
serenity and sobriety one normally associates with her songs.
Here, in a deviation from the fence-sitter attitude one discerns
in Lata's fast-paced numbers, she lets her emotions fly, making
her sound volubly liberated without being impish (à la 'Bhai
battur' in Padosan).

The early 1970s witnessed the beginning of Pancham's fascination
for Asha Bhonsle's voice, and the song 'Dil to lei gawa' was an
experiment where her ability for vocal callisthenics was put to
the test. One of Pancham's definite wild moments where he
makes Manna Dey chant gibberish and mouth Tarzan calls, the
song is also noticeable for its African feel, with a motley of
sounds and rapid beat patterns. This genre of music was tried
out by other Hindi film composers in the 1970s, but it was
probably beyond imitation; it began and ended with Pancham.

O.P. Ralhan's last film to garner a good box office response
was Talash. When Pancham heard the plot as Ralhan narrated
it to SD, he was noticeably upset as he was working on a film
with an almost identical story. The film with 'an identical
story', started in 1966, was released years later as Phir Kab

Milogi (1974), and it was a surprisingly awful offering from Hrishikesh Mukherjee. The Lata–Mukesh classic *'Kahin karti hogi'*, the pivotal song in the film, was 'discovered' following the song's re-release in 1986 in a twelve-pack album titled *Yaadon Ki Manzil* by HMV. Pancham had tamed a typical Spanish matador tune called *'Lonely bull'* and turned it into a soft romantic number with a dream-like feel. Music lovers would surely have preferred being gored to death than having to listen to the distorted remix of the song by Anamika.

Though Sasadhar Mukherjee and his kin had worked regularly with S.D. Burman, the only instance of Pancham working full-time with the Mukherjees was when Subodh Mukherjee, Sasadhar's brother, signed him for *Mr Romeo* (1973). Directed by Subodh Mukherjee's son Subhas Mukherjee, one remembers a few posters of the film and that's about it.

What went wrong with *Mr Romeo*, apart from the fact that as a film it hardly made any sense? Both the Asha–Kishore duet *'Yahan nahi kahungi'* and the Lata–Kishore duet *'Na soyenge na sone denge'* were framed as question–answers, where the melody was sparkling and the rhythm vibrant. The short guitar prelude in the former and the use of the suspended fourth chord in the latter lent an orchestral elegance to the songs. The thoughtful usage of Kishore Kumar for a solitary reprise in the antara of *'Na soyenge'* brought back shades of the reluctant male partner in *'Neend churake raaton mein'* (*Shareef Budmaash*, 1973). *'Ja re ja main tose na bolun'* was an experiment designed for Lata Mangeshkar, with short phrases of notes woven in a complicated mesh of beats. *'Hey, mujhe dil de'*, the peppy Kishore–Asha duet, with Bhupendra and Pancham coming in patches, was zesty and swift. With variations in rhythm, it delivered a knockout punch. The finely disguised application of the tune of *'Mera kya sanam'* from S.D. Burman's *Talash* in the refrain was deliciously Pancham-ish. One can also trace back the tune of *'Mera kya sanam*' to the sax solo in the second antara of '*Din dhal jaye*' from *Guide*. Asha Bhonsle's '*Isi shahar ki kisi gali mein*' was a novel way of a girl refusing marriage, a number in the singing–talking–shouting mould based on the bossa nova, with Asha's voice recorded in an overlapping double track in the last stanza.

Regarding the overlaps between Pancham's and his father's tunes, this is what Manohari Singh had to say, especially about the song '*Hey, mujhe dil de*': There was a certain working relationship between father and son, and both influenced each other. Baap bete mein aisa chalta hi tha. The tune of "*Mera kya sanam*" could have been created from the sax piece in *Guide*. I know who was more instrumental in the orchestration as I handled the arrangement of *Guide* and *Teen Deviyan*. But the credit should always be given to the official composer.'

Kishore Kumar's solo '*Dil toota re*' was a trifle loud and did not fit too well in the film. The Bengali version for a Puja album, with Pancham singing the blues, was experimental, but Sachin Bhowmick's lyrics '*Ke kande*' were pedestrian and irritating.

Most of the stylizations in the form of colouring of chords, application of harmony, chord inversions and leading bass notes were there in the right proportion in the songs for the film. Was the music, then, too avant-garde for its time? Was the audience not accustomed to this genre of sound or the seldom-used question-answer style in the duets? Pancham was experimenting with the dialogue-interspersed songs characteristic of Western musicals — something unfamiliar to an audience brought up on a diet of conventional, mushy, symmetrical notes and lyrics.

'The word "different" is used very loosely today. With Pancham, "different" was really different,' avers Amit Kumar. *Mr Romeo*'s music was different.

5

Pancham's journey in the first half of the 1970s was an exotic musical drive on an uncertain personal highway. He had legally separated from Rita, and it is rumoured that his relationship with Asha Bhonsle was pretty unsettling for his parents, especially for his mother Meera. He had shifted from Hotel Caesar Palace to Odena building in Khar, where the terrace flat was witness to some of his less-heard compositions. One such song was '*Jeena toh hai par aai dil kahan*', featured on a hero as unlikely as Manu Narang.

Manohar Lal Narang was a businessman and hotelier who was in the news in Bombay during the early 1970s, and also during the mid- and end-1970s when he shifted his place of operation to England. Given the glamour the film profession entails, Manu Narang too chose film production and acting as an alternative career with *Paanch Dushman* (1973), re-released almost a decade later as *Daulat Ke Dushman* (1982). Billed as a film with an anti-smuggling propaganda, it made smuggling appear as easy as cycling and as boring as angling. The music, however, was an underground favourite with Pancham seekers throughout 1970s and '80s. Kishore Kumar sparkled in the solo '*Jeena toh hai*' – which had subtle shades of Simon and Garfunkel's '*The sounds of silence*' – as he did in '*Jo bhi hua hai*' and '*Jaana hai hamen toh jahan*', the latter song mildly similar in form to '*Meri bheegi bheegi si*'. '*Jeena toh hai*' is mainly conspicuous for its avant-garde form, with the mukhra starting on the minor chord and ending on the major chord of the root.

'*The sounds of silence*' seemed to enamour Nadeem–Shravan far more. They quietly photocopied the original tune note by note in '*Pal do pal ki zindagi*', the title song of *Maine Jeena Seekh Liya* (1982).

The early 1970s saw a gradual shift in film genres. Romance was waning in favour of violence-laden cop stories, espionage dramas and whodunits. The demand for brawny leading men grew, and composers had to adjust the music to fit in with the changing scenario. Pancham was now composing for a higher percentage of action-based films like *Madhosh, Goonj, Double Cross*, etc. One thriller Pancham did around that time was *Benaam* (loosely based on Hitchcock's *The Man Who Knew Too Much*), for which he teamed with director Narendra Bedi after *Jawani Diwani* and *Dil Diwana.*

Bedi also roped in Pancham for another film, a Wild West saga. Straddling genres was not exactly what composers would have loved, but in the 1970s, Pancham accepted films with diverse music requirements, from painting the dark hues of a film noir to laying out the canvas for the brightness of the Western.

The film was Narendra Bedi's *Khhotte Sikkay* (1974), a mix of *The Magnificent Seven* (1960) and *The Good, the Bad and the Ugly,* with Feroz Khan appearing in an all-black attire as The Man With No Name, riding a wild stallion on the road to nowhere. It was probably the country's first curry Western, and Pancham's warm-up for *the* curry Western which was to be released on the heels of this one.

By a strange coincidence there was a 'khota sikka' in that too.

12

The Film of the Millennium and the Aftermath

'Dead ember', 'thematically, it's a gravely flawed attempt', 'an imitation Western ... neither here nor there' were some of the critical responses that welcomed the film. The actor originally chosen to essay the villain had refused the project as he was busy with another. The director was being sued by actor–producer Joginder for allegedly having copied the theme from his film *Bindiya Aur Bandook* (1973). Actor MacMohan grumbled to the director about the length of his role in the final edited version, considering all the work he had put in. The film took almost two-and-a-half years to complete and went rupees three lakh over budget.

Upon its release on 15 August 1975, the movie was termed a commercial disaster. It was lucky to have landed a Filmfare Award for editing by M.S. Shinde.

Over time, the film managed to win a few more laurels: the highest-grossing Indian film ever for one; running for over five years at Minerva, the largest cinema hall in Bombay. This was the first movie to release a disc containing its dialogues alone; in addition to the hundreds of thousands of music records released by Polydor that had already been sold.

Ramesh Sippy's *Sholay*.

'The film of the millennium' was the BBC's verdict.

'The greatest star cast ever assembled', the posters say till this date.

'The greatest story ever told', the tag line claimed.

True, if one considers the way the story has been told.

Javed Akhtar, reminiscing with Nasreen Munni Kabir, agrees that *Sholay* was based on John Sturges's film *The Magnificent Seven*.

The lead characters Veeru and Jai, though, may have been modelled on *Butch Cassidy and the Sundance Kid* (1969). Dharmendra's drunken scene atop the water tank had its predecessors in Kishore Kumar in *Chacha Zindabad* (1959) and Anthony Quinn in *The Secret of Santa Vittoria* (1969). The tossing of the coin to one's advantage was, in all likelihood, inspired from Henry Hathaway's *Garden of Evil* (1954) or Marlon Brando's *One-Eyed Jacks* (1961).

But what about the music?

The audience might have expected deafening trumpets and an eighty-five-piece band hammering away throughout the 188 minutes as a reminder that *Sholay* was an action movie. What was heard, however, was palpably different.

The concept of songs in movies is peculiar to this part of the subcontinent. Songs do not add character to cinema and, as per classical definitions, distract from cinematic expression, unless of course one is talking of a musical. It is the quality of the background music or its absence that underlines the character of the film, rather than the songs.

Sholay's background music was central to the film's narrative core, its fifth dimension, along with Thakur, Gabbar, Veeru and Jai.

When Thakur's family is wiped off by Gabbar, à la the massacre by Henry Fonda in Sergio Leone's *Once Upon a Time in the West* (1968), the only sounds heard are gunshots, punctuated by the languid hooves of a horse slowly trotting down the hill and the elaborate creaking of a lawn swing. The scene is not so much about action as it is about terror.

During Jai's funeral, one only hears the crackling of dry firewood and the harmonica.

In the famous 'Kitne aadmi the?' scene in which Gabbar torments his failed men over a game of Russian roulette before shooting them, the singular banshee wail – created by a combination of the organ by Kersi Lord, the cello by Basu Chakravarty, an indigenously designed hydrophone, and a pre-recorded tape loop – stands out.

The Gabbar theme plays when Thakur is confronted by the dead bodies of his family, followed by the violin ensemble which highlights Thakur's blind rush into the ravines to seek Gabbar. The violins that have risen to a crescendo stop abruptly as the dacoits capture Thakur and tie him up, his arms outstretched. The synthesized piece of music, double-paced, creeps in again. With the banshee wail in the background, Gabbar approaches Thakur … and then a scream. Cut to the present as an involuntary squeal escapes Thakur's throat and his shawl falls off with the empty sleeves of his kurta flapping in the wind. All that is allowed here is the gentle whistling of the wind in the background, which becomes slightly louder to underline the shock of this unbelievable cruelty.

In the final scene in which Veeru is ordered to hand over his quarry to Thakur, the lietmotif again creates the eerie feeling.

In the scene where Basanti is chased by dacoits, Pancham

opts for the rather unusual tabla for the background, rather than the violins or accordion that one is used to hearing in such sequences.

In an interview published after Pancham's death in the film magazine *Movie* (February 1994), Ramesh Sippy said, 'Pancham came up with some innovative ideas for *Sholay*'s background music. I remember one particular score that he gave for the buggy chase scene in the film. He used only a tabla, a dholak and a ghungroo coupled with horse hooves. It was very simple, but it gave a tremendous effect to the whole sequence.'

It is a widespread misconception that Pandit Samta Prasad was the sole tabla player during this sequence. Kersi Lord clarifies: 'Film music is light music, and it is mostly about adaptation. Pandit Samta Prasad was an expert tabla player, but his domain was classical and not light music. It was Maruti Rao Keer on a second tabla, giving the "theka", guiding Pandit-ji to play the piece that defined Hema Malini's flight for life.'

During the night when the village is asleep, a solitary man sitting on the steps of Thakur's courtyard shares his solitude with his mouth organ, while a young widow turns off the kerosene lamps on the balcony one by one, as she prepares to turn in for the night. The uncomplicated strains of the instrument weave a bond between the two characters – a nomadic thief and a young woman whose dreams died one horrific afternoon.

'The basic tune was probably suggested by Basu Chakravarty. Amitabh was to play it on screen,' says Bhanu Gupta who played the harmonica. 'On observing the actor's obvious non-synchronous lip movement with the actual notes, director Ramesh Sippy, a stickler for detail, preferred to shoot Amitabh's profile, retaining the impression that it was Amitabh actually playing the instrument.' He continues, 'Once, I had come to Bombay for some important work and was driving fast when a traffic policeman stopped me and asked for my licence. I thought it would be futile to argue with him, so I just told him that I was a musician and I was going for a recording. The policeman was not moved, so I asked him if he had heard the harmonica piece in the film *Sholay*, stating that it was I who had played it. I was let off immediately!'

Pancham's restraint throughout *Sholay* in delivering just as much as the screenplay needed was his strength. Vibrant guitar chords, the French horn and percussion, including a tabla tarang, accentuate the two horsemen's ride from the railway station towards Ramgarh in the opening scene. As they canter past open fields and villages, through swaying greenery, the chords and the beat of the music alter accordingly to a very folksy and rustic tone, ending with Dakshina Mohan Tagore's taar shehnai before it cuts back to the initial chords on the acoustic guitar and the French horn in the final lap as the horsemen reach their destination at Thakur Baldev Singh's bungalow.

There is a certain twang in the acoustic notes that is reminiscent of the Wild West. The hollow sound of the horn is ominous – a sense of the impending war in the gorges of central India. The French horn, nicknamed 'jalebi' by sound recordist B.N. Sharma because of its unique shape, has been used sparingly in Hindi movies, and never really to this effect.

Even today, this coveted road tune continues to be played on popular demand during various stage shows by Manohari Singh, Ramesh Iyer, Kishore Sodha and team.

Sholay's title track was recorded at Rajkamal Studios which had India's first six-track recording system. After the recording, Kersi wanted to hear it. But recordist Mangesh Desai kept refusing, till he played it at the behest of Pancham. It turned out that there was a defect in the recorder and the piece had to be recorded again. Kersi also remembers that he brought the mini moog just before the recording of the title track of *Sholay*, around 1973.

The title track has also been dubbed in the film at a note higher than what was actually recorded. Bhanu Gupta's statement about the chord confirms this. 'Pancham had the tune in mind and asked us what chord could be used so that the entire effect could be generated using open strings. Bhupi and I suggested using D. For the recording, R.K. Das, a guitarist who used to play mainly with L-P, also joined us. You can say that it was an eighteen-string guitar with three of us.'

In the film, the title track is on D-sharp scale. It would not be incorrect to say that many of Pancham's songs are at a higher scale in the film than on the audio format. Variations in frequency due to power fluctuation plagued recording studios in Bombay, especially Film Centre which was in Tardeo, a residential area.

The songs in *Sholay* were all situational, and except for '*Mehbooba mehbooba*', all had something to narrate. '*Yeh dosti*' was a statement on male bonding. In Indian society, this expression is common. In the West, this might have been wrongly construed as a gay affair, a licentious relationship then. '*Jab tak hai jaan*' had Hema Malini dancing to save the hero, like in Raj Khosla's *Shareef Budmaash* (1973) where she had to dance to '*Mohabaat baazi jeetegi*' composed by Pancham. '*Koi haseena jab rooth jati hai toh*', the first song to be approved for the film, had the hero wooing and successfully winning the heroine's affections. '*Holi ke din*', probably one of the most celebrated Holi songs in Hindi cinema, ends with Gabbar attacking Ramgarh, shaking the villagers out of their celebratory mood.

There are elements in the songs that have the composer's special touch. Randhir Kapoor recalls: 'One day I entered Pancham's house to find him with his assistants, blowing air into half-filled beer bottles. For a minute I thought he had gone loony. When I asked him what he was up to, he replied that he was trying out a new sound. That's the sound you hear in the beginning of the song "*Mehbooba mehbooba*".'

Basu Chakravarty was responsible for recreating this sound during the recording, and it was accompanied by the madal, followed by the rabab with the Urdu dholak (dholak played by holding it upside down) as percussion.

The thirty-eight-second-long third interlude in 'Jab tak hai jaan' could have been a songlet in its own right, and there is little doubt whether Googoosh, the Iranian singer, would really consider the song a plagiarized version of her song 'Jomeh'. The bonhomie of 'Yeh dosti' sparkles, more so since it is also a duet between Manohari Singh's whistling and Bhanu Gupta's harmonica. The song triggered off a series of songs on male bonding in the 1970s. Pandit Ajoy Chakrabarty describes the song as a classic example of how a simple tune can be packaged to run the entire gamut of emotions – from the joyous to the deeply poignant. The interlude of 'Koi haseena' uses the notes Pa, Sa and Komal Re, similar to the first three guitar notes in the prelude of 'Chingari koi bhadke', a similarity that even seasoned listeners fail to observe. It seems that Pancham took a leaf out of Pudovkin's book on cutting and editing in films, and positioned the same note pattern in two different tunes, resulting in drastically different interpretations.

A Chaar Bhaand (a qawwali-like folk form popular in central India) song, imported by Anand Bakshi and sung by Kishore Kumar, Manna Dey, Bhupendra and Anand Bakshi, was not used in the film.

The final scene at the railway station had the title music being used once more, but the French horn was replaced by Manohari Singh's whistling. For some reason, it sounds very different this time as it stirs up something deep within, opening up a valley of indefinable sadness, making one wonder at the senseless violence, at the pitiable loss that Veeru and Thakur have suffered. The train rolls out of the station bearing Veeru and Basanti to some unknown, faraway destination, to a new life, as the film's credits start to roll across the screen.

Thirty-five years after it was released, *Sholay* remains the most enigmatic action musical ever made in India.

The media response to the music of *Sholay* wasn't flattering to begin with. During its time, *Sholay* was criticized as a film devoid of good songs, except '*Mehbooba mehbooba*', which gave R.D. Burman a new identity – that of a lead singer.

One possible reason for the cold reception could have been that, initially, the music album did not disappear from the shelves quickly enough, till the dialogue long-play records hit the market. This led to conjecture that the music lagged behind the script. Matters worsened when Pancham was labelled a plagiarist for using the tune of Demis Roussos's '*Say you love me*' as the mukhra of '*Mehbooba mehbooba*'. As a matter of fact, the tune had been recommended to Pancham by Ramesh Sippy, who had, along with his wife Geeta, heard the song at his brother Ajit's house in London and taken an instant liking to it.

One does not expect the public to be privy to such information since it has surfaced after years of research. Unfortunately, at that time, the damage was done, and the tag of being a plagiarist stuck to Pancham for the rest of his life.

If the undeserved flak wasn't bad enough, just a few months after *Sholay*'s release, Sachin Dev Burman passed away on 31 October 1975, after battling coma for months. In an instant, Pancham had lost his father, mentor, and so much more. 'Dada Burman had spent his last days with his son at Odena, as Meera boudi had been tending to senility with occasional outbursts of violence,' recalls Sachin Bhowmick. Pancham completed his father's final rites and then, as the heir to the Burman legacy, picked up the unfinished strings of *Mili* (1975).

'Sachin-da had recorded the tunes for all the four songs for the film in a spool and handed those over to me just prior to being hospitalized,' lyricist Yogesh recalls. 'Pancham helped in getting the songs recorded. Among the four, one song, "*Dusht rakshas*", was not used. During the recording, a particular assistant was trying to act smart, quoting the absence of a proper beat in *"Aaye tum yaad mujhe"*, but Kishore Kumar snubbed him right away.'

An unkind joke circulating in bourgeois Bengali circles at the time went that S.D. Burman had been so shocked by the loudness of '*Mehbooba mehbooba*' that he suffered a fatal stroke.

The truth is that the once-disapproving father had come round to admire his son's talent. In an interview given to Shankarlal Bhattacharya in the *Hindustan Standard* on 19 March 1972, when asked about his son, SD had said, 'I should not say much about him; it could smack of nepotism. He is imaginative and very creative. He is bent on experimentation. I believe he has a great future.'

S.D. Burman's funeral journey was facilitated by the Bombay Police for Rahul Dev Burman, who had performed with his team for the police force a few months earlier.

Dada Burman was probably being the good coach: outwardly stern but, deep down, proud of his son's success. Indeed, one morning, after he came back from a walk, he proudly recounted how bystanders at Juhu had identified him not as S.D. Burman but as R.D. Burman's father. (This was when *Hare Rama Hare Krishna* was playing in town.)

2

After composing for eighteen films in 1974, Pancham's releases dropped to eleven in 1975, and to ten each in 1976 and 1977. Pancham told Sanjeev Verma in an interview for the *Sunday Observer* on 31 May 1992: 'I have had a slack period thrice. First in the mid-1960s, then in the mid-1970s, when, after *Sholay*, everyone was ignoring me . . .' The third period that he doesn't mention in this quote was in the mid- to late-1980s.

What was the reason? Surely, S.D. Burman's death could not have been a valid reason.

The post-*Sholay* world saw consolidations take place all over the industry. The film had set new standards for multi-starrers and big-budget productions which only the big houses could afford. *Dharam Veer*, Manmohan Desai's answer to *Sholay*, was one such film. As a result, low-budget films were slowly edged out of the competition. This was also the period when Amitabh Bachchan ruled the industry like a colossus. *India Today* carried a cover story about Bachchan's string of successes, titled 'The One Man Industry'. As business savvy as he was talented, Amitabh consolidated his position with Prakash Mehra, Manmohan Desai and Yash Chopra, commanding a fee as high as Rs 25 lakh in 1980. Pancham could not break the grip that Kalyanji–Anandji, Laxmikant–Pyarelal or even Khayyam had on these producers' clubs. This denied him the opportunity to be a part of commercial masala films that benefitted from the brand image of their stars and the publicity machinery of their producer–directors who at times averaged more than one film per year.

Call it carelessness, call it boredom, call it a strategic move, Pancham became reluctant to accept offers from directors whose films had not done well in the past and gradually began palming off such offers to his assistants or suggesting fresh names to unsuccessful directors who approached him. In the process, he ended up distancing himself from old friends like Mahmood whom he had pestered for an opportunity years ago. In an interview published in the February 1994 issue of *Movie*, Mahmood said, 'Nasir Husain ne meri puri team le li (Nasir Husain took away my entire team). And Nasir was a bigger producer than me and sab uske saamne jhuk jaate the (people bowed before Nasir who was a bigger producer). When I would call Pancham or Suresh Bhatt (dance director) they would not come on the line. In the mid-1970s, I took Rahul's assistants (Basu and Manohari) as my music directors for *Sabse Bada Rupaiya* (1976). Then no contact with Pancham for the next twelve years till we met last month. And then it was like old times.'

Despite this physical distancing, Pancham's music, albeit through his assistants, remained very much a part of Mahmood's world. He sang the title song of *Sabse Bada Rupaiya*, '*Na biwi na bachcha na baap bada na maiyya*', the perfect blues song in the history of Hindi films, where all the notes corresponded to the hexatonic blues scale. Though Basu–Manohari scored the music for *Sabse Bada Rupaiya*, Pancham's influence was unmistakable, particularly in this stunning composition.

Kailash Chopra, Prem Chopra's brother, had produced *Nafrat* (1973) with Pancham as the composer. After the film bombed, Kailash Chopra had to make do with the services of Sapan Chakraborty for his next film *Jab Andhera Hota Hai* (1974). Pancham joined him once again for the shelved *Devdas*, but this was possibly due to the influence of Gulzar who was slated to direct the movie.

A maverick composer's poorly thought-out business strategy and even more ordinary sense of market forces were becoming apparent. He had missed capitalizing on *Sholay*'s success, distanced his old alumni and had lost the toehold among the big boys. Other than Bhupendra, most musicians in Pancham's inner circle, including Pancham himself, lacked the skills to market themselves. To add to these uncertainties was the presence of a discomfiting element called Sapan Chakraborty.

3

In an interview with Pavan Chawla, published after Pancham's death in the *Independent* on 8 January 1994, Pancham had said, 'I was at a stadium, I think, watching a football match. And I had a transistor with me to follow the commentary. While flipping across stations, I caught a song sung by Kishore Kumar and Asha Bhonsle. It was from the film *36 Ghante* (1974). I immediately became a fan of Sapan and contacted him.'

Pancham was, at times, remiss with facts. He frequently made errors when talking about his films. In Sandip Ray's documentary on Kishore Kumar, *Zindagi Ek Safar* (1989), he quoted *Abhimaan* instead of *Mili* when talking about the song '*Badi sooni sooni hai*'. He even confused the year of SD's heart attack in separate interviews, saying 1961 in one (*Filmfare* 16–30 June 1984) and 1963 in the other (*The Independent*, 24 October 1992).

Not only had Sapan Chakraborty written the lyrics for Pancham's Puja songs in 1972, his assistants Basu, Manohari and Maruti had worked as assistant music directors in *36 Ghante* as well as *Naya Nasha* (1973), Chakraborty's first film. The *Hindi Film Geet Kosh*, Volume 5, mentions him as an assistant as early as *Paraya Dhan* (1971).

What some of Pancham's associates recollect is his disproportionate patronage of Sapan. He had promoted Sapan to the stature of assistant music director in *Zehreela Insaan*, and continued with him in prestigious ventures like Shammi Kapoor's *Manoranjan* and Gulzar's *Khushboo*. His sudden entry into Pancham's inner circle – which had developed over the years through an unselfish struggle and years of music making by Basu, Manohari, Maruti, Bhanu, Amrutrao, Devichand, Bhupendra, Homi, Chandrakant, Kancha – raised eyebrows.

Sapan could market himself well, a trait that Pancham might have found useful given the post-*Sholay* lull. Flattery came naturally to Sapan, as exhibited in his use of RD's name in the line '*Raaste mein, R.D. Burman ka ek gaana ga raha tha . . .*' of the song '*Ek ladki le gayi dil*' in *Naya Nasha*. Many people associated with RD have lashed out at Sapan, alleging that he exploited Pancham, taking advantage of his gullibility.

4

Producers Vinod Shah and Harish Shah, together with director–cinematographer Ravikant Nagaich, continued their association with Pancham for yet another curry Western-cum-Indianized Bond thriller (the industry had really begun to overdo it) named *Kala Sona* (1975), which had Feroz Khan as the beleaguered protagonist trying to pin down the aptly named heroin king Poppy Singh played by Prem Chopra. Tshering Phintso Denzongpa (christened Danny by fellow FTII-ian Jaya Bhaduri) who had debuted as a singer under Pancham's father in *Yeh Gulistan Hamara* (1972), sang for Pancham in a duet *'Sun sun kasam se'*. *Kala Sona*'s release saw the return of Asha Bhonsle's sizzling numbers, which had been missing in 1975. *'Koi aaya aane bhi de'* included typical Pancham touches like the sound that accompanies the opening of a door and double-track recording with Asha Bhonsle's voice superimposed on her own. *'Ek baar jaane jaana'*, a folksy tune which might have been the inspiration for fusion artist Ananda Shankar for his composition titled *'Hill Train'*, was part of the thrilling climax where the heroine bamboozles the villains with her charm to rescue her brother.

Part of the background music was a flute piece that would later re-emerge in the form of *'Tum kya jano, mohabbat kya hai'* in *Hum Kisise Kum Naheen*.

Kala Sona, however amateurish the film, had songs that were built into the script – folksy, part-electronic numbers that managed to blend with the mood of the ravines and the patches of greenery masquerading as poppy fields.

In a surprise move, Pramod Chakraborty's *Warrant*, which released the same year as *Kala Sona*, had no Asha numbers, not even when the heroine tries to wriggle out of the villain's den; *'Main tumse mohabbat karti hoon'* had Lata Mangeshkar doing the honours. For the first time ever, Pancham used a bhangra beat, for *'Ladi nazariya ladi'*, a Lata–Kishore duet.

For a Dev Anand–Zeenat Aman starrer, *Warrant*, like *Heera Panna*, had few songs – just four in all, the most popular of which was '*Ruk jana o jana*', a Kishore Kumar solo that also found a place in Vidhu Vinod Chopra's graduation film in FTII, *Murder at Monkey Hill* (1976).

The title music of *Warrant* was a synthesized version of the title music of Robert Clouse's *Enter the Dragon* (1973), a sign that Pancham had either started concentrating less on films he did not perceive as important and borrowed a piece in totality

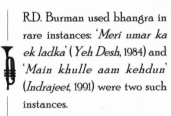

R.D. Burman used bhangra in rare instances: '*Meri umar ka ek ladka*' (*Yeh Desh*, 1984) and '*Main khulle aam kehdun*' (*Indrajeet*, 1991) were two such instances.

for the background, or had left the task to somebody else. The former is unlikely, given the Pramod Chakraborty–Dev–Zeenat combination.

It is possible that Pancham may not have been involved in the title track for *Warrant*. Many a times, producers would insist on a particular tune and it would be recorded from canned music. But letting producers interfere much more than required in the music-making process was unpardonable. Small mistakes and carelessness often snowball and lead to disastrous results. Despite ruling the Hindi film music world in the 1970s, Pancham contrived to sour his own fortune. The background score of *Khhotte Sikkay*, for example, a concoction of themes from *The Good, the Bad and the Ugly* and *For a Few Dollars More*, was a let-down given the fact that Pancham had the best brass band in the business and could have built around the core theme with his own stylization. However, considering that the background of *Khhotte Sikkay* also had the tune of the song '*Tum mile pyar se*' from Feroz Khan's previous hit *Apradh* (1972), composed by Kalyanji–Anandji, it might have been Khan who was actually calling the shots for the background music.

5

Actor Biswajeet was one among the first-time producers who sought Pancham during the 1970s. If his directorial debut *Kehte Hain Mujhko Raja* (1975) had not been a nightmare, Kishore Kumar's comical *'Bam bam chike'* – which Kishore had sung partly as a phrase in the song *'Duniya mein ameeron ko araam nahi milta'* in the film *Kaneez* (1949) – might have fared better. The Asha Bhonsle solo *'Jiya mein toofan'*, the Hindi version of the Bengali hit *'Pora baanshi shunle ae mon'*, was remarkable in its multilayered configuration, with Rekha doing a Jaya Bhaduri-in-*Anamika*. The impish *'Liyo na babu tanik piyo na'*, another of Pancham's conversions, this time from his Bengali hit *'Mahuaye jomeche aaj mou go'*, was constructed around a folksy tune and had notes which seemed to clamber over each other.

Ritesh Mukherjee, son of singer–composer Hemanta Mukhopadhyay, roping in Pancham for his production *Mazaaq* (1975), was interesting as Hemanta himself was a composer of very high repute and was still in demand in his native Calcutta. *Mazaaq* had a sweet-yet-saucy Asha Bhonsle solo, *'Takra gaye do badal ambar pe'*, where the interludes were in the form of dialogues by lead actor Vinod Mehra. This unconventional stylization might have been Pancham's salute to Hemanta Mukherjee's song *'Zara nazron se keh do jee'* in Hemanta's home production *Bees Saal Baad* (1962).

Meanwhile, Randhir Kapoor was not having a great time as a comedy hero. Bhappie Sonie's *Bhanwar*, Prakash Mehra's *Khalifa* and Ashok Roy's *Dhongee* turned out to be his short cuts on the way downhill, all in the same year. The only thing that tempted people to set forth towards the hall was their music.

Mili Bhattacharya recalls, 'I was humming a number sung by Purna Das Baul called *"Menoka mathaye dilo ghomta"*. Pancham inquired whether he could exercise the liberty of remoulding it into a Hindi film song. I told him to go ahead. After a few days, when Pancham was in Calcutta, he said, "your song has been recorded". I was later made to savour the taste of his creation "*Hai re hai tera ghungtaa*" [*Dhongee*] with its plethora of percussions and very distinctive sounds.'

With *Khalifa*, actor-turned-lyricist Gulshan Bawra, who had replaced Anand Bakshi as the lyricist for the film, joined the Pancham bandwagon. Their relationship would deepen with time. From the film, '*Dil machal raha hai*' became the trademark Pancham song. It was racy, pulsating with emotion, varying in pitch and intonation with the shot divisions, and digressing from one pattern to another, with a diabolically different antara on a higher octave, all enmeshed in a 4 x multiple matra pattern.

'The Teentaal, which is a sixteen-matra beat is almost the same as four bars of common time in Westerm music,' Kersi Lord explains. 'It is also a universal beat. How you play around with the beat is important. It can be 1-2-3-4 repeating itself in cyclic patterns. It can also be 1, gap, 3-4 and repeat. You can break the pattern into 3 x 4 + 4, like 1-2-3, 1-2-3, 1-2-3, 1-2-3, 1-2-3-4. It still adds up to sixteen, which is nothing but 4 x 4. This is a composer's innovating playpen and a test of his rhythm section. You can create many patterns within the form. Pancham would keep experimenting with various beat divisions within the given framework ... 4 bars and you would find Pancham.'

6

Narinder Bedi's *Maha Chor* (1976) which brought Sapan Chakraborty into prominence was one of Pancham's lows during this period. Sapan's name appeared as the arranger in the film's publicity booklet (confirmed by Manohari Singh) though it did not feature in the credits. The film also marked the beginning of the rift between Rajesh Khanna and Narinder Bedi. The songs were some of the rare instances where the antaras –

something that RD usually excelled in – sounded dreary and
jaded. In Kaka's slide after *Namak Haraam*, at least the songs
stood out and were placed on a pedestal they richly deserved.
There was nothing to be salvaged from *Maha Chor.*

Neetu Singh claimed that the Asha Bhonsle–Anand Bakshi duet in *Maha
Chor*, '*Suno banto baat meri*,' inspired B.R. Chopra to plan a Punjabi film
named *Sohni Mahiwal,* which was to be produced by Rajesh Khanna. Khayyam
was to write the music. The mahurat too was held in Chandigarh, but the
project was shelved.

Along came the life-after-death tale, *Mehbooba* (1976), which
renewed the combination of Shakti Samanta, Rajesh Khanna,
Pancham, Lata Mangeshkar and, of course, Kishore Kumar.
Here, experiments were out. The music was vintage 1971, the
year of *Kati Patang* and *Amar Prem,* a deep dive into classicality.
The tandem '*Mere naina saawan bhadon*' presented Raga
Shivranjani in a manner that was symphonic, haunting, modern,
yet traditional, to suit the different time periods in which the
versions were set.

Manohari Singh says of the composition: 'Nobody could use
Shivranjani as evocatively as Pancham did in "*Mere naina
saawan bhadon*".' Singh's statement was perhaps based on the
observation that the raga was used in the traditional mould by
most composers of the day, though composers Shankar–
Jaikishan's usage of this raga conquered generation barriers.
But unlike Pancham, they were more conventional, with even
their most well-known Shivranjani number, '*Jane kahan gaye
woh din*' (*Mera Naam Joker*, 1970), sounding like a semi-classical
dhun. Incidentally, composer Salil Chowdhury gave the raga a
twist in the song '*O mere saathi re*' composed in 1980 for *Aakhri
Badla* (1989), where, despite the melody sticking to the norms
of the raga, the arrangement was chord-based.

'*Mere naina saawan bhadon*' was recorded by Lata Mangeshkar first and then by Kishore Kumar who was given Lata's recorded version to work upon. 'Initially, Kishore-da said that this was beyond him and that he could not sing this number,' Pancham said in an interview. 'I persuaded him saying, "What are you saying? Where can I go looking for another singer just for this number?" He relented, suggesting that I record the Lata version first. He then listened to Lata's version for at least seven days, a tribute to his sincerity. When the final recorded version emerged, it did not sound as if it was memorized at all. It sounded very original.'

Kishore Kumar, in an interview with Pritish Nandy in the *Illustrated Weekly of India* in 1985, after having received the Lata Mangeshkar Award from the Madhya Pradesh government, cited '*Mere naina*' as one of his top ten favourite songs. This was the second Pancham nugget after '*Chingari koi bhadke*' that featured in Kishore's list.

'*Gori tori paijaniyan*' was based on a mix of ragas like the Kamod, Malhar and

Curiously, at the time of the movie's release, Kishore Kumar told his son, Amit: "'*Mere naina*' is fine, but look at the compositional elegance of "*Jaaneman jaaneman*" (*Jaaneman*, 1976). L-P have done a brilliant job there.'

Vrindavani Sarang and set to Addha taal, played on the tabla by Amrutrao Katkar and Maruti Rao Keer. The semi-classical song is also notable for its use of instruments which vary from the pakhawaj to the veena, from the violin to the Bengal drum. Manna Dey relished this number immensely, not only because of its strong base in classical music, but also for its presentation in the shorter format of the film song.

Singer Shurjo Bhattacharya, who sang for Pancham in the film *Purushottam* (1993), was present at the recording of '*Gori tori paijaniyan*'. He recalls: 'Manna Dey's presence in the recording studio would normally create the ambience of a military base camp. An emotional man with a tough exterior, he had great respect for Pancham. During the song rehearsals, Pancham was laying out phrases for Manna babu and asking him to choose the ones he liked, and to apply his classical erudition to embellish the phrases. Manna Dey, on the contrary, was telling Pancham, "Pancham, it is your song; you decide what should be done." The mutual respect which was evident during their interaction was remarkable. Another vital input to the song was from Gopi Krishna, the dance director who was finalizing the taal. It was essential for visualizing the dance sequence for Hema Malini.'

'*Aap ke sheher mein*' is a Lata Mangeshkar solo that deserved more acclaim. In an innovative mukhra–antara arrangement, Pancham keeps listeners wondering where the song really begins. It starts off with the sher '*Aap ke sheher mein*', gets into the metre at '*Ke jashn-e-shadi hai*' and rises with the mental agony of the dancer, falls and winds itself mysteriously with '*Main tawaif hoon mujra karoongi*' – another instance where Pancham rejects convention while using Raga Bhairavi. The film also had a song based on Raga Maru Behaag, '*Jamuna kinare aaja*', a Lata Mangeshkar solo which was left out in the final version of the film.

The breezy, light and easy Lata solo '*Chalo ri*' and the Lata–Kishore duet '*Parbat ke peechhe*' provided a contrast to the classical tunes in *Mehbooba*. For its exceptional music, *Mehbooba* should have done much better at the box office. An overweight Rajesh Khanna and an equally flabby Hema Malini helped nobody's cause. Even a reincarnation failed to cure Kaka of his wooden expressions and Hema Malini of her grunts.

In an interview given to Shonali Sabhrewal in the *Times of India*, Bombay, on 9 November 1989, Pancham mused: 'What I have never understood is why a good score in a bad film is forgotten. Before *Mehbooba* was released, its songs were a craze; once it flopped, it was out of sight, out of mind.' In another interview to Sanjeev Verma in the *Screen Observer*, on 31 May 1992, he said: 'Of my songs, the one which remains a favourite for the way it was conceived and executed is "*Mere naina saawan bhadon*". People laughed at the film, but I was thrilled with the song.'

In an informal discussion in the Tolly Club, Kolkata, in 2001, Shakti Samanta differed: 'Reincarnation stories generally run in our country. Look at *Madhumati*. I realize that *Mehbooba* did not run, but I do not feel the songs were picturized badly. As much as I agree that the songs of *Mehbooba* were brilliant, only audiences know the chemistry of a hit or a flop. There can be no set formula. I can give many examples from big houses where two films with almost the same storyline met with drastically different results at the box office.'

Pancham's woes were multiplied further during the making of *Mehbooba*. He had one of his innumerable 'childish' quarrels with Kaka. This time, the squabble did not end in a 'Bharat Milaap' – a term coined by common friends to notify a session that usually went high on Scotch and after which the two stars generally made up.

Samanta failed to bridge the growing gap between his two cornerstones, and in walked Laxmikant–Pyarelal for his next film with Rajesh Khanna, *Anurodh* (1977). Pancham lost the Samanta household for a brief period. But clinging to an overdrawn Kaka turned out to be Samanta's critical error in judgement.

Vijay Anand's *Bullet* (1976) followed closely on the heels of *Ishk Ishk Ishk* as Pancham's next album for the Anand brothers. Incidentally, *Bullet* was produced by Vijay Anand under the banner Navketan Productions, and was supposed to be a celebration of Navketan's twenty-five years.

Despite a slick script, closely echoing James Hadley Chase's *Just Another Sucker, Bullet* misfired. Signs of Dev's eroding image perhaps, as the film had polish, Vijay Anand's trademark tribute to Hitchcockian elements, and some funky music. In this crime thriller, where police officer Dev Anand (instead of the scribe Harry Barber in the novel) – appearing under his real name Dharam Dev – is framed by swindler Kabir Bedi, Pancham's background score was expectedly sharp, especially in the Dev–Kabir confrontation scenes. Given the genre, the songs had a secondary role to play in the film. This was also the first colour flick from Navketan without a romantic duet.

Lata Mangeshkar was fascinating in her rendition of the effervescent yet touching '*Jab tum chale jaoge*', the only song that talked about romance, while Kishore Kumar deftly negotiated the notes of the theme song '*Bullet bullet*' – the picturization of which also brought Dev in contact with his heroine to be, Tina Munim.

Two other songs are worth a mention as they reveal Pancham's penchant for experimenting with sound, keeping in mind a song's situation. '*Peene ke baad*', with its one-off scale change using woodwind, the staccato brass fillers, the continuing guitar strums, the piccolo/flute arpeggios and the occasional offbeat rhythm, replicates the psychedelic, near-surreal feel of a nightclub-cum-marijuana den. '*Chori chori chupke chupke*', the Kishore–Asha duet, was the most popular song in the film. Its intoxicating and well-mixed dose of warbling, laughter, deliberate drawls, bossa nova, staggered rhythms, electronic sounds, eerie sax fillers, etc., brings forth images of spinning rooms, blurred night lights, empty roads, the stars close enough to clutch, the inky sky flirting with the pale moon, a 'who-is-that-man-following-me' eeriness, the cold comfort of a lamp post at the street corner . . .

This was nirvana, Pancham style.

13

A for ABBA,
B for Boney M

The mid-1970s saw Pancham being sidelined by big production houses, dogged by unfair negative publicity, and ignored by the establishments that instituted awards. Though this did frustrate Pancham, it hardly hampered his creativity, and he composed some of his best music during this period. In the process, he was helped by friends he could rely upon – Nasir Husain, Ramesh Behl, Gulzar, Gogi Anand and R.K. Soral, among others.

In 1977, Nasir Husain put an end to a four-year wait. Maternal nephew Tariq and his guitar were back; Rishi Kapoor became the eighth hero Nasir directed in just nine films; and Indian audiences were introduced to actress Sunita Kulkarni, rechristened Kajal Kiran. The cello and hydrophone music used as the Gabbar lietmotif in *Sholay* was back too – superstition or mere coincidence? What remains amusing is that the price on villain Amjad Khan's head remained at Rs 50,000, like in *Sholay*, with no adjustment having been made for inflation! Or, maybe, like the music motif for Gabbar, this too was superstition.

Like its predecessor *Yaadon Ki Baaraat*, this film had two parallel story tracks – one of revenge and one of love. Pancham used heavy brass as well as a lot of synthesized sounds to create the soundtrack for the film which was based on an entertaining screenplay by Sachin Bhowmick, *Hum Kisise Kum Naheen*.

The film had ten songs (one recorded but unreleased), a high number given the context of the late-1970s when most productions did not exceed six.

In contrast to the 1960s, the singing hero in Nasir Husain's films had shifted from the meadows to the stage to woo the audiences. The Kishore Kumar solo '*Bachna aye haseeno*' starts with George Fernandes's trumpet announcing the arrival of a star dressed like Elvis. Kishore modulated his voice to add the rough grains characteristic of Rishi Kapoor and the song fits his persona. The number is replete with jazz notes, is high on brass, and has three antaras, one of them with Asha Bhonsle humming. The interludes are extravagantly coloured and this track is almost like a mini medley in length, with even HMV's Long Play record being unable to accommodate Pancham's grunting in the tailpiece of the song. Pancham's understanding of the situation emerges nicely as the rhythm of the interlude slows down abruptly before the third stanza; the sound levels fall to accommodate a few moments for the hero to become sentimental. This song has lived two generations at last count, going a long way in ensuring the commercial success of the eponymous Ranbir Kapoor starrer.

'I want this sound. Recording is in seven days' time,' declared Pancham when he heard someone try to start a car whose battery was dead. 'How do we produce this sound, Pancham? Vocalize it?' was the question. 'That's what you need to figure out,' replied the composer.

'I played this on the mini moog synthesizer,' Kersi Lord recalls. 'It is a three-octave instrument and I had a very long portamento sliding from one note to another, controlled with the leg. [Portamento was not possible on keyboards till the introduction of synthesizers.] A VCF [voltage-controlled filter] was used since a VCO [voltage-controlled oscillator] would have given a siren-like sound. In keyboards, the lower note has slower pulse even with LFO [low frequency oscilliation] on. Higher will go faster. So I played the lowest note [which is the slowest] with the filter on. And gradually shifting to the higher [and faster] notes with the portamento taking over.'

This technique was used for the intro tune of the Rafi–Asha duet '*Ye ladka haye Allah*', one of Rafi's four songs in this film. *Hum Kisise Kum Naheen* helped Rafi anchor himself in the face of the Kishore Kumar hurricane; he picked up his last Filmfare Award and the National Award for best singer for the song '*Kya hua tera wada*', a duet with junior artiste Sushma Shreshta.

Working under the a-demand-a-day director and the punishing schedules meant that musicians spent a lot of time in the recording studios. Kersi Lord pays a compliment to Pancham's ability to hold together a team that was willing to put in its best: 'It was a challenge working for him, always. But I used to enjoy that. We used to work for him normally twelve to fourteen hours a day, but never felt that we were working. It was a relaxed atmosphere . . .'

With '*Kya hua tera wada*', Pancham was back in the domain of simple melody. This time it was wedded with riffs on the electric guitar by Bhupendra and an exquisite piece of fiddling by Uttam Singh. The base tune of the song was derived from a violin prelude to '*Tum mujhse roothe ho*' in *Phir Kab Milogi* and remodelled into a full-fledged song enjoying towering popularity during its time.

The arrangement for the Raga Kalavati-based qawwali, '*Hum kisise kum naheen*' – Pancham's best-known qawwali (though he had previously composed songs resembling the style, an example being '*Na khidki na jharokha*' in *Shareef Budmaash*), recorded at Mehboob Studio – was done by Amrutrao.

'I was asked by Pancham to arrange the qawwali as both Basu and Manohari were abroad at that time. Interestingly, this score was one of the few songs in which I ever played the tabla. Also accompanying on tabla was Iqbal Khan. The vibrant dholak was by Sattar, Abdul Kareem Khan and Chandrakant. This song, I think, helped in giving Pancham a new dimension,' says Amrutrao.

Rishi Kapoor remembers Laxmikant being sceptical about the qawwali when he described it to him, but acknowledged it later when it became a hit. 'I featured in two super hit qawwalis that same year, the other one being "*Parda hai parda*" in *Amar Akbar Anthony*.'

The dance competition – a medley of songs stretching over ten minutes, where two competitors sing and dance on a dance floor made to represent the two heads of the Cuban drum, bongo – is the highlight of the film. The medley stands as a definitive moment in the film, a benchmark of coordination during song construction and picturization. It begins with a flurry of brass, starting with a war cry on George Fernandes's trumpet generating a muffled but metallic sound using a cup to cover the bell (the open end of the trumpet). Notes on the bass guitar are a constant companion. Ivan Muns, not a regular with Pancham, played the trombone. The intro music crescendos with a '*Wakao!*' and a roll of the drums, then merges seamlessly into Rafi's '*Chand mera dil*' bridged by soft strokes of the guitar.

Opinion differs on who played the electrifying bass guitar during the opening notes of the prelude. The common belief is that it was Tony Vaz. However, Shankar Iyer, a music enthusiast who is also associated with the music magazine *Swar Alaap*, confirms that in a private gathering in June 2009, Manohari Singh clarified that it was Charanjit Singh and not Tony Vaz. One of the perpetual roadblocks in researching Hindi film music is the sheer lack of documentation. Even within the Pancham team, Amrutrao was the only member who started the tradition of meticulously keeping records of who played what in the songs – till he was snubbed by Guruji Maruti Rao. While the Western world has abundantly emphasized the need for documentation, the lack of foresight in the Bombay film music industry has made going behind the curtains an impossible task. One wishes the disciple had held his way against the master, in this case at least.

Coming back to the medley, the tune of *'Chand mera dil'* was a modified version of *'Jeena toh hai'* from *Paanch Dushman*. It is packaged so masterfully that it is difficult to spot the similarities.

According to prominent quizzer, music fanatic, film buff and director of Kolkata Knight Riders, Joy Bhattacharjya, *'Aa dil kya mehfil hai tere kadmon mein'*, which follows *'Chand mera dil'* in the medley, was the iconic career high for Kishore Kumar. "'I am the king" seems to echo in the track throughout. It is a voice which is extra wide. It hits you straight in the belly. With a voice like that, anything and everything else is made to sound secondary,' he says. The most popular track in the medley followed next. Packed movie halls would wait for Tariq, wearing a red gauzy headband, to plonk himself on one knee; the audience would erupt in raptures, throwing coins at the screen as Pancham demanded *'Tum kya jano, mohabbat kya hai'*. It starts with a brief *'Oooooo'*, a stylish reminder of his first solo hit as a singer in *Sholay*. The final track, *'Mil gaya'*, the only duet in the medley, was at the receiving end of accusations of plagiarism. True, the song is a lift from the ABBA classic *'Mamma Mia'* but a former associate of Pancham's recalls that Husain prevailed upon the composer who agreed, although reluctantly. The fact that 'Honey Honey', another ABBA number, can be heard in the background just before 'Kya hua tera wada' is testimony to Husain's fascination with the acronymic Swedish group. In any case, Pancham's arrangement was jazz-based, whereas 'Mamma Mia' is pop music; the two tracks were constructed on two totally distinct metres.

In a television documentary on Pancham, Nasir Husain recalled the medley: 'During the making of Hum Kisise Kum Naheen, I had been to London. There is a famous store named Tiffany, where I found teenagers flocking around the disco which was popular during that time. To my amazement, I found that people who were dancing to one song continued even when the next one started. In fact, the crowd would appreciate when the new track replaced the earlier one. When I came back to India, I told RD that I have a situation for a dance competition in my film, where I want to employ not one, but three or four tunes. As always, Pancham would be prepared for experimentation. We arranged four songs, all in different tunes and rhythms. Before the recording, some of R.D. Burman's friends warned him of the risk involved in this, as the shifts between the songs were so fast that the melody would fail to register in the minds of the viewers. Pancham said, "Who else but you, Nasir Sahib, would attempt such a bold experiment? Let's try it out, if it does not work, we shall replace the four tunes with one; maybe this would lead to some losses on account of shooting." Out of the four songs, one was by RD. Later I found that the songs were so popular that even people who had seen the film eight to ten times would enter the theatre to view only the qawwali and the dance competition and come out.'

Hum Kisise Kum Naheen, it seemed, was Nasir's answer to the increasing presence of ABBA and Boney M on the Indian music scene. 'We can do it too, and do it better,' he seemed to say to his audience. And Pancham, his trusted comrade since *Teesri Manzil*, helped him deliver on that promise in what was the biggest grosser that year.

Unfortunately, this was also Nasir Husain's last hurrah. His next three films flopped and he handed over the baton to his son Mansoor Khan eleven years later. Few directors in Indian cinema have been able to mix music so well with commercial masala films. But then, he had R.D. Burman by his side.

2

In the 1970s, 'a' for apple had been replaced by 'a' for ABBA and 'b' for Boney M. At least one Long Play record of each of these two groups at home symbolized and was proof of westernization: 'We listen to English music.' It didn't matter that neither group was English. Though ABBA had partly influenced Pancham's music in *Hum Kisise Kum Naheen* and also in *Love Story* (1981), in an interview with the Bengali magazine *Alokepath* in September 1993, he opined that both ABBA and Boney M were very good groups, but did not have longevity.

The 'English' group Pancham did draw inspiration from was the Beatles. Having taken up the challenge at a party at producer Debesh Ghosh's house to retrofit a Beatles tune for the Indian milieu, RD returned with '*Humne kabhi socha nahin*' (*Jeevan Mukt*, 1977) and '*Tumne yeh theek socha tha*' (*Imaan*, 1974), both based on the hit '*Norwegian wood*'.

This wasn't the first time he had used the Beatles to compose his own tracks. The interlude of '*Aap se miliye*' in *Pyar Ka Mausam*, where Manohari's sax plays the reprise of '*Raju chal Raju*' from Pramod Chakraborty's *Azaad* (1978), was a mix of Frank Sinatra's '*When I was seventeen*' and the Beatles' '*A taste of honey*', a fact ratified by Amit Kumar as well. However, '*Raju chal Raju* was characterized by the beat structure of a man riding a stallion, and finds Pancham trademarks like shifts between major and minor chords and the use of the suspended fourth chord, à la the theme of *Sholay*.

Krishna Shah's bilingual *Shalimar* (1978) could have been a James Bond flick set somewhere in the Orient, like *Octopussy* (1983), had it not been for the Hindi and a misplaced Lata solo. The film had elements of a Hollywood action movie: no emotions, matter-of-fact dialogue delivery, and comfortable physical intimacies. The background score might have been designed to cater to both the Hindi and the English audience, while the songs were essentially for the Hindi version. The background music, with its mix of jazz to tribal to Carnatic, was representative of Pancham's awareness of the need to innovate to impress an international audience.

As Basu, Manohari and Maruti were away in the US, Kersi Lord stepped in to do the background score for *Shalimar* at Pancham's request. In an interview with the authors on 18 April 2009, Kersi Lord spoke at length about the instruments and recording equipment used for *Shalimar*. 'This was the first time we had done a background score in stereo. This was at Film Centre, which was not equipped for stereo recording then. So we had to modify. Two mikes were kept with Sunil's [Kaushik] guitar amplifier and Pancham was handling the "Left-On, Right-Off" switches inside. He needed to be attentive, else one mistake and everyone would have had to play all over again. One rhythm section was on the right channel [Franco Vaz] and the other on the left channel [Vancy D'Souza]. For the bass guitar, I used a Y-connector. I took an "Out" from Tony's bass guitar and split it into two "Out"s – one went into an amplifier on the left side and the other into an amplifier on the right. The main sound can be heard in the virtual [pseudo] centre. We used the only stereo mike for the string section

[violins]. The two tracks available had been used and one track
was needed for the vocal section. So I told Abu [from the police
band], the guy who played the French horn, to walk across the
studio even during recording as there was no multi-tracking.
The saxophone was played by Rao Kyao, a Portugese saxophone
player [born Joao Jorge Ramos, who had come to India around
that time]. Pancham was okay with Rao since Manohari was
away in the US. I had to match the music with the film; so my
conducting was important. The bass guitar and percussion were
playing a slow eleven beat while the two electric guitarists,
Bhupi and Sunil, played the fast five-and-a-half beats twice. I
was fond of Carnatic music, so my Lehkari was based on
Carnatic. The *Countess' Caper* [the background score picturized
on Sylvia Miles who was playing Countess Rasmussen] was
written to sync with the countess doing lots of capers [vaulting
over the barriers on her mission to steal the Shalimar]. The
flute was played by Pandit Hariprasad Chaurasia. Homi Mullan
played the accordion for a change [he had played it in *"Ek din
bik jayega"* (*Dharam Karam*) too]. Rao Kyao was used for this
piece and the song *"Naag devta"* as well.'

Though Kishore Kumar's solo 'Hum bewafa' edged out Asha
Bhonsle's 'Mera pyaar Shalimar' in the popularity charts, the
Asha solo probably deserved a better deal. With a 'faraway'
echoing effect befitting the island setting given to the rendition,
'Mera pyaar Shalimar' has a prominent bass riff and a cascading
violin motif that sounds like waves breaking in succession. It is
heard at various points in the film and creates a sinister effect.

Pancham engaged the services of Usha Uthup in the opening
song sequence in 'One, two, cha cha cha'. This song was a rage
with college students and there were instances of people going
to the theatre only to come out in a quarter of an hour, after
'One, two, cha cha cha'.

Except Lata's finely wrought (but out of place in a film like this) *'Aaina wohi rehta hai'* and *'Hum bewafa'*, the other songs could be mistaken as part of the background scores, so finely were they woven in. As a film, *Shalimar* was badly paced, and was taken off theatres in two weeks. But it gave a glimpse of how RD would have sounded in a Hollywood production. The English version retained Pancham's score, without the songs.

3

Sangam (1964), *Love in Tokyo* (1966), *Night in London* (1967), *Ankhen* (1968) and even the little-heard-of *Around the World* (1967) – Bombay film producers have been bringing picture postcards of the world to the cinema halls since film-making began. Television was barely two years old in India when Shakti Samanta took his audiences on a package tour of Cairo, Lisbon, Venice and Rome. Planned in 1968, Samanta's film had to wait ten years to find its way to the shooting floor. Based on a story by Vikramaditya, *The Great Gambler* (1979) starred Amitabh Bachchan in a double role – Jay and Vijay, twins separated after birth. One, a crook. The other a police officer.

The stopovers in Egypt, Italy and Spain were part of the screenplay, and Pancham had no trouble incorporating them into his compositions, having been exposed to the music of these countries from a young age.

'Raqqasa mera naam' was an Egyptian belly dance sequence inspired by Middle Eastern folk, replete with bottle blowing. Asha was paired with Mohammad Rafi, in the latter's only song in this film.

Cut to Venice. Sharad Kumar was the voice of the boatman who sang in Italian while Asha Bhonsle translated it into Hindi as *'Do lafzon ki hai'*. The soft romantic feel of the song, as the gondola floats across the Venitian waterways, seemed more suited for Lata Mangeshkar's voice. Notable for the wonderful use of the bass and electric guitars, this is still considered *the* melody from the film. Samanta had a penchant for boat songs, and it is likely that he considered it the natural successor to '*Raat ke humsafar*' from *An Evening in Paris* and '*Chingari koi bhadke*' from *Amar Prem*.

Meanwhile, the twin Bachchan was romancing his heroine Neetu Singh in the duet '*Pehle pehle pyar ki mulaqatein*' elsewhere in Europe; a track with prominent strumming on acoustic guitars. The song is interspersed with lyrics without tune, almost like dialogues with a lilt that lends the moment a light, airy mood as opposed to '*Do lafzon ki hai*', which represents a temporary getaway for the couple trapped in a web of international crime.

With the two club sequences '*O diwano dil sambhalo*' and '*Tum kitne din baad mile*', RD was on a roll. Both the Asha solos were representative of the Pancham who liked to experiment with the arrangement of notes. In '*Tum kitne din*' the notes climb progressively, only to drop down to the root. '*O diwano*' is high-pitched, with a beautiful trumpet refrain in the mukhra; the connecting line between the antara and the mukhra is comparable to the tune of the mukhra, played at a different scale.

The Great Gambler also had a couple of interesting background score packages in addition to the songs. One was a Helen dance item which had a secret code embedded for the 'traitors' in the way the light flickered in the background. The other was the Amitabh–Shetty fight sequence inside an abattoir in the Lido, Venice. A bloodshot-eyed Shetty repeatedly swinging his butcher's axe at the hero inside a cold storage that had cattle meat impaled asymmetrically all over was considered too violent, and the movie was awarded an 'Adults Only' certificate.

Pancham's music was popularly certified as terrific.

4

In an interview (*Showtime*, July 1992), Pancham spoke of going through a lean period just after *Sholay*, followed by hits: 'Then came *Yaadon Ki Baaraat* and *Kasme Vaade* [1978] and things were comfortable again.' Surely Pancham meant *Hum Kisise Kum Naheen* and not *Yaadon Ki Baaraat* as the latter had come two years before *Sholay*. *Kasme Vaade* found Pancham back in his familiar circle with Ramesh Behl, Gulshan Bawra and Randhir Kapoor. Gulshan Bawra, in the music album *Untold Stories*, recounts the incident when Pancham walked into his house one evening, singing 'Sarson ka saag pakana, Anju [Bawra's wife]' in a tune which later became the title track of *Kasme Vaade*. The tune of the first two lines of the mukhra seems to have a faint resemblance to Gregorian chants, and a connection could be established to a South African stage musical, *Ipi Nitombi* (1974).

'The original tune envisaged for the qawwali in *Hum Kisisse Kum Naheen* was one of Pakistani origin, which Nasir Husain Sahab was impressed with. But it was subsequently used for *Kasme Vaade* – this was "*Pyar ke rang se tu*", sung by Asha Bhonsle and Anand Kumar C.,' Gulshan Bawra recalled in a conversation with us. In an ironic cascade of sorts, a song recorded for this film, '*Gumsum kyon hai sanam*', which had a delightful merging of the sax with Asha Bhonsle's vocals, did not fit in anywhere in the screenplay. 'So this song was given to Vishwamitter for his film *Bhala Manush* [1979] since the lead cast was the same: Daboo and Neetu,' Mrs Madhu Behl says. In the meantime, though, the track had been recorded and released, a rare occurrence of a song featuring in the Long Play record of one film and on-screen in another.

Kasme Vaade was a huge success with its music topping the popularity charts. Those were Amit Kumar's initial days and this film helped his career too. 'For "*Aati rahengi baharen*"

[Kishore Kumar, Asha Bhonsle and Amit Kumar],' Bawra said, 'Pancham used the tune of *"Happy Birthday"* only to weave a song around it. This tune was played on the harmonica by Bhanu Gupta. Pancham also made Amit Kumar sing in an exaggeratedly lively manner, to fit in with the image Ramesh had for Daboo. After *"Bade achche lagte hain"* [*Balika Badhu*], I think this was Kishore-da's son's biggest hit during that period.'

It is rumoured that Nasir Husain had rejected the tune of *'Aati rahengi baharen'* for *Hum Kisise Kum Naheen.* Amit Kumar, in a dreamy flashback thirty-four years later, recalls his first hour of glory under the sun with Pancham: 'I came to Bombay from Calcutta in 1970. In 1972, I went with my father to East Africa and to the US with Bhupi, Charanjeet, Buggie Lord [Kersi's brother], Devichand, et al. I was also a percussionist. At that time, both my father and Pancham were on top. I used to be a special guest in Pancham's sitting sessions. In 1974, I was party to the rehearsal of a fun song sung by my father and Manna Dey. Pancham suddenly asked me to sing a song and I, not ready for the occasion, sang *"Jhumroo"*, albeit badly. On the way back, my father, disheartened by my performance, asked me why I did not concentrate. I replied that I was not prepared and a touch nervous too. Earlier, L–P had come to me with an offer to sing for Rishi Kapoor in *Bobby* [1973], but I had not taken it seriously. That evening, despite my lacklustre *"Jhumroo"*, Pancham-da called up my father and told him to send me across for recording. My father asked him in a lighter vein as to why Amit and why not him, and Pancham-da replied that he needed a raw voice and that Kishore Kumar was already over forty. Next day, I went to Pancham-da's place and he made me rehearse *"Bade achche lagte hain"*. After a series of rehearsals, Pancham-da took me with him in his car to Film Centre and the song was approved by director Tarun Majumdar and producer Shakti Samanta. This recording happened at the end of 1974 or early 1975. It was used in *Balika Badhu* [1976] and it became extremely popular and continued to grow in stature over time. I came to be known as Amit Kumar. Though I had sung a few songs earlier, this song was released first. I owe the credit to Pancham-da for giving me an excellent launching pad.'

Pancham had the ability to tap the potential of new artists, and often gave them the space needed to excel. '*Bade achche lagte hain*' had all the ingredients to make it a success: simple yet beautiful lyrics and a dew-fresh melody. A poignant piece of violin by Uttam Singh was used to set the mood of the mukhra and to act as a cue for Amit. Pancham himself pulled the song together, joining the mukhra and the antara with a wailing '*O majhi re, jaiyo piya ke desh*'. The monosyllabic '*Aur?*' was by Sushma (later known as Purnima). *Balika Badhu*, written by Bimal Kar, tells a touching story of love in pre-Independence days. Filmed partly in the Birbhum district, Tarun Majumdar captured the period admirably, amidst the idyllic portrait of rural Bengal with its paddy fields, mangroves and autumn sky. Pancham, it seemed, had left all his favourite instruments, electronic and Western, behind at Sealdah Station.

Shakti Samanta, in an informal interview in Kolkata, said, '*Balika Badhu* was made on a small budget, but the film did exceedingly well. During the making of the film Girija, my brother, suddenly passed away, and I dedicated the film to his memory. Tarun Majumdar was the director for the original Bengali version too. The Bengali version made Moushumi Chatterjee a star; my version perhaps made Amit Kumar a star.'

5

After *Amar Prem* and *Mehbooba*, Pancham's next chronologically important classical port-of-call was Gulzar's *Kinara*. The transition from *Parichay* to *Kinara* was almost seamless, though the latter was slightly heavier on the ears. Gulzar's first film as official producer seems to be heavily influenced by Douglas Sirk's *The Magnificent Obsession* (1954). 'Baap ka maal' was how Pancham referred to the score of the film. Three songs in the film – '*Ab ke na sawan barse*', '*Koi nahi hai kahin*' and '*Meethe bol bole*' – were based on his father's compositions. He even used the phrase '*Din dhal jaye*' in the antara of '*Ab ke na sawan barse*', harking back to the original tune SD composed in *Guide*.

Kinara led to allegations that Pancham was parading his father's tunes as his own when in fact he openly acknowledged his good fortune in finding quite a few of his father's compositions suitable for song situations in the film. Like a jazz musician, Pancham would pick up a spark from an original tune, Indian or Western, and colour it with his own interpretations. His flair in presentation and musical detailing were what lent individuality to the end product.

'There are but only seven notes. However much you learn Indian classical music, you have to be colourful,' Pancham told Amit Kumar. 'You have to take inspiration to survive. Take a phrase into your head and scribble with it. Go with it. It will loop back in the second phrase.'

'That was his style. His knack,' Amit says.

All the songs in the first half of *Kinara* – '*Naam gum jayega*', '*Ek hi khwab*' and '*Jaane kya soch kar nahi guzra*' – are original Pancham tunes, and even his fiercest critics would vouch for the fact that these three tunes stand out in the film much more than the ones he borrowed from his father. *Kinara* was also the only film where Gulzar used two of his poems which had already been set to music by a different set of composers. '*Jaane kya soch kar*' had been recorded as a non-film song by Sabita Chowdhury to a musical score by Salil Chowdhury. Pancham set the lyrics to a metre radically different from the original Salil composition.

The progression of the song was similar to Raga Kalyan; it became one of Kishore Kumar's greatest hits during its time.

According to Pankaj Rag, author of *Dhunon Ki Yatra* and the director of FTII at present, the second poem, *'Ek hi khwab'*, was initially written for the film *Mera Yaar Pocketmaar* and set to music by composer Kamal Rajasthani in the early 1970s. Kishore Kumar was greatly impressed with the newbie composer and reportedly gave him Rs 500. Unfortunately, the film was shelved and the track was never released. Gulzar reused the lyrics and Pancham set it to a different tune to be sung by Bhupendra in *Kinara*. In Vishwas Nerurkar's book *Qatrah Qatrah*, Gulzar mentions that Pancham got stuck for want of a metre in the word *'chabiyaan'*. Finally, the song was recorded with minimal instruments and singer Bhupendra playing the lead guitar himself – probably the only instance of the singer playing the lead guitar during a song.

From the sublime to the ridiculous: the tune of *'Meethe bol bole'* was used as a parody with the lyrics *'... Jamuna ke teer, Laila ko dhoonde'* in another song – the first-ever credited RD–Kishore duet: *'Ye duniya kya hai duniya'* – in Gogi Anand's *Darling Darling* (1977). The bossa nova was back in *'Woh aurat hai, yeh hai sharab'*, Kishore's perfect portrayal of the drunken lout. New heights were reached in secondary percussion when Amrutrao was told to strip off his shirt inside the recording studio so that Pancham could play a fast-paced series of beats with his hands on Amrutrao's back as a part of the interlude in the Asha–Kishore duet *'Raat gayi baat gayi'* in *Darling Darling*.

'It so happened that this song was composed based on a guitar progression we were working on at that time,' says Bhanu Gupta, talking about *'Aise na mujhe tum dekho'* from *Darling Darling*. 'The number was recorded by Kishore. This was the time when Pancham's tunes had started to be passed on surreptitiously to other composers. We knew about people who could stoop down to this level, but there was no proof. Well, a few days later, Kishore-da was recording the title song for another film with another composer at a different studio. A well-known diva who was also present during the rehearsal of *"Aise na mujhe tum dekho"* realized that the tune which Kishore was singing was very similar to the song she had heard him rehearsing with RD. The singer pointed out the stark similarity to Kishore and he too was taken aback. The composer was then asked for an explanation, but he was in no position to defend himself. This led to the diva refusing to sing for that composer for over a year.'

There is a more generic story that runs in the background of this incident. A trend had emerged in Hindi film music in the 1970s, which, if we put it straight, could be summed up as influenced deeply by Pancham's scores and his arrangement. This was perceptible in the work of contemporary composers. Bappi Lahiri for one was composing greatly in minor scale, using the electric guitar for arpeggios, using percussions more than basic rhythm instruments, and using deep bass lines, also cutting down the clutter by reducing the use of dholaks, the daflis and violins. Songs like *'Chalte chalte'* (*Chalte Chalte*, 1976), *'Mana ho tum'* (*Toote Khilone*, 1978), *'Jalta hai jiya mera'* (*Zakhmee*, 1975), *'Yeh naina yeh kaajal'* (*Dil Se Mile Dil*, 1978), *'Muskurata hua gul khilata hua mera yaar'* (*Lahu Ke Do Rang*, 1979), *'Pyar maanga hai tumhise'* (*College Girl*, 1978), *'Aankhon mein tum'* (*Tere Pyar Mein*, 1978), etc., were songs which seemed to be inspired by Pancham's style.

However, Bappi was not the sole composer who mimicked the Pancham sound. Sapan–Jagmohan, Rajesh Roshan, Vijay Singh, Hemant Bhonsle (musican and pilot – son of Asha Bhonsle), etc., too were deeply influenced. One can hear the bossa nova flourish in the Sapan–Jagmohan composition *'Tumhi rehnuma ho'* from *Do Raha* (1971). The Kishore Kumar–Ranu Mukherjee

duet *'Jawani mere yaara'* from *Call Girl* (1974) has emphasis on
off-beats, on the seventh and the ninth notes, and definitely
sounds like Pancham's composition. Though Rajesh Roshan's
tutelage was in the L–P school, the mystic sound, the use of
long-drawn notes, and the sudden surge of the bongo, conga
and the tumba in albums like *Julie* (1975), *Priyatama* (1977) and
Doosra Aadmi (1977) were more in the Pancham mould. Vijay
Singh and Hemant Bhonsle did not have a long innings as
music composers; their music seemed to be profoundly influenced
by Pancham. In his native Bengal, Suparnakanti Ghosh (son of
composer Dr Nachiketa Ghosh) was a follower too, though his
tenure as a composer was limited. Pancham was, in a way,
inspiring a whole new generation of musicians.

Once in a while, even old-timers seemed to be inspired
by Pancham's style and orchestral elegance. One can track
down the divine use of the blues scale in Madan Mohan's
compositions – as in *'Tum jo mil gaye ho'* (*Hanste Zakhm*, 1973),
in *'Aaj mujhe jal jaane bhi do'* (*Rehnuma*, unreleased) or in *'Raat
ujiyari dil andhera hai'* (*Chalbaaz*, 1980). Pancham's trademark
bossa nova rhythm surfaced in Salil's work as well, a
representative song being the unreleased *'Hum kho gaye'* sung
by Lata Mangeshkar from an unreleased film.

It was apparent that the mainstay of Pancham's work in the
1970s included experiments with arrangement, which set
precedence for other composers. However, Pancham, with
customary modesty, admitted in an interview (in the *Sunday
Observer*, 31 May 1992): 'I feel that I am not a good arranger
and I need help from my assistants on blending sound.'

Musicians associated with Pancham interpret this statement
differently. Bhanu Gupta and Ramesh Iyer agree that though
Pancham was well-versed in Indian notations, he did not care
to write staff notations and left that part to his assistants. But
the envisioning of the sound, the comprehensive fitting of the

pieces of the jigsaw was all his. 'He would mix sound himself. The huge sound mixer in Film Centre had come for Pancham. His tracks have that crystal-clear sizzling sound that is not there even today with all the technology,' says Amit Kumar.

Pandit Ajoy Chakrabarty wonders at how Pancham used so many sounds. 'Pancham-da used to generate music out of sounds like that of rain, through instruments like a spoon and a glass. The way he handled sounds is a textbook in itself. He created new sounds.'

'Once Bhupinder-ji told me about a bunch of keys that fell on the guitar while he was playing. Pancham promptly recorded that sound. He would record any sound,' recalls Chhaya Ganguli.

Baba Desai, brother of ace recordist Mangesh Desai, adds, 'Pancham did everything, from redesigning preludes and interludes to overruling anything and everything which sounded discordant to him. He was the master of ceremonies during the final take.'

6

The late 1970s was when the Gulzar–RD partnership really flourished, both in films directed by Gulzar and in the ones for which he wrote songs. And their offerings contained one of the finest songs recorded for children in Hindi films. After 'Sa Re ke Sa Re' in Parichay, Lata's 'Ek din hasana' in Benaam and 'Aaye re aaye re' in Doosri Seeta, Pancham's next children's special arrived in masterji's chitthi. With the saucy half-pants mimicking 'Teri gathri mein laga chor' (Dhoop Chaon, 1935) and the radio ad jingle of VIP underwear–banian, and banging on the classroom benches in lieu of primary percussion, 'Masterji ki aa gayi chitthi' (Kitaab, 1977) was about impressionable schoolboys breaking into an impromptu musical during tiffin break.

'What on earth has he purchased? Sounds so off-tune,' was

people's reaction to Pancham's 'impulse' purchase on one of his trips to the US. 'Any instrument, if used well, produces a good sound,' RD pointed out to his critics. He was referring to the flanging instrument which he had bought. Ramesh Iyer, in a live show and later in an interview with us at his Kandivali residence, explained what flanging was actually about. 'It all began when the same song was being played simultaneously on two different systems. Somebody's hand accidentally fell on one of the systems and it started running slowly. The sudden change in the overlap pattern of the same tune produced a sound that was called flanging. The delay was simulated electronically in a contraption that was then named the flanger. A guitar when connected to the flanger produces a minor distorted sound which is very different in character.'

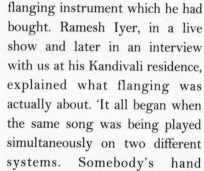

The term 'flanging' is said to have been coined by John Lennon while trying to understand the technology behind Artificial Double Tracking (ADT) in 1966.

Pancham went ahead with what was the first-ever use of the flanging instrument in Hindi films in 'Dhanno ki aankhon mein', a groovy track picturized inside a steam engine. The guitar connected to the flanger keeps playing as a motif throughout and is practically the only instrument in the track, save infrequent sharp notes on the tabla and the flute to generate the sound of the whistle of a train engine.

'Normally no singer can sing this. Or no normal singer can sing this,' Gulzar said in the radio programme *Meri Sangeet Yatra*. 'Pancham taught me how the rendering of a song determines its character.'

Kitaab was based on *Pathik*, a novelette by Samaresh Basu. The story chronicled the experiences of a child who had run away from home. Pancham lent the film a touch of rural Bengal with '*Mere saath chale na saayaa*', inspired by the Bengali folk song *'Janam dukhi kapal poda ami ekjona'*, and *'Hari din toh beeta'*, literally translated from Chunibala Devi's song *'Hari din toh gelo'* in Satyajit Ray's *Pather Panchali*.

Kitaab was also the first film in Pancham's career which did not have any major singers, barring Rajkumari, a well-known singer in the 1950s, who was summoned from oblivion for *'Hari din toh beeta'*.

Using untested voices and rookie musicians demonstrated Pancham's confidence in his ability to harness raw talent. He also believed in giving his musicians the freedom to contribute their two-bit to the composing process. Dada Burman, on the other hand, preferred working with a set team and being directional. Their styles differed, but each Burman's preference worked like magic for him.

Based loosely on an actual incident of rape in Bombay, *Ghar* (1978) was perhaps the most representative Pancham–Gulzar combo since *Aandhi* because of the intensity and depth of its music and its Lata–Kishore gems. Partly directed by Gulzar, who took over when director Manick Chatterjee was injured in a car accident, the film is commonly considered Gulzar's creation, who also wrote the songs.

The song *'Phir wahi raat hai'*, the tune of whose first line was inspired by *'Sing, sing a song'* by the Carpenters, has the husband trying to alleviate the trauma his wife is suffering after being raped. He tries to inject the normalcy of marital conjugality into their lives to soothe her injuries, both psychological and physical. Delicate in its rendition, almost like a late-night breeze on a summer night in the hills, the melody resonates in Kishore Kumar's voice.

Pancham contributed to the Lata–Kishore pantheon with the playful *'Aap ki aankhon mein'*. It used very few instruments, allowing the two great singers free rein. Gulzar has pointed out that Kishore mispronounced the first word in the antara as '*lab hile*' when he was supposed to sing '*jab hile*'. Since the rest of the take turned out fine, the composer and lyricist decided to let it be.

'After an acoustic lead, the muted rhythm joins to lead to the opening lines of the number,' Ranjit Gazmer says, describing the use of the madal in the Lata–Kishore duet '*Tere bina jiya jaye na*'. 'I played the madal, not one, but many. Here was the catch. Pancham had used multiple madals tuned in different scales and I had to play them alternately with the changing chords during the prelude.' Gazmer also remembers Pancham wanting a metallic sound of percussion. After evaluating possibilities of visiting Darjeeling to procure the same, a metal madal available locally was used.

Bhanu Gupta adds, 'I was playing the guitar, and initially the percussionist did not know which madal to play when. With every stroke on the guitar, I had to nod my head to indicate which madal to play.'

The song begins with a subtle touch of the bossa nova, shifts to a different metre, and uses the Teevra Madhyam in the antara to give the feel of a shift in scale. The shift in scale illusion is again created when the antara terminates on Sa, four major notes below Pa – which was the starting note of the mukhra.

Madhu Behl confides that the prominent strokes of the acoustic guitar may have been sparked off by the sound created by the rhythmic flooring of the brakes of Pancham's car on a late-evening drive by the Behls and Pancham.

Using common instruments to extract diverse sounds, taking risks with unfamiliar instruments, using natural sounds within tracks and experimenting with rhythm and mixing had become Pancham's favourite plaything. His passions outside of music were cooking, harvesting green chillies (he had around 200 varieties in his garden at Marylands, the flat he shifted to in the

1980s), driving fast cars and savouring single malt whiskey.
Born a prince, he could not be far away from fine living either.
His favourite perfume was *Grey Flannel* designed by Geoffrey
Beene which, with the essence of lemon, geranium and cedar
wood blended with notes of musk, violet and sage, had the same
meticulous mixing that Pancham used in his music.

7

Gol Maal (1979) was another feather in the Pancham–Gulzar
cap. In what was a relatively quiet year, it was Pancham's
biggest hit. Choosing Kishore Kumar's voice for Amol Palekar
was probably a gamble, as large as the one director Hrishikesh
Mukherjee took in casting Palekar as a suave and resourceful
gent. Amol's earlier roles in films like Basu Chatterjee's
Rajnigandha (1974), *Chhoti Si Baat* and *Chitchor* (1976), and
Bhimsain's *Gharonda* (1977) had been that of a simpleton who
struggles with most things in life – job, home, women. In a
continuation of that perhaps, one of the 'double roles' he essays
in *Gol Maal* has shades of that simpleton.

Both gambles paid off. A hilarious script with exceptional
performances by Palekar, Utpal Dutt, Dina Pathak and David
Abraham, *Gol Maal* remains the slickest comedy–musical of all
times. Kishore Kumar's '*Aanewala pal*', with a haunting trumpet
build-up by George Fernandes, is one of the most searched for
songs on saregama.com even after thirty years. The title track,
'*Golmaal hai bhai sab golmaal hai*', saw the return of the flanger.
Rekha, Zeenat and Amitabh as themselves, and the mention of
Pele and Lata – all greats thrown into a daydream of a young
crowd full of enthusiasm was what '*Sapne mein dekha sapna*' was
about. Adding to the fun quotient was Gulzar's play with
words. In one stanza of the song, which mentions Lata
Mangeshkar, Gulzar wrote: '*Ek din dekhi chhoti si ek sapni, woh*

jo hai na Lata apni', cheekily changing *'sapna'* to *'sapni'* to
maintain the rhyming pattern. Riding on the compositions'
vibrancy and Kishore Kumar's voice, Amol Palekar's
transformation from the soft-voiced romantic to the suave city
slicker was complete.

Continuing his association with Hrishikesh Mukherjee,
Pancham also composed for *Jurmana* (1979). No two films could
be more different. But Mukherjee constantly alternated between
frothy comedies and heart-tugging tear-jerkers right through
the 1970s, though the latter often failed to make as big an
impact as the former. And as with all films which flop, the
melodies in *Jurmana* were lost in obscurity, though Lata
Mangeshkar did popularize *'Saawan ke jhoole padé'* in her stage
shows abroad. *'Chhoti si ek kali khili thi'* – which had a faint
resemblance to Tagore's *'Basante phool gaanthlo'* – was a feast of
percussion and had a swaying feel. The Raga Kalavati-based *'Ai
sakhi Radhiké'* – the Bengali version of which, *'Bolo ki achhe go'*,
remains among Pancham's best-sung songs – however languished.

If *Jurmana* featured Amitabh Bachchan in his less obvious
angry man avatar, another film where Amitabh played the
hopeful middle-class man was Basu Chatterjee's *Manzil* (1979).
Based on Mrinal Sen's *Akash Kusum* (1965), it ran into production
problems and took around five years to complete. For the most
part, it appears that Pancham was hardly involved with the
background score of the film, which was created from Salil
Chowdhury's stock music (uncredited). With *'Rimjhim gire
saawan'*, *Manzil* brought Pancham and Yogesh Gaur together.
The song, composed in two versions, one shot in the middle of
a downpour in Bombay and the other picturized as a mehfil, was
a melody which started a relationship. Like the Gulzar–Pancham
association, the Yogesh–Pancham combo ran strong with other
releases in the 1970s like Asrani's *Chala Murari Hero Banne*
(1977) and Sudhendu Roy's *Jeevan Mukt* (1977). It was during
the course of *Hamare Tumhare* (1979), F.C. Mehra's answer to

Basu Chatterjee's *Khatta Meetha* (1977), that a misunderstanding cropped up between the composer and the lyricist.

'At that time, I was working with Pancham and F.C. Mehra for two films simultaneously, *Hamare Tumhare* and an Indo-Russian venture *Alibaba Aur 40 Chor* [1980],' Yogesh recalls. 'The songs of *Hamare Tumhare* had been recorded and I was supposed to join Pancham for the sittings for the second film. One day, as soon as I entered his music room, Pancham's assistant Sapan Chakraborty said something unpleasant about me to Pancham in Bengali. Sapan did not know that I understood Bengali. I said to Pancham, "I know Bengali. I cannot do your film. Please take Bakshi Sahib instead. Thanks for the opportunities." I left.'

Pancham and Yogesh later reconciled their differences and worked together on a few projects.

Sapan and Yogesh had earlier worked in Nabendu Ghosh's film *Dagdar Babu*. Started in 1976 and based on Phanishwar Nath Renu's story *Maila Aanchal*, this was one among the many films of Pancham that were abandoned midway. Pancham, desperate to foster-parent Sapan as a singer, had caringly composed nine songs for his assistant.

8

Pancham's second Bengali film was *Troyee* (1982), a decade after Salil Sen's *Rajkumari*. Though the release year of the film was 1982, the music was judged hot during the winter of 1979. It was vibrant, trendy and urban – Pancham's detailing was rare for a Bengali film made in the late 1970s. From the magical duet '*Aaro kachha kachhi*' where he keeps Kishore Kumar and Asha Bhonsle guessing about where to start the second line of the mukhra, to the piano accordion-based '*Katha hoyechhilo*' which he based on Martin Denny's '*Enchanted Sea*', Pancham almost urbanized Bengali film music around that time. Among the pulsating songs of *Troyee*, Bhupendra's soulful solo *'Kobe je kothay'* is a late revelation, where Pancham sets sail on a voyage of distressing loneliness with two 'Ni's, in the last notes of the third and fourth lines of the antara, for support. The tune was later used in the track *'Ae zindagi hui kahan bhul'* in *Namumkin* (1988).

Sapan Chakraborty debuted in Bengali films with *Troyee* in which he was involved as a lyricist. By Bengali standards, his lyrics had as much depth as a housewife's grocery list. According to radio jockey and music buff Siddhartha Dasgupta, Sapan's lyrics were a shame. 'I doubt if people of his calibre would have ever dared to enter S.D. Burman's music room,' says Dasgupta.

Pancham also scored for another high-profile Bengali film, *Kalankini Kankabati* (1981), starring Uttam Kumar, Mithun Chakraborty and Sharmila Tagore. Pijush Bose, the director, had passed away during the shooting and it was left to Uttam Kumar to complete the project. Tragically, Uttam Kumar too passed away before the film's completion, resulting in a film low on post-production value. The music had the best of both worlds. The Asha–Kishore duet *'Adho alo chhaya te'* found Pancham in his Occidental avatar. The Parveen Sultana solo *'Bendhechhi beena gaan shonabo'* was among his best classical-based compositions. The tune was used later for the Lata Mangeshkar solo *'E ri pawan'* in Hrishikesh Mukherjee's *Bemisaal* (1983), which, however, did not have the punch of the Bengali version.

Troyee and *Kalankini Kankabati* were a 'homecoming' of sorts for two men associated with it. Two men who were returning after a triumphant voyage on the Bombay seas: Pancham and Mithun. Nobody in Bengal had the heart to point out that the films were not really that good.

It was Shakti Samanta who, along with a cape-and-Spanish-hat-clad Amitabh Bachchan, helped further consolidate Pancham's position in Bengali films with *Anusandhan* (1980).

Book Three

SUN IN GEMINI

A young laurel tree, broken by the wind and withered.

The natives will be of a hopeful and honourable character, full of plans for the future, but will lose many opportunities through misfortunes unforeseen. Their affections will be sincere, but fate will be against them in this respect, and few things in their life will come to maturity. Expected honours will be snatched from them.

14

Old Boys' Alumni

Vir Sanghvi, in his article 'Why the Seventies were the real Sixties', reasoned that though the 1960s is rated as the most influential decade in the second half of the twentieth century by the Western media, it meant little to India. It was the 1970s, with changing equations in almost all domains of popular culture, which really had an impact on society and on popular psyche. Regarding the music, he said, 'Even the music changed. There is little nostalgia for the playback singers of the Sixties [Mukesh, Manna Dey, Mahendra Kapoor, Mohammad Rafi, etc.] but Kishore Kumar remains as popular today as he was during the Seventies. Rahul Dev Burman crawled out from under his father's shadow after *Aradhana* [1969, they collaborated on the score] and the Seventies were his decade [starting with the two brilliant but completely different scores for *Hare Rama Hare Krishna*, 1971, and *Amar Prem*, 1971] and his Seventies' songs are still recorded by new singers every month.'

As Vir points out, it is acknowledged by social scientists and the media that Pancham was one of the archetypal harbingers of the 1970s.

'Pre' and 'post' are commonly used axes of time to refer to any event or person: pre-Independence, post-war, post-9/11. However, 'the Pancham Seventies' ought to be classified as a brand and not a period in a calendar. Strictly speaking, his 'Seventies' began in 1966 with *Teesri Manzil.*

The 1980s meant just a flip of the calendar for Pancham. He was in the process of consolidating his team with new faces who turned into regulars: santoor player Pandit Ulhas Bapat, guitarists Sunil Kaushik and Ramesh Iyer, drummer Franco Vaz and jazz pianist Dambar Bahadur Budaprithi, a.k.a. Louis Banks, whom Pancham had seen performing at the Blue Fox on Park Street, Kolkata, one evening. Banks's recruitment to the Pancham family was swift, almost comparable to the Sicilian mafia in its execution. No wonder he referred to Pancham as his 'Godfather'.

Louis Banks's father Bobby Banks was a jazz musician. He often shared the finer details of the alto sax with Manohari Singh.

Such instantaneous recognition of musicians' worth and laying out the red carpet for them was second nature to Pancham. This was in sharp contrast to his father who was extremely choosy and sceptical about taking in new faces without a detailed grilling process. In a television interview, Brajen Biswas once described the way the senior Burman had initially thrown cold water on his aspirations of playing the tabla with him, without even giving the blind musician an opportunity to exhibit his expertise.

All the new musicians Pancham enrolled, talk with infectious enthusiasm about Pancham's music recordings. 'If it was Pancham-da's recording,' Sunil Kaushik says, 'we knew for sure that it would be completed on schedule and we could have the evening to ourselves. He used to give us a lot of freedom, but somehow had total control. I do not recall his recordings running into overtime.'

Film-maker Tarun Majumdar who had opted for Pancham for his only Hindi venture, seconds the statement: 'Apart from factors like music and knowledge of Bengal, one of the reasons I went to Pancham was because he would not let the budget overshoot.'

There are stories about some composers encouraging overtime because it meant additional payment for the musicians who were expected to canvas for the composers in return.

Meanwhile, Pancham carried on working with old-timers like Hrishikesh Mukherjee, Sanjay Khan, F.C. Mehra, Vinod and Harish Shah, R.K. Soral, Ramesh Sippy and Gulzar, among others. He also developed new partnerships with Ravi Chopra, actor-turned-film-maker Danny, and Gulzar's erstwhile assistant, Meeraj.

The new decade also saw Pancham act as the launch pad for many young acting aspirants. It began with the sons of stars who had almost had a parallel career in Hindi films: Rajendra Kumar launched his son Kumar Gaurav in *Love Story* and Sunil Dutt introduced Sanjay Dutt in *Rocky*, both in 1981. Within a couple of years, Dharmendra and Dev Anand too launched their sons with *Betaab* (1983) and *Anand Aur Anand* (1984) respectively.

Pancham's music contributed immensely to the success of at least three of these debut vehicles. Dev Anand's son came a cropper at the box office. It is another matter that the music was the saving grace of a by-now characteristic shoddy film from the former matinee idol.

Before he debuted as the male lead in *Love Story*, Manoj Kumar Tuli, a.k.a. Kumar Gaurav, worked as Raj Kapoor's assistant in *Satyam Shivam Sundaram* (1978), and had taken a six-month course in acting at Roshan Taneja's institute. *Love*

Story had no acknowledged director since, following the alleged fallout between producer Rajendra Kumar and director Rahul Rawail, the name of the director was removed from the credits.

Rajendra Kumar had never had Rahul Dev Burman as the music director in any of his own films and mostly shared the credit for his success with Shankar–Jaikishan and Naushad. 'I think it was Ramesh Behl who monitored [influenced] a bit. Rajendra Kumar and Ramesh were somehow related,' feels Amit on how Pancham may have been chosen. A tradition-bound individual from the old school, it was expected that Rajendra Kumar would get a like-minded person to compose for his son's first film.

So, if choosing Pancham over other composers for his son's launch came as a surprise, the choice of Amit Kumar as the voice of Kumar Gaurav was even more startling. Amit had not quite been able to build on the success of *'Bade achche lagte hain'*. 'In *Love Story*, there was this "Kishore ka ladka, mera ladka" equation between Rajendra Kumar and my father,' says Amit Kumar. Akin to the equation between two middle-aged, nostalgic friends seeing their sons go to the same university that they went to.

Pancham's self-flagellating assessment of a song he composed for *Love Story* was that it sounded as soporific as a bhajan. That both versions – the Amit Kumar solo and the Amit–Lata duet – of *'Yaad aa rahi hai'*, a song where flautist Pandit Ranendranath (aka Ronu) Majumdar debuted, actually turned out to be one of the biggest success stories of that period is a sign that Pancham was his own worst critic. Later, Pancham acknowledged *Love Story* as one of his big scores. 'Look Amit, this is the way things turn out in life. One of my worst compositions, but it's a hit,' was his take on the success of the song.

Sunil Dutt, a Pancham follower since the days of *Padosan*,

and someone who had used Pancham once for his production
Nehle Pe Dehla (1976), had planned a grand launch for his son
Sanjay with *Rocky*. Sanjay had first faced the camera as a
silhouette in his father's mono-act film *Yaadein* (1964) and later
played a child artist, lipping a qawwali, in *Reshma Aur Shera*
(1971). He reportedly had a traumatic childhood that included
being kidnapped by dacoits during the filming of *Mujhe Jeene
Do* (1963). He was well into drugs when *Rocky* was under
production and turned the blind corner into addiction following
his mother's death in May 1981.

The droopy-eyed Sanjay Dutt provoked nothing but laughter
in the early 1980s. Gangly, wooden and gawky, his dialogue
delivery was a disaster and his physical movements seemed to
be in a state of complete disarray. Sunil Dutt too disappointed
by playing it safe with the film. There was no sign of the
boldness of offbeat topics (*Mujhe Jeene Do* and *Reshma Aur
Shera*) or an interesting screenplay (*Yaadein*). A regulation
Hindi masala film suffering from an inexperienced leading pair,
Rocky surprisingly broke even, riding mainly on the music.
Pancham in his interviews tended to overlook films which were
not big successes, and is likely to have missed quoting *Rocky* as
one of his best works of that period. The compositions for *Love
Story* were in the conventional mould, and on a good day, could
have been attempted by other composers. The Pancham touch
was visible only in patches, such as in the rhythm technique for
the Asha Bhonsle solo '*Kya ghazab karte ho jee*'. But *Rocky* was
an out-and-out Pancham special, identifiable within the first few
notes of any song, including the Asha solo '*Geet sunoge huzur*',
which, in spite of being a customary mujra, was devoid of the
clutter associated with the genre.

Rocky had six tracks out of which two Lata–Kishore duets –
'*Kya yahi pyar hai*' and '*Hum tumse mile phir juda ho gaye* – are
enduring hits. As was the disco number '*Aa dekhe zara*', which

people have started listening to once again post the release of the Bipasha Basu–Neil Nitin Mukesh flick of the same name.

Bhanu Gupta, who had a hand in fashioning 'Kya yahi pyar hai', says, 'I was fiddling around the chords for G-minor scale and it struck me that I could use D-seventh in lieu of it. Gradually, a tune emerged based on the chord progression, and I asked Pancham to try it out. When I had told him that I had based it on a G-minor progression, Pancham was puzzled and asked where the G-minor was in the song. I told him that it is not there, only touched upon once in the antara. Later, when Lata Mangeshkar was rehearsing the song, she praised Pancham, but he told her, "Don't thank me, thank Bhanu."'

This song marks a shift from voices to instruments. In mid-1980, when it was recorded, Lata Mangeshkar was over fifty, and the vocal stress at higher octaves was beginning to show, something that became more prominent with her advancing age. Another fifty-year-old, Kishore Kumar's voice had coarsened too, so much so that the heavy bass seemed to dominate everything else at times. This hampered the free flow one associated with his voice. Consequently, the Pancham songs of the 1980s with Kishore Kumar and/or Lata Mangeshkar tended to be restrained and sober. This was a key departure from his more jazzy scores in the 1960s or the '70s where he would let his imagination run wild, with musicians and singers often improvising on the spot.

A seminal song like 'Kya yahi pyar hai' finds a Pancham who has adjusted himself to the demands of electronically generated sounds and shorter, lesser-drawn notes. This arguably placed more restriction on his unshackled style, but he used this opportunity to experiment more with the arrangement. Apart from the very prominent use of multiple guitars and chord inversions, one finds the use of brass and woodwind to fashion a hollow, tranquil feel.

This song was the calm after the storm of 'Bachao, aao mere

yaroon aao', a song composed by Pancham for a Sanjay Dutt who loses control at the unexpected sight of Tina doing aerobics in skimpy clothes.

Manohari Singh's soprano sax in *'Kya yahi pyar hai'* largely contributed to the sombre, resonating sound that went so well with the background of Kashmir. In the Bengali version sung by Asha Bhonsle, Singh plays the English flute, and the effect is rather diluted in the absence of the sax.

'Hum tumse mile' was a breezy tune, more fluid than *'Kya yahi pyar hai'*, but lacking in the 'hollow echo' factor which singled out the latter. It was moderately paced, had delightful strumming and persuasive use of the flanger and the moog, along with trademark trumpet pieces by George, creating a signature melody of sorts. Lata Mangeshkar's *'La la la . . .'* in particular imparted a very buoyant, almost schoolgirl-like feel to the song.

The track had its share of helpful controversy as posters, hoardings and the Long Play record carried a shot from the song, featuring Sanjay Dutt in a swim trunk leaning over Tina Munim lying flat on a motorcycle. Interestingly, in the film, the names of both the hero Sanjay Dutt and the villain Shakti Kapoor had the initials 'RD'.

Love Story and *Rocky*, both released in 1981, created a precedence of star sons being introduced with the orchestra-backed compositions of Rahul Dev Burman. Another norm was re-established: Pancham could compose as per the requirements of the producer or director and still come up with diverse scores as in *Love Story* and *Rocky*. It also shut out the water-cooler critics' prissy opinions that rhythm and brass were the only two sections Pancham considered important.

Tailing the windfall of *Love Story*, Pancham was signed on for Kumar Gaurav's next film *Teri Kasam* (1982). The film was probably one of the first where the Indian censors passed a kissing scene. The story primarily dealt with marital discord and the ramifications thereof. The score of *Teri Kasam* was built on the same lines as that of *Love Story* – voice-oriented and melody-based – although one would have wished Amit Kumar to be a trifle more dedicated to holding the tune, the absence of which often turned a pleasurable listening experience into a drag.

In this, his third decade as a composer, Pancham had secured acceptance into the new brigade of actors. Sunil Dutt, in an interview to Ali Peter John after Pancham's demise (*Screen*, 14 January 1994) said, 'He understood youth like no other music director did.'

Karan Shah and Neelam's debut film *Jawani* (1984) was another example that vindicated Sunil Dutt's statement. '*Tu rootha toh main ro doongi sanam*' turned out to be a radio favourite. Lyricist Gulshan Bawra has described how taxing writing the lyrics for this seemingly undemanding metre was. The Roland Jupiter keyboard played by Charanjit Singh, programmed to repeat a pattern of notes – one of the first instances of its kind in Hindi films – functions both as a melody and a rhythm instrument. For a song embossed with electronic sounds, Pancham keeps the movement uncharacteristically simple, and incorporates the trademark Franco Vaz drums pick-up to break the monotony. Asha's voice modulation makes her sound like the teen she is singing for. The part that stands out in the Asha Bhonsle–Amit Kumar duet is the hand clapping effect, achieved using an electronic penumbra. It is not a surprise that '*Tu rootha*' is the track Neelam is most remembered for.

If Pancham were an amulet, newcomers might have wrapped him round their arms, such luck he seemed to bless beginners with. Anup Ghoshal made his Hindi debut film as singer in first-time director Shekhar Kapur's *Masoom* (1982); Abhijeet Bhattacharya did the same in Bengali with the film *Aparupa*

(1982) and in Hindi with an impressive solo *'Mai awara hi sahi'* in Navketan's *Anand Aur Anand*. 'People fail to realize that I was the only singer to make my debut under R.D. Burman, the first prominent male singer to ever do so,' Abhijeet says. However, Kumar Sanu too debuted (as Sanu Bhattacharya) under Pancham as one of the singers for a song in the film *Yeh Desh* (1984).

2

Probably riding on the flickering luck that *Amar Deep* (1979) had brought him, Rajesh Khanna signed more films in Madras, one of which was Bharathi Raja's Hindi remake of his 1978 Tamil thriller, *Sigappu Rojakkal*. Named *Red Rose* (1980), it was almost a frame-by-frame copy of the original, including the sequence of *'Kiski sadayein mujhko bulayein'*, a song Pancham fashioned brilliantly, taking inspiration from *'The windmills of your mind'* from *The Thomas Crown Affair* (1968). *Red Rose* was a psychological thriller with the hero playing a psychic misogynist; it had only two songs including *'Kiski sadayein'* in which Pandit Ulhas Bapat plays the Irani santoor (the Irani santoor is thirty-six inches wide and smaller compared to the normal one, he points out). Pancham's background music was chic — it included humming by Annette and Usha Uthup, the intermittent use of the bossa nova — and fitted the urban nightlife of the late 1970s like a glove.

Pandit Ulhas Bapat had learnt the tabla for most part of his growing-up years, but took to a different instrument which was string-based but still percussion by definition. A printing technologist by qualification, he made his debut for R.D. Burman by playing the santoor in the background music of *Ghar*. He went on to play with Pancham till his last film. 'I played for Pancham-da from 1978 to 1942 [*1942: A Love Story*],' he says.

As a throwback to Pancham's days of assistantship in the Navketan camp, Rajesh Khanna's cigarette lighter had chimes generated by the glockenspiel, à la the one played by Kersi Lord in *Hum Dono* (1961). However, this might have been a synthesized version.

Though Pancham's association with Feroz Khan did not extend beyond *Khhotte Sikkay* and *Kala Sona*, Sanjay Khan, the younger sibling who had roped in Pancham in 1973 for his directorial debut *Chandi Sona* (1977), continued with him for his next film *Abdullah* (1980) as well. Made during the time of the alleged Sanjay–Zeenat Aman wedding, *Abdullah* generated enough gossip to sustain magazines for weeks; but the film bombed. However, the music bloomed, partly due to an overexposed Zeenat Aman in the film, say, in the song *'Bheega badan jalne laga'*. Pancham's music in the film was, in essence, similar to *Chandi Sona*, replete with Middle Eastern elements. Pancham's work with Sanjay Khan even in the most nondescript of films – *Saas Bhi Kabhi Bahu Thi* (1970), *Mela* (1971), *Trimurti* (1974), *Chandi Sona* (1977) – always had an air of exclusivity. In *Abdullah*, the strings section played a fundamental role in creating the desert-like ambience; the transitory use of the brass and the multilayered percussion added mirage-like contours to the tunes. Ramesh Iyer recalls, 'The sound of the desert wind, heard in the track as well as in the background of the film, was created mainly by rubbing a rubber-cased stick on the rim of a bowl filled with water and by rubbing a bare finger on the rim of an empty wine glass of fine quality. This was recorded, amplified and mixed. We made many new sounds at that time. These have become standard software products now.'

The part-lullaby, part-devotional song, *'Lallah, Allah tera nighebaan'*, had Pancham tweaking the mukhra of two of his road songs *'Jaane-jaana jao kal phir ana'* (*Samadhi*) and *'Dekho hum dono ki yaari kya kehna'* (*Double Cross*) and using them as the first lines of the mukhra and the antara respectively. It was incredible, as Pancham created the feel of the Phrygian dominant scale characteristic of Middle Eastern melody by using two radically dissimilar tunes. Doel Gupta, daughter of Badal and Mili Bhattacharya, recalls about the same song, 'Pancham Kaku was a fascinating raconteur of stories. He had explained to me in detail about the song *Lallah*. And when the part about Raj Kapoor's crucifixion came about, I was literally in tears. I think he understood the scenarios very well, and this helped him compose songs with the feeling required.' Remarkable for its tranquility, Kishore Kumar's '*Aye khuda har faisla*' finds the mukhra and antara being bridged with a high-pitched cry of '*Allaaaah*'.

The desert saga continued with Umesh Mehra's *Alibaba Aur 40 Chor* (1980), an Indo-Russian venture, the only one of its kind Pancham worked for. The film is famous for the Kishore–Asha duet '*Jadugar jadu kar jayega*' and for the eerie background score for the 'khulja sim sim' section, created by recording the sound produced by dropping stones and assorted utensils from a height, mixing the same, and playing the mixed sound in reverse. Asha Bhonsle's '*Khatooba*' (again a word coined by Pancham), replete with warbling, is a song in demand today.

During the 1970s, Pancham had started the trend of warbling, using monotonic notes like Pa Ra Pa, often at different octaves, in pockets where proper lyrics could not fit into the metre, like in '*Jab andhera hota hai*' (*Raja Rani*), '*Dekho mujhe dekho*' (*Humshakal*) and '*O saathi chal*' (*Seeta Aur Geeta*). This carried on to the 1980s too. In Harish Shah's film *Dhan Daulat* (1980), Pancham began a song with the notes Pa Ra Pa, dovetailed the tune with the bossa nova, incorporated changes in the scale while shifting between the voices of Asha Bhonsle and Kishore Kumar, and presented '*Woh unki nayi hai duniya*'. Under normal circumstances, Pancham would have used instruments like the alto sax or the trumpet, but by using human voices, especially Asha Bhonsle's voice, Pancham was perhaps making a statement regarding sustaining a style that he had patented and was bringing both the style and Asha into sharper focus post his marriage to her.

Musicians agree that Pancham was fascinated by Asha Bhonsle's range and created songs with her in mind during most of the late 1970s and the 1980s.

In an interview to Ardhendu Nayak in the *Statesman*, Calcutta, on 30 July 1994, Asha said that Pancham and she had formalized their off-studio relationship on 7 March 1979. Lata Mangeshkar, Kishore Kumar, Bharati Mangeshkar (Hridayanath Mangeshkar's wife) and Babu Bhai Desai (an acquaintance) were the witnesses.

Mili Bhattacharya recounts, 'My husband [Badal Bhattacharya] was present during the occasion. To offset the risk of controversy and the hurt that it might cause to Meera Dev Burman [because of the culture shock it came with – her son getting married to a lady who was six years older to him and widowed], the event was very low-key with no publicity at all. Just to be doubly careful, the film roll had been removed from the camera [probably by Kishore Kumar] that Sapan Chakraborty was clicking away on.'

In startling contrast, Sachin Bhowmick gives another angle to the whole event: 'From what Pancham told me, there was no marriage or anything like that. Asha had taken Pancham with her to a temple in Darjeeling one night [when he was] in a drunken state. Garlands were exchanged. There is no photo or any registration.'

3

Harjaee (1981) was the last instance when Ramesh Behl cast Randhir Kapoor as the male lead. Pancham's melodies in this

film were lost in the debris of its failure, despite comforting
words by well-wishers that this film may turn out to be a
'surprise package', as Bubbles Behl (Ramesh Behl's wife) puts it.
Today, thanks partly to HMV's packaging and the general
'rediscovery of Pancham', melodies like the Kishore Kumar
solos *Yeh rut hai haseen* and *Kabhi palkon pe aansoo hain*, Lata
Mangeshkar's *Tere liye palkon ki jhalar bunu* and the Kishore–
Asha duet *Kherishu varishu* have stunned many with their depth,
leaving listeners wondering how such brilliant compositions
could have languished for a decade in the wilderness.

The Kishore Kumar solo *Yeh rut hai haseen* finds Pancham
mixing the Orient delectably with the West. In this major-
scale-based song where all the santoor-laden notes are shuddha
(barring the sporadic use of the Teevra Madhyam), the violin
ensemble creates a crescendo in the prelude, and the synthesizer
and the guitar gradually take over. The sporadic use of the
Komal Dhaivat by the sax in the second interlude creates a
fatalistic feeling in the song which is the hero's last attempt at
winning the love of his beloved. *Kabhi palkon pe aansoo hain* has
all the seven major notes in the mukhra, and the use of three
minor notes in the antara depicts the darkness that comes with
death looming large. *Tere liye palkon ki jhalar bunu* uses the
major seventh chord, coupled with chimes generated from a
bell-tree – an instrument made from cycle-bell caps of different
diameters strung vertically – and is laced with notes from
Pandit Ulhas Bapat's santoor. Representative of the Pancham
songs of the early 1980s, where the rhythm was softer and
subtle, this track gained critical and popular acclaim later, even
though Lata's timbre had lost some of its lustre of the mid-
1970s.

In April 2009, four months prior to his death, Gulshan
Bawra, one of the lyricists of *Harjaee*, recounted how another
song in the film was created: 'We had gone for the shooting of

a film in Kashmir and dusk had fallen over the Valley. Near a
ropeway, I heard two locals call out to each other in a language
I did not understand. One of the silhouetted men seemed to ask
a question and the other seemed to reply in the affirmative. My
panic swelled as the only recognizable word sounded like
"shoot". I interpreted this as "Should I shoot?" and "Yes, shoot"
respectively. I hurried away from the scene, understandably
quickly. A couple of days later a friend of mine in Bombay
clarified amidst relieved laughter that what I had heard was
"Kherishu?" and *"Varishu"* which meant "How are you?" and the
reply "I am fine". When I told the two words to Pancham, he
asked, "Which language is this? Russian?" "No, this is Kashmiri,"
I replied. An amused Pancham used the words for an Asha
Bhonsle–Kishore Kumar duet and the song *"Jeevan me jab aise
pal . . . Kherishu, Varishu"* was born.'

   Good music notwithstanding, *Harjaee* was a disaster of gigantic
proportions, with distributors unwilling to even accept the film.
'Daboo's bulky persona did not convincingly pass for a terminal
cancer patient,' Madhu Behl says, probably one reason for the
film's debacle. But Randhir Kapoor has no regrets. '*Harjaee* had
brilliant songs. It was probably Pancham's best score for me
and I live by it,' he avers in his typical ebullience.

   Randhir and Pancham's ill luck continued with *Jaane Jaan*
(1983), known as *Nikamma* when production started in the mid-
1970s, which faced multiple production problems till it was
released as late as 1983. It took down with it a truckload of
melodies which could have been instant hits had they come at
the right time. Tracks included the theme music of *Khel Khel
Mein* made into *'Tere bina main kuch bhi nahi'*, and *'Tere bina
kabhi ek pal'* the Hindi version of Asha Bhonsle's dainty Bengali
solo *'Shondha belaye'*, a song that Pancham had composed while
enjoying the evening air with Asha near Dhakuria Lake in
Calcutta.

Pancham's Bengali songs habitually suffered from the handicap of inane lyrics. Non-film music has a limitation in the sense that there is no situation sketched for the tune to capture the essence. The genesis of the song situation was, hence, often Pancham's brainchild. He did go overboard at times, like when designing the song 'Daak pathale kaal sokale' (in Pancham and Asha's 1980 Puja album) which drafts the story of Flight No. IC 108 from Bombay to Calcutta. But more often than not, he compensated by giving a lot of thought to the arrangement and providing offbeat tunes. The result was that the songs had a long shelf life. Hindi film producer–directors too would wait patiently for Pancham's Puja songs, and negotiate for tunes from the repository.

Amit Kumar recounts an amusing anecdote leading to the birth of a song: 'Around the late 1960s, Pancham-da had gone to Beirut. Once he returned, he asked my father to come over to the Sun 'n' Sand Hotel for a floorshow by belly dancers from the Middle East. Pancham-da had apparently invited the dancers and they were supposed to show up at the hotel at 7 p.m. My father and Pancham-da waited till there was a "no show" from the dancers. My father, disappointed, told Pancham-da: "Pancham, Shey to elo na [she didn't show up]." Pancham-da caught on to the line and the fabulous sentimental song "Shey to elo na" was composed.'

4

With ideas borrowed from a late-night viewing of Gilbert Cates's The Promise (1979), Yeh Vaada Raha (1982) was Ramesh Behl's follow-up to Harjaee. Kapil Kapoor, son of actor Kamal Kapoor and Ramesh Behl's brother-in-law, was given the task of directing the film. Kapil, one of the assistants in the Rose Movies team, had also served as an assistant to director Narendra

Bedi from the days of *Benaam* (1974). The songs of *Yeh Vaada Raha* are some of the best from the 1980s, and find an ever-enthusiastic Pancham at work. This is what Viju Katkar, Amrutrao's son and a key member of the Pancham team after 1979, remembers of the title track '*Tu, tu hai wohi*': 'The number starts with a prominent bass guitar by Tony Vaz. Then the sax picks up, after which one hears whistling by Manohari Singh. Ravi Sundaram and Kishore Desai create very fine interludes on the mandolin. The Pancham touch comes in the form of two quick claps followed by a sound made by clicking the tongue against the roof of the mouth after "*Mil jaaye is tarah*".'

'The title song of this film remains one of my most favourite ever,' says Rishi Kapoor.

Pancham had told Gulshan Bawra how grandly he would orchestrate the tune using a lot of instruments in a style hitherto untried. Generally, in the 1980s, courtesy multi-tracks, Pancham would have ensured that the deep, low-frequency notes came out clear and were not lost in the cacophony that is so characteristic of a large orchestra. This has been corroborated by his musicians. Blasco Monsorate revealed that Pancham was very particular about the brass positioning in his orchestra and used to keep a separate track for the trombone. Ditto for the bass guitar.

'With this film, we decided on taking Rishi Kapoor,' Madhu Behl recalls. 'We had it in mind that the faces [of the two heroines] might change after plastic surgery but the voice should remain the same. As a result, Jaya Bachchan's was the voice connecting the two faces of the heroine[s] pre- and post-plastic surgery in the film. I also feel Rakesh Roshan modernized *Ye Vaada Raha* into what we saw as *Khoon Bhari Maang* [1989], and, later, *Kasme Vaade* into *Kaho Naa ... Pyar Hai* [2000].'

Films like *Harjaee, Love Story* and *Teri Kasam* were devoid of elaborate instrumentation, while *Rocky* and *Yeh Vaada Raha* carried an arrangement style that was high on instruments. Over the years, Pancham had acquired the ability to compartmentalize his mind in order to multitask effectively, and films like *The Burning Train* (1980) and *Satte Pe Satta* (1982) had him delve into the domain of experimentation in new sounds.

One of the new sounds was using the vocoder, an instrument that modifies voice input into a metallic voice output. This gadget had been around during the time when moog synthesizers were introduced, but was not used in Hindi film music. Inspired by the German group Kraftwerk, who used the vocoder for the album *The Man Machine* in 1978, Pancham became the first person in Bombay films to use the instrument in the title music of Ravi Chopra's *The Burning Train*. This vocal input to the contraption was a one-liner '*The Burning Train*' sung by Pancham and Annette Pinto. The vocoder found its way into Pancham's background scores, and also into songs, such as in the interlude of '*Aa dekhe zara*' (*Rocky*) and the Amit Kumar solo '*Hum bhi toh hain talabgaron mein*' (*Dhuan*, 1981). Dakshina Mohan Tagore, a regular accompanist in Pancham's team, who played the taar shehnai, had earned the nickname 'Dukhi Dada' because he mostly got to play only for maudlin background scores in tearful scenes. In this Amit Kumar track, the lyrics '*Dukhi Dada, Dukhi Dada*' with a metallic output on the vocoder formed a part of the interlude. The uncredited singer of the phrase was Bhupendra! This comical innovation still evokes laughter among the former members of Pancham's team.

In *Satte Pe Satta*, it was the use of human voices that formed an integral part of the arrangement in most of the songs. Seven heroes and seven heroines meant multiple playback singers. 'I want a lot of noise,' was Pancham's demand. Sapan Chakraborty, Basu Chakravarty, Anand Kumar C., Ramesh Iyer, Gulshan

Bawra, Sunil Kaushik, all chimed in with their vocals to support Kishore and Bhupendra.

'How can I write for a song with so many voices? I'm used to something else,' Gulshan Bawra had protested to Pancham. 'Yes, you can,' was all the composer had to say in return. Bawra promptly jotted down what he deemed suited the script and it worked like magic.

During a rehearsal of *'Pyar hamen kis mod pe le aaya'* (which Pancham had composed with the dummy lyrics *'Roop tera mastana hoga re'*), Gulshan Bawra chipped in with a spontaneous *'Haaye'*. Pancham was so taken with the sound that he asked Gulshan to reproduce the word exactly in the final take.

The number *'Pariyon ka mela hai'* was partly inspired from the theme of *Zorba the Greek*. Guitarist Sunil Kaushik recalls, 'The prelude of *"Pariyon ka mela hai"* was the result of some casual, good-humoured horsing around by Bhupendra and me on a tune by Bhanu-da. Pancham was listening to the same, and maybe he found it musical too, and inquired what it was. Bhupi said, "This is for my guru [Bhanu Guptaji]." Pancham asked us to replay the stuff so that he could consider using it. In the final take, Tony played the bass, I played the chords and Ramesh Iyer played the lead notes with a wailing effect. Bhupendra wasn't there for the recording, so the two of us played it.' The 'synchronized sound of boots kicking wooden tables' made for an unconventional element in the song, according to Viju Katkar.

In the scenes involving the impostor Babu (Amitabh in a double role), the signature tune was created by 'sampling' (recording the sound and playing it in a continuous loop) the sound of Annette Pinto gargling with water in her throat. In an interview, director Raj N. Sippy applauded Pancham for coming up with the signature tune for the grey-eyed Amitabh Bachchan. This loop has found its way into other films too.

The tracks of *Satte Pe Satta* took time to climb the popularity charts, probably because unlike the standard Hindi film song, which is often independent of the visuals, these were intrinsic to the screenplay and had to be enjoyed with the visuals of the film. *Satte Pe Satta* remains a film where all the songs, barring '*Zindagi mil ke bitayenge*', are situational, like in Hollywood musicals. Pancham, like Amitabh, played a 'double role' in the recording of '*Zindagi mil ke bitayenge*'. He sang and played the harmonica notes as well. Shuttling from the voice cubicle to the orchestra area to play the instrument must have mandated 'a high energy level' as Gulshan Bawra put it.

The music of the film was a mix of tunes and styles from all over the world: the march song of the Royal Canadian Air Force during the Second World War ('*Zindagi mil ke bitayenge*'), German gypsy song ('*Dilbar mere kab tak mujhe*'), Irish folk tunes, and portions from Pancham's own songs ('*Mausam mastana*' could have been inspired from the tune of '*Ai meri jaan*' from *Puraskar*, and a guitar riff in the second interlude of '*Tune cheen liya*' from *Bandhe Haath*). Despite the nondescript valley that featured dominantly in the long shots, the film actually had a subterranean cosmopolitan feel, and Pancham liberally incorporated inputs from world music and worked around the same, giving it a local flavour.

The same cannot be said of Rahul Rawail's *Betaab*, though it remains one of Pancham's more popular films from the 1980s. The story of the film revolved around the happenings on a ranch. In many ways the locale was similar to that of *Satte Pe Satta*. But it appeared as if Pancham had deliberately simplified the score so as to cater to the average listener brought up on Indian sounds and flat 2–4 beats on the dholak and the tabla. Still, *Betaab* galloped home with five big hits. Punjab da puttar Sunny Deol and Punjab di kudi Amrita Singh debuted in style as the Bhowanipur regiment in Calcutta marched into theatres

to capture the release-day tickets. However, apart from the
simplicity of the tunes, which made them hummable, the songs
did not have the structural tautness and multilayered expanse
one associates with Pancham. Shabbir Kumar's insipid singing,
often off-key, further added to the woes of the Pancham fan who
might actually have wanted the songs to flop instead! That
would probably have saved many the trauma of having to listen
to Shabbir Kumar for the better part of the decade. Perhaps this
was one of Pancham's urges to create original tunes which
catered to a more rural audience, something which was not
really his strength.

Singer Sonu Nigam played the young Sunny Deol in *Betaab*. In the 1980s,
Pancham's association with Rahul Rawail, which started with *Gunahgaar* (1980),
was prolific. Apart from the uncredited *Love Story* and R.K. Films' *Biwi O Biwi*
(1981), the partnership resulted in films like *Arjun* (1985) and *Dacait* (1987).
Dacait had a Punjabi version too.

But he compensated for the mundane score, and in style
too – with the title track of the film, which remains the most
and perhaps the only sought-after piece of music from the film.
'The title music was a grand affair of forty violins led by Basu
Chakravarty, four brass and woodwind instruments led by
Manohari Singh, castanet and donkeys' jaws by Homi Mullan
and Viju Katkar, and with me on a singular lead acoustic
guitar,' Ramesh Iyer says enthusiastically. 'The acoustic guitar
lent an effect of good old Western movies. The hugeness of an
expansive outdoor with mountains, running streams, cowboy
shoes and untamed horses needed percussions like the timpani
and broad brass sections to give it a very Texan/Mexican feel.
There was no scope for anything electric.'

5

After the demise of Madan Mohan, who was Chetan Anand's musical mainstay since *Haqeeqat*, Chetan needed a composer for *Kudrat* (1981) and though *Kudrat* was not produced by Chetan Anand, Pancham volunteered to write the music in what would be like a sentimental pilgrimage of the Burmans to the original Navketan shrine. Meera Dev Burman gave her son permission to use SD's composition '*Hai kije kori ae mono niya*' and recast it as '*Tune o rangile kaisa jadu kiya*', to be sung by Lata Mangeshkar. Pancham's experiment in *Kudrat* was with '*Hamein tumse pyar kitna*', used repeatedly in the film, cutting across time. Apart from the solos by Kishore Kumar and Parveen Sultana, Asha Bhonsle and Annette too hummed the tune at different points in the film.

Parveen Sultana was the first singer from the classical school to win the Filmfare Award in 1981 for her rendition of '*Hamein tumse pyar kitna*'. (Amit Kumar won the best male singer for *Love Story* the same year, making it a double whammy for Pancham.) Small-time singer Chandrasekhar Gadgil also became an overnight singing sensation in his hometown Pune after the title solo '*Dukh sukh ki har ek mala*'. Pancham, as usual, did not feature in the Filmfare Awards.

'It's to R.D. Burman's credit that songs composed by him have got both the playback singer awards. This year, RD's *Love Story*, *Kudrat*, *Harjaee*, *Rocky* and *Basera* were musically much acclaimed and it's a pity that he did not feature in the awards; in fact, he has been providing us with innumerable melodic tunes for a decade now and is yet to win a single Filmfare Award,' Vinodkumar M. Nayak, a reader, wrote in the 'Letters' section of *Filmfare*, 16 July 1982.

Not that Pancham needed the endorsement of any curvy statuettes. In any case, the credibility of the very process of the *Filmfare* award selection was questioned. There are recorded reports of composers purchasing multiple copies of *Filmfare*, filling out the readers' choice forms and mailing it to a response team that did not stop to wonder why thousands of responses had come from the same postal precinct. 'R.D. Burman never cared for these awards. His team was above all this,' confides Nandu Chavathe.

The thoughts in Nayak's letter, representative of thousands of others, perhaps prodded the *Filmfare* jury into hurriedly handing out two successive awards to RD in an attempt to save its own skin.

6

Basking in the glory of the resounding success of *Ek Duje Ke Liye* (1981), Kamal Haasan teamed up with Pancham for the first time in Barkha Roy's *Sanam Teri Kasam* (1982). The storyline, similar to films by Nasir Husain, especially *Phir Wohi Dil Laya Hoon* (1963) and *Pyar Ka Mausam*, lacked the warmth and the zing of a Nasir Husain production. Nevertheless, it was a hit. Maybe it was riding the Kamal Haasan wave, and the disco wave which had crept in too. Though Pancham and his musicians claimed not to have espoused the disco wave, it was something they could not totally avoid.

The film had one archetypal Pancham song, '*Jaan-e-jaan o meri jaan-e-jaan*'. In the music CD *Untold Stories*, Gulshan Bawra narrates how Pancham, after viewing the film *Xanadu* (1980), used the keyword Xanadu ('*Xaanadoooo, O Xanadu*' was the dummy lyric to be replaced by '*Jaan-e-jaan O meri jaan-e-jaan*') to compose the duet. Sunil Kaushik describes this as a number which Pancham orchestrated deftly, successfully encapsulating the conflict between the lead actors. It was also a rare instance of 'Bhupi playing the bass guitar', remembers Sunil. Gulshan Bawra also referred to the 'cooking' spree that went on during the creation of the title song '*Kitne bhi tu kar le sitam*'. Amrutrao narrates the story of the African instrument resso resso, or rather the evolution of the instrument in the context of Hindi film music: 'The first resso used was made of gourd. It was in use since the 1950s, I think. This unorthodox instrument made out of a humble plant had infused magic into "*Mere saamne wali khidki mein*" in *Padosan*. During a journey for a stage show in Surat, everyone, in their hurry to alight from the train, forgot that piece of luggage. With the loss of the "lauki", a makeshift resso was manufactured out of bamboo, till 1982 when the first metal resso came into being as a Pancham invention for the songs of *Sanam Teri Kasam*.'

The music of *Sanam Teri Kasam* received good reviews, from both critics and viewers. Khalid Mohammed described the film as 'appealing primarily because of a finger-snapping score by R.D. Burman and Kamal Haasan's spontaneous reaction to it' in the 1 July 1982 edition of *Filmfare*.

Even Shalini Pradhan, known for her acidic reviews of Hindi films in general – even *Mili* and *Abhimaan* failed to graduate beyond a single star (poor) rating – had kind words for Kamal and Pancham. 'It is just him [Kamal Haasan] and R.D. Burman's music.'

The music was among the five nominated for the Filmfare Award in 1982. Barkha Roy, actress Reena Roy's sister and the producer of *Sanam Teri Kasam*, later told a TV channel on 27 June 2009 that Pancham was apprehensive about it winning, considering he had given much better scores earlier, which had gone unrewarded.

Pancham won the award, breaking a jinx. It was his twenty-fifth year in the composing rooms of Bombay, and he had not won a Filmfare Award for *Amar Prem, Kati Patang, Aandhi, Mere Jeevan Saathi, Yaadon Ki Baaraat, Hum Kisise Kum Naheen,* and countless others, which had scores much superior to *Sanam Teri*

Kasam. The award, when it came, was more an acknowledgement of *Filmfare*'s culpability in neglecting him all these years. Pancham's act at the awards function included capturing centre stage and belting out songs like *'Samundar mein nahake'* from *Pukar* and *'Jaana o meri jaana'* (*Sanam Teri Kasam*).

In an interview to Chaitanya Padokone in the *Mid Day*, Bombay, on 21 July 1983, Pancham remarked on his win: 'I really lost all hopes and consoled myself by reminding myself that what is more important is rewards and not awards. My fans are my rewards. The winner *Sanam Teri Kasam* was not exactly one of my best films – it was more of an electronic frenzy. Nevertheless, I was thrilled when I was informed about my trophy. That night, I wept with joy.'

In retrospect, Pancham might have been right as there was at least another contender for the award, Khayyam's *Bazaar* (1982), arguably the best score that year, and it is a shame that it went unrewarded. It was almost poetic justice. Six years ago, Khayyam's score for *Kabhi Kabhie* (1976) had been voted by the *Filmfare* awards committee over the score of *Mehbooba*.

Pancham's happiness was marred by a dark cloud. Narendra Bedi, director of *Sanam Teri Kasam*, passed away suddenly in October 1982, at the age of forty-seven, unable to enjoy the success of his film.

Around this time, Pancham shifted to Avanti apartments, across the street, from Odena. This flat proved lucky for him as his second Filmfare Award-winning composition was written during his short stay here.

15

Cracks on the Wall

Sanam Teri Kasam filled a void in Pancham's living room, but the early 1980s did bring their quota of speed breakers, which led him to gradually sever ties with producer–director combos who had been part of his dream run.

Ramesh Sippy's *Shaan* was the most ambitious film of the early 1980s and was sold for a record value of Rs 10 million per territory. Inevitable comparisons with *Sholay* followed. Due to a very large and costly star cast and high production values involving lots of technology including helicopter shots in Somerset, England, the film barely managed to break even. Down the years, after several reruns and telecasts on television, *Shaan* is now considered the highest-grossing film of 1980 by the Internet trade channel, http://ibosnetwork.com.

However, the public perception of the film has remained the same. *Shaan* was branded a flop. Pancham's music, funky and electronic, failed to get the adulation it deserved then. '*Jaanu meri jaan*' was initially left out of some prints, and '*Mitwaa tere liye jeena*', one of the few duets featuring Lata and Asha, was also left out of the film.

Pancham experimented widely in the film. The background music was startling in the use of human voices. Usha Uthup's voice, used in the background, was also used for the brass-dominated title song which was somewhat along the lines of the title songs of James Bond films. Percussionist Amrutrao was made to digest loads of salted savouries and the resultant burp was used in '*Dariya mein jahaz chale pasha*'. In both the earlier Ramesh Sippy films, Pancham had alternated between the voices of Kishore and Manna. Here, Rafi was back, replacing Manna. '*Yamma yamma*', the climactic track, would be Pancham's only duet with Rafi. Pancham had expected to re-record it since Rafi's voice was not in its best shape during the recording. That day never came. Mohammad Rafi passed away sometime after it was recorded.

The death of Rafi at the age of fifty-six was a blow for the film industry. A mild-mannered person with absolutely no vices, he had been the epitome of discipline and perfection. Loved across generations, spanning five decades, his passing away was the end of an era. Rafi's presence in Pancham's compositions was like that of an esteemed guest – infrequent, but fondly remembered. The Pancham book would be a few pixels less colourful without the tales of *Teesri Manzil*, *Caravan*, *Mela* and one-off scores like '*Zamane ne maare*'.

Film-maker Tarun Majumdar remembers an untold story about Mohammad Rafi: 'In *Balika Badhu*, the song "*Yeh chudiyaan nahin hatkadiyaan hain*" was based on the poetry of Mukunda Das, and was written as part of the freedom movement. When he came to know about the roots of the song, Rafi refused to accept money for the recording.'

2

The pièce de résistance of *Shaan* was the title song, '*Pyar karne wale pyar karte hain shaan se*', conceived, according to Manohari Singh, during the planning of the film's background score. A representative song of the Pancham–Asha Bhonsle pantheon, Pancham's deep knowledge of the singer's range made the difference. Pancham was probably *the* composer to comprehend that Asha required some space to demonstrate her ability for vocal callisthenics. The song's antara, where the lyrics were spaced out, gave her the freedom, just what she needed to explode into a flurry of melodic notes.

The recurring beat in the song could have been inspired, in part, from '*I feel love*' by Donna Summer, but the song in itself was multidimensional, a grand mix of Asha's voice and a host of instruments, and bore no resemblance to the Donna Summer hit. But once again Pancham was accused of borrowing, just as the trumpet piece in '*Bachna aye haseeno*' was thought to be inspired by the opening bars of the Osibisa song '*Oja awake*'.

Right through his career, this was probably one question that Pancham had to defend himself against in most of his interviews, and he often clarified that inspiration was part of the game in any field of art and that his rule was to use one line and recreate an entire song out of the same, something that most composers did. Some faced flak, some came out unscathed. Secondly, the accepted norm was that copying from Indian music was justified. It was often labelled divine. Issues cropped up when somebody was inspired by the West. Singer Sivaji Chatterjee narrates an incident: 'One day, Pancham-da made me listen to Western music from 11 a.m. to 6 p.m. in his living room. It was surprising to see that he knew all the songs inside out. "You see, Usha (Uthup) and I have sung these songs many times over. These are in my blood," he told me. Hearing a tune and importing it is one thing. To internalize Western forms of music from one's formative years and to make it a part of one's DNA is another.'

Pancham's stand against charges of plagiarism was matter-of-fact; he did not go all out to copy tunes if given the chance to operate on his own terms. He might have needed a start, only to help him trudge along, and crafted music from the perspective of an entranced dreamer, creating his own, personalized world out of the flickers of inspiration he captured from anything he found musical. A classic example of the case could be the dazzling Bengali song 'Pora baanshi shunle ae mon aar' (Hindi equivalent 'Jiya mein toofan' from Kehten Hain Mujhko Raja [1975]) parts of which seem to have been inspired by the title song of Goldfinger. It would take an extremely seasoned ear to even spot the similarity, let alone identify the same. On the flipside, there were aberrations, like 'Meri jaan meri jaan' (Do Chor), based on 'Fall in love' by Cliff Richard or 'Lehra ke dagar' (Jeevan Mukt) which was inspired from Ron Goodwin's title song for Those Magnificent Men in Their Flying Machines (1965). Here, the inspiration extended marginally beyond the first line.

Music is first and foremost a permutation and combination of twelve notes; and there are bound to be similarities between even two disparate sources. Surely, the Boney M members were not thinking of Kazi Nazrul Islam's composition 'Jaltaranger jhilimil jhilimil dheu tule shey jaye' when writing the music of 'Rasputin', and yet the similarities between the two are uncanny. Neither was Peter Green listening and improvising on the taan of 'Laut ke aa' (Rani Rupmati, 1957) when creating the framework for 'Black Magic Woman'. The first line of Sajjad's classic composition and Suraiya's last Hindi film song 'Yeh kaisi ajab dastaan ho gayi hai' (Rustom Sohrab, 1963) sounds similar to the first line of the theme of Charlie Chaplin's City Lights (1931), although it would be safe to say that Sajjad was not inspired by City Lights. If one tries to dissect Pancham's composition 'Aisa *ho toh, kaisa hoga'* (*Ratnadeep,* 1979), one might just find the first four notes corresponding to '*I am pretty*' (*West Side Story*), and the notes of Raga Manj Khamaj too!

Coming back to *Shaan,* critics got free target practice. One periodical compared it to *Sholay* and said that the former at least had two good songs, '*Yeh dosti*' and '*Mehbooba Mehbooba*', while *Shaan* had none.

But, as usual, opinions of film reviewers were inconsistent and they conveniently missed the point that *Shaan*'s music was like a decorative adjunct which failed to gel with the shallow narrative. Sippy, in trying to blend crime, romance, comedy, emotion and James Bond, had tried too hard and fallen flat. RD took the rap.

Ramesh Sippy had started *Shakti* (1982), loosely based on the Tamil film *Thanga Padhakkam* (1974), simultaneously with *Shaan*. The contract with producers Mushir–Riaz was that *Shaan* would be completed first, closely followed by *Shakti*. However, the film got delayed due to Amitabh Bachchan's ill health during the course of the project and took around five years to complete. The Salim–Javed team had envisioned *Shakti* as a film without any songs, but Ramesh Sippy was adamant that it be otherwise. As a result, the songs did not have a role to play in the narrative, much like in *Deewaar*.

Commercially, *Shakti*, despite being a far more sincere effort by Sippy, did not provide the expected returns until much later.

Plagiarism and inspiration in music have been in vogue for quite some time. Previously, there was hardly any stigma attached to the same. A startling example would be the 'Fandango' in Mozart's *The Marriage of Figaro*, which was in fact a note-by-note copy from a movement in C.W. Gluck's ballet *Don Juan*. This surely does not make Mozart any less a composer. There are many such instances of inspiration and pure plagiarism in all forms of music, including classical music.

The blame for the film's failure was laid squarely on Ramesh Sippy, and to some extent, Pancham too. Apart from *'Jane kaise kab kahan'*, a Lata–Kishore duet which turned out to be extremely popular, there were no other tracks in the film that the audience could hum along. However, it was undeniable that Pancham had written a very subdued, albeit effective background score, especially for the father–son face-off scenes and the fight sequence between Dilip Kumar and Goga Kapoor.

The early 1980s were indeed unpredictable, to the extent that even Amitabh Bachchan and Ramesh Sippy could not guarantee enough horsepower to pull the film through.

Director Tinnu Anand, shifting from Rajesh Roshan in *Duniya Meri Jeb Mein* (1979) to Pancham, ended up with the moderate hit *Kaalia* (1981), while Ramesh Behl's *Pukar*, a film about the liberation of Goa, went down without so much as a whimper. Today, *Kaalia* is repeatedly reincarnated on weekends in the various homages paid to Amitabh Bachchan. One of the most popular retro numbers in any pub or disco is *'Jahan teri ye nazar hai'*, inspired by Persian pop singer Zia Atabi's *'Heleh maali'* (1977). Amitabh Bachchan and Pancham worked on the number together after Amitabh suggested the original Persian tune. Apparently, the song was filmed on the sets of Prakash Mehra's *Namak Halaal* (1982), which was also being shot around the same time.

Ramesh Iyer, who played the rhythm guitar in this song, says, 'This song has some typically complex chords by Boss, similar to "*Bachke rahna re baba*" [*Pukar*]. The prelude starts with a 3/4 beat at a slower pace, breaks, and then restarts at a completely different rhythm. In its interlude, this number also has the sequencer played by Louis Banks in the portion where Amjad Khan spins his partner around the dance floor.'

The other Kishore song that became popular was *'Tum saath ho jab apne'*, which had Asha Bhonsle chipping in with her humming. The minimal use of Asha's voice was similar to *'Ek paheli hai tu* (*Heera Panna*) and '*Socha tha maine toh aye jaan meri*' (*Chandi Sona*).

Due to an alleged face-off between Amitabh Bachchan and Kishore Kumar, Pancham took over the playback for Amitabh in *Pukar*, except for '*Tu maike mat jaiyo*', which Amitabh sang himself. Pancham gave expression to his wild imagination and contributed with his uncharacteristic voice, coupled with trademark grunting, huffing and puffing. His cameo in '*Bachke rehna re baba*', with a purported inflection as if straying offbeat and recovering remarkably is one of the highlights of the song. Pancham's demand for a 'pumping styled' rhythm on the guitar in the song also challenged the best guitarists in the industry.

Other composers too wanted Pancham to sing their compositions; Laxmikant for one had asked RD to sing '*Gore nahin hum kale sahi*' (*Desh Premee*, 1982), but Pancham refused.

S. Ramanathan's *Mahaan* (1983), after a great initial run due to the pre-release publicity and the popularity of the songs, also bombed. Not even three Amitabh Bachchans and Lord Pashupatinath's blessings could redeem it. This is not to demean the music of *Mahaan*; the songs are remembered even today, in and out of discos. The Pancham–Asha duet '*Ye din toh ata hai ek din jawani mein*' with its racy rhythm and wild whiff was a rage during its time; so was the Kishore solo '*Jidhar dekhun teri tasveer*', a perennial favourite of those in love, and the Kishore–Asha duet '*Pyar mein dil pe maar de goli*'.

It was Kersi Lord again who had to generate the sound of a tracer bullet electronically, fulfilling Pancham's requirement for 'that specific sound'. '"*Pyar mein dil pe*" had six gunshot sounds,' points out Shankh Banerjee, an unabashed Pancham info-hunter from Delhi. The film, however, shows Amitabh Bachchan firing

The RD–Asha duet '*Yeh din toh ata hai ek din jawani mein*' is notable for the malapropism as RD sings 'dil' in place of 'din' – all along in the song.

ten shots from his revolver. The extra gunshots seem to have got the producers themselves. *Mahaan* was a towering flop.

3

There was one more producer itching to join the flop brigade, and he did, with *Zamaane Ko Dikhana Hai* (1981). Untouched by failure since his debut *Tumsa Nahin Dekha*, a cocky Nasir Husain had boasted after *Yaadoon Ki Baaraat*, 'Wait. I will give you a flop.' And he duly kept his promise.

The failure of *ZKDH* was a mystery to producer–director Nasir Husain who did not know how to react. In an interview with the film magazine *Cine Blitz*, September 1985 issue, he said, in response to whether film-making relied on gimmicks or formula, 'If film-making relied on gimmicks, a formula film like *Zamaane Ko Dikhana Hai* should have done extremely well. I spared no efforts on the production values of the film. Each set cost me ten lakhs. My most ambitious project exploded into nothing.'

Lead actor Rishi Kapoor said in *Filmfare*, 1–15 August 1982 issue: 'It is difficult to say why the film failed. When a film flops, people start telling you so many reasons; when a film is a hit, they become blind to its faults. It is difficult to analyse what went wrong. Maybe in totality it did not impress. Nasir Husain had initiated the trend in disco music, but between the last film of his and this one, there was a big gap. The trend he initiated, others kept alive. They repeated it so often that they killed the originator's identity. People found nothing new in it.'

Pancham's response to the film failing, in the *Sunday Observer* on 31 May 1992 was baffling. 'Though quite frankly, I wasn't happy with *Hum Kisise Kum Naheen*; but with *Zamaane Ko Dikhana Hai*, I felt great again. The picture did not do well but people felt that Pancham had done something good again.'

As with a majority of Pancham's interviews, the intent was not very clear. *Hum Kisise Kum Naheen*, by all accounts, was a far better film and score than *Zamaane Ko Dikhana Hai*, which did not really have the fanciful song situations so intrinsic to a Nasir Husain film. Also, the songs of *Zamaane Ko Dikhana Hai* were undone by too many elements and zany sounds, and appeared gaudy and compromising on melody. The spirit of *Hum Kisise Kum Naheen*'s dance competition was badly missing. The background music too had repetitions; the Amjad Khan motif from *Hum Kisise Kum Naheen* was reused, and, as if by force of habit, the *'Chura liya hai'* tune was heard again. While in *Hum Kisise Kum Naheen* it served to introduce Zeenat Aman's cameo, here it was inserted without any reason. Overdone, bloated, insensitive, catering to the frontbenchers, *Zamaane Ko Dikhana Hai* was surely the lousiest film Nasir Husain had made till then. The fact that there were no songs by Kishore Kumar didn't help the film's cause either.

Newbie producer Mithun Chakraborty got a standing count in *Boxer* (1984). Films on sporting themes had not yet arrived in India, surprising for a country that won the Prudential Cricket World Cup in 1983. Mithun went back to the tried-and-tested imitation of John Travolta, giving Bappi Lahiri the opportunity to liberally Indianize tunes borrowed from the West. The music of *Boxer* did seem to have been done in a hurry. *'Dekho idhar'*, a solo by Kishore Kumar, is characterized by a trademark guitar duet by Ramesh Iyer and Sunil Kaushik, an aspect of Pancham's craft which reached its apogee with the prelude of *'Chehra hai ya chand khila hai'* (*Saagar*, 1985). The film had singer A. Hariharan debuting under Pancham with *'Hai mubarak aaj ka din'*. Popular during its time, *'Hai mubarak*

aaj ka din' had Pancham rehashing the tune for the antara of
'*Bachao*' (*Rocky*). Unlike the S.P. Balasubrahmanyam–Pancham
combo, the Hariharan–Pancham association did not last for
more than five songs of which only two, including '*Ganapati
bappa morya*' in Sunil Dutt's *Dard Ka Rishta* (1982), were
released.

Amjad Khan's directorial debut remained incomplete for a
long time. Ironically titled *Adhura Aadmi* (1982), the project
had commenced in the late 1970s. Amjad had almost completed
his second film *Chor Police* (1983) by the time his first was
released. Neither of these films influenced film trade, though.
Pancham and Amjad were buddies from the days of *Sholay*, and
Pancham composed two of Lata Mangeshkar's best solos in
these films: '*Tum se hi toh shuru hai*' for *Adhura Aadmi* and
'*Tumse milke zindagi ko yun laga*' for *Chor Police*. Remembers
Yogesh, the lyricist for the film: 'I was summoned for the
recording of *Adhura Aadmi* quite suddenly and the producer
came and picked me up in his car. I was very nervous and kept
penning the lyrics sitting inside the car en route to Film
Centre. Upon reaching, I made a clean copy of the verses and
recited them to Pancham-da who liked them instantly.'

The failure of the films had a direct bearing on the music
sales and it took these songs two decades to come to the
limelight, through an HMV compilation called *Tumse Milke*.

Pancham's career graph was now getting increasingly
chequered; with the highs and lows in worryingly identical
proportions.

4

The middle-of-the-road cinema movement of the 1970s spilled
over into the early 1980s, and with Salil Chowdhury, the default
composer for such films, in semi-retirement in Bombay, directors

Hrishikesh Mukherjee and Basu Chatterjee relied on Bengali stories and Pancham's music.

Hrishikesh Mukherjee had started *Bemisaal* (1982) for producer Debesh Ghosh with the lead pair of *Jurmana*. In the meantime, he also directed the sequel to *Gol Maal* – *Naram Garam* (1981) – with Amol Palekar and Miss India Swaroop Sampat. Basu Chatterjee too had moved away from Sarat Chandra after the debacle of *Apne Paraye* (1980) to his comfort zone, comedy, with *Shaukeen* (1982), based on a story by Samaresh Basu.

Pancham scored the music for all three films. Each one is remarkable in its own right. '*Mere angna aaye re Ghanshyam*' (*Naram Garam*) was a beauty in Addha taal; '*Kisi baat par main kisi se khafa hun*' (*Bemisaal*) was a westernized Bhairavi where Pancham added frills like stroking a glass with a spoon as the prelude to the song; '*Waheen chal mere dil*' (*Shaukeen*) found Suresh Wadkar consolidating his position as one of the top singers of the time.

Shaukeen was arguably India's second adult comedy film after Hrishikesh Mukherjee's *Sabse Bada Sukh* (1972). It featured three old men and a leggy young girl in Goa. The men fantasize about her, using their lusty imagination to prop up their otherwise inert libidos. Singer Chirashree Bhattacharya had been trying out her luck in Bollywood and was able to secure her place in history, joining the likes of Devika Rani, by accompanying Ashok Kumar in a duet '*Chalo haseen geet ek banayein*'. 'It was originally recorded by Sapan Chakraborty but then Dada Moni [Ashok Kumar] refused to allow Sapan's voice. He threw away the cassette and went ahead and sang it himself,' recollects Yogesh, the lyricist of the film who had by now made up with Pancham after the misunderstanding during *Alibaba Aur 40 Chor*.

Gulzar's fascination with Bengali and world literature

continued with films like *Angoor* (1981) based on Shakespeare's *Comedy of Errors,* and *Namkeen* (1982), which was based on Samaresh Basu's *Akaal Basanta.*

Pandit Ulhas Bapat remembers an incident: 'I once told Pancham-da that I wished to play something that I had recorded on a cassette for him. I did not tell him what it was as I had meant it to be a surprise. "Chal meri gadi mein," he said. Basu-da and Manohari-da were in the car as well. On Pancham-da's car audio system I played him the "meend" slur which is a style of playing that gives a continuous sound on the santoor. Otherwise, santoor gives only staccato, straight notes. I had invented "meend" on santoor. On hearing it, he exclaimed like a child: "Kya baat hai! Santoor pe meend kaise kiya?" He replayed it ten times. A couple of months later I got a call. This was for playing in the track *"Hothon pe beeti baat"* from *Angoor.* In Film Centre when the meend innovation piece arrived, he loudly exclaimed to Asha-ji and everyone else, "Dekho ye ladke ne santoor mein meend laya hai!"'

Namkeen was arguably the apex of the Pancham–Gulzar combo in as much as the film appeared right out of the neorealist tradition. The background music melted into the Kulu hillsides and the melodies had the perfect balance of emotion and rusticity. The choice of scales for the Raga Manj Khamaj-based mujra *'Badi der se megha barse'* sung by Asha Bhonsle and the UP folk-inspired nautanki *'Aisa laga koi surma'* sung by Alka Yagnik – the songs were set at a key higher than what is perceived normal for a Hindi film song – was appropriate for the genre. The higher scale was introduced keeping in mind the fact that voice throwing was essential for courtesans and nautanki dancers who hardly had the advantages of modern-day acoustic systems. The meend style on santoor was used again, in the background, and it was played by Pandit Ulhas Bapat.

Two songs from the film, both used in the background, have

a discernible multilayered sound. While the tunes have a touch of the rugged hills, the arrangement is a judicious mix of the Orient and the West. The Asha Bhonsle solo '*Phir se aaiyo badra bidesi*' talks of fragile aspirations, of dreams which are bound to be broken. Pancham merges the sound of the distortion of notes on the guitar with the voice, creating a drawling effect and also adding to the weight of the sound. The percussion fashions a periodic thumping sound, amplified by the reverb, forecasting impending doom. 'This was picturized in the dense fog, rain and biting cold of Rohtang Pass where it was impossible to stand for more than two minutes. Shabana, with only a shawl, sincerely braved the weather in which one could turn blue. And she was inspired by Pancham and Asha as well,' Gulzar says, paying a tribute to them.

With '*Raah pe rehte hain*' Kishore Kumar added another remarkable road song to his repository. Fashioned in the style of hill songs, Pancham also added the tune of '*Hum dono do premi*' (*Ajnabee*) to the interlude. The imagery conveyed by the lyrics is remarkable, and Gulzar draws parallels between the life of a truck driver and the gypsies, as in the lines: '*Aise ujde aashiyaane, tinke ud gaye/ Bastiyon tak aate aate, raste mud gaye/ Hum thehar jaye jahan, usko shahar karte hain*'. A probable extension of '*Ek akela is shehar mein*' (*Gharonda*, 1977).

In the early 1980s, Pancham also found patrons in the assistants from the Hrishikesh Mukherjee, Gulzar and Yash Chopra camps, people who were branching out on their own. Anand, aka Uday Kumar Singh, a small-time comedian, remembered best as Amol Palekar's paan-chewing friend in *Gol Maal*, produced *Naram Garam* and *Zameen Aasmaan* (1984). Meeraj, Gulzar's assistant, directed a fairly realistic version of Dulal Guha's *Mere Humsafar* (1970) as *Sitara* (1982). Ramesh Talwar's *Basera* (1981) was his rendezvous with Pancham, a meeting facilitated by producer Ramesh Behl. This relationship with Talwar, unfortunately, did not extend beyond a few films despite *Basera* being sated with the Pancham sound, from the near-ethereal *'Jahan pe basera ho'* re-forged from *'Phire esho Anuradha'*, to the very hip and trendy, yet sublimely melodious *'Tumhe chhodke ab jeene ko jee toh nahin'*.

The middle-of-the-road family films became Pancham's strength in the early 1980s. The music in these films has a charming, innocent quality, a naiveté that makes them universally appealing. Songs like *'Thodi si zameen thoda aasmaan'* or *'Yeh saaye hain, yeh duniya hai'* from *Sitara* are comparable to the best in this category across eras. Without taking direct recourse to folk songs from the north or the east, Pancham developed his own version of folksy music, delicate, and at the same time, fresh, never consciously attempting to create a rustic atmosphere. These songs talked of nature, of human bonding and dreams, but did not creep into overt sentimentalism. The distanced approach gave the music more acceptability to the elite section of the audience too.

Pancham won his second Filmfare Award for *Masoom*. Shekhar Kapur's debut film as director was one of the many deviations from mainstream Hindi cinema for Pancham. *Masoom*, based on Erich Segal's novel *Man, Woman and Child*, was about children. Unlike other Hindi films, the children behaved more or less like children, barring some hamming which may have been kept intentionally to woo the audience. Shekhar Kapur was able to extract the best from the youngest members of his cast by making them feel that they were actually playing a game. The adult cast members were seasoned thespians, Naseeruddin Shah, Shabana Azmi and Saeed Jaffrey. The film's music, compassionate and warm, complemented its fascinating interplay of characters and relationships. The title track may remind one of Satyajit Ray's background music, with its primarily flat notes arranged in multiples of three. Exaggeration in any form was avoided, which made the note movements terse and economical, as if to portray, in Pancham's own words, (as told to Chaitanya Padokone in *Mid Day*, 21 July 1983) the 'pangs of a guilty conscience of an errant father'.

Pancham was a natural communicator with children. Madhu Behl says, 'Pancham did not have any children, and it created a vacuum in his life, so much so that he had also expressed the desire to adopt our son Goldie.' Present-day singer Shurjo Bhattacharya who, as a kid, had been to Pancham's place, remembers Pancham spoiling him with boxes of imported chocolates. Doel Gupta, however, differs: 'I won't say he was fond of kids. Pancham Kaku was never comfortable with kids jumping around his place. But somehow he shared a very deep bond with us. With Pancham Kaku in town, it was no school, all fun. Almost like a feast.' Bhanu Gupta recounts an interesting conversation with the composer: 'One day Pancham told me, "I have a request which you shall not refuse. Promise me that I shall bear all the expenses of your daughter's marriage." I was too moved to even answer. This was not a false promise. Pancham did take the entire ownership of my daughter's marriage.' Sromona Guha Thakurta remembers: 'I called him Pancham-da. It was difficult to say whether he was like an elder brother or a father. I think he could slip into both the roles with consummate ease.'

Hence, it wasn't surprising that Pancham would give his best to a film like *Masoom*, more so when the lyricist was Gulzar, another sorcerer when it came to writing for children. Pancham experimented with as many as eight playback singers, five of whom were new, for the five songs in the film. Anup Ghoshal, a singer of semi-classical songs in West Bengal, who had scaled musical peaks with Satyajit Ray's '*Goopy Bagha*' films, made his debut in Hindi films with '*Tujhse naaraz nahin zindagi hairaan hun main*', giving the output a Kishore Kumar-esque resonance.

Unconfirmed reports suggest that Satyajit Ray had asked Kishore to put in a word in Anup's favour to Pancham. This dream breakthrough in Bombay and a subsequent Bengal Film Journalists' award for the song notwithstanding, Anup Ghoshal's career could not sustain the heights this song helped him attain. In the radio programme *Meri Sangeet Yatra*, Gulzar shares, 'I used to write a book every year as my daughter kept growing. The idea of my poetry for children was to instigate their imagination with phonetically funny words for them to play with like *"Aapa ki aapdi pani me jaa padi"* or *"Khanna ki khannadi"*. *"Lakdi ki kathi"* was penned in those days.'

Child singers Vanita Mishra, Gurpreet Kaur (daughter of violinist Uttam Singh) and Gauri Bapat sang the effervescent *'Lakdi ki kathi'*. 'She was just a four-and-a-half-year-old kid. Pancham wanted a child singer; so I told him that I'll bring my daughter. After listening to her, Pancham gave her a solo piece which was the starting line sans metre,' remembers Uttam Singh. 'Pancham said, "Uttam, God bless you. She is fantastic."'

Arati Mukherjee, pursuing her career in her native Calcutta despite the grand success of *Geet Gata Chal* (1975) and *Tapasya* (1976), received her first Filmfare Award for *'Do naina ek kahani'*.

'I first sang for Pancham in a Bengali film called *Aparupa*,' Mukherjee says, talking of her association with RD. 'During the recording, actor and film-maker Rajendra Kumar was present as he was doing a film with Pancham at that time. I think it was *Love Story*. Anyway, Rajendra Kumar liked my voice. Pancham asked him, "How would she fit in within our Bombay film music?" Rajendra Kumar said, "Why not? It is you composers who are scared of using new voices. Why don't you try her out for one of your songs?" A few weeks later, Pancham gave me contracts for singing in two films, *Rusvai* [1983] and *Masoom*.

For the *Masoom* song, Pancham was being nagged by another singer who kept questioning him about his decision to use a new voice for the film. Pancham gave the excuse that this was an art film and the producer had no money. Before the sitting, Pancham explained the song to me in detail. He structurally broke it into finite elements, making it simple for me to grasp. After a few rehearsals, it was okayed in a single take. Pancham kept a second take as a back-up in case one was needed. I came back to Calcutta, not realizing that I had actually recorded a best-seller. A few months later, I received the news that I had won the Filmfare Award for the song. Pancham and I were supposed to do more songs together. We did some, but the prized idea of recording songs for the Pujas did not materialize. I had also sent him some poetry by Subhash Mukhopadhyay. But God knows why he kept silent. Later, I came to understand that Pancham did not have the power to wield the baton. Puja songs for female singers other than a particular crooner were a no-no; it was as if he was bound by some external control.'

This sneakily points to the alleged Mangeshkar monopoly in the Bombay film circuit. True as the rumours may be, there is no denying the musical talent of the sisters. On the professional front, Pancham often faced the difficult choice of assigning songs to Lata and Asha. When asked how he chose between them, Pancham said that it was like debating on who was greater – Don Bradman or Gary Sobers! Though, in the *Times of India*, Bombay, 29 September 1985, he did say, 'Still, there is no doubt that Lata-ji is supreme. When she sings, she forgets about herself, her home, and there's a complete changeover of personality. Though she may not admit this, she becomes a mother, or a sweetheart before the microphone.'

His admiration for Lata was reflected in his work of the 1980s, albeit sporadically. He did not have a Lata equivalent for every '*Phir se aaiyo badra bidesi*', but there would be the periodic mesmerizer like 'Aisa sama na hota' from Zameen Aasmaan. Directed by Hrishikesh Mukherjee's assistant Bharat Rungachary, the film was a disaster, as a result of which the brilliance of the number surfaced only much later.

In 1986, Pancham scored and sang for Bharat Rungachary's TV serial *Subah*, which was focused around the evils of drug abuse among youngsters.

Robin Bhat, a finance specialist settled in the US, a self-confessed fan of Hindi film music spanning K.L. Saigal to Kumar Sanu, has this to say about the first instance of him hearing the song while driving on a highway: 'We all have indelible memories of our very first hearing of a song which we like. In my case, never since that day has a song had such an impact. I was driving along a highway, playing a Lata romantic songs disc when I heard *Zameen Aasmaan*'s "*Aisa sama na hota*". So stunned was I by this number that I literally had to pull over in the emergency lane, stop the car, put on the hazard lights and listen to it, in rapt attention. The journey simply had to come to a standstill for a few minutes. As it happened, the place where I stopped was close to an Air Force base, where some fighter jets were doing their practice runs. It was a spectacle of pure power, synchronized formations, the breathless beauty of swoop-downs and near-vertical ascendancy, all done without any seeming effort, even though underlying all this was split-second control and precise planning; all in all, a majestic display of flawless perfection, almost an art form. It then struck me that RDB-for-Lata and Lata-for-RDB in this song shared the very same attributes! So here I was, watching this aerial spectacle and playing this Lata song over and over again, on a highway, one complementing the other.'

Pancham, as an experiment, had mixed flutes in '*Aisa sama na* hota' – Pandit Ronu Majumdar's bamboo flute and Manohari Singh's recorder (English flute) – carving a hilly tune. Ramesh Iyer's bass guitar notes were contrasted by sharp and deliberate offbeat strokes on Kancha's madal. The transition from mukhra to antara found the ephemeral use of the suspended fourth chord. The title song of *Zameen Aasmaan*, *'Ye faasle ye dooriyan'*, was no lesser a wonder. It had the typical Pancham–Lata sound of the early 1980s, maybe a tad shrill, but dreamy nevertheless.

5

Though Pancham's music did make an impression on a section of the city-bred Generation X, a few film critics remained reluctant to accept his greatness. They probably had their own agenda, and while praise flowered aplenty for some composers of the 'good ol' days', the Pancham sound, crafted mostly for the likes of Gulzar and Yogesh, found limited takers. Like most good art, however, these found gradual acceptance and are now benchmarks against which much of Hindi film music is judged.

But, amidst all this, there was a hint of disparity from one track to another that was gradually beginning to show. While one had got used to around 80 per cent of RD songs in each film in the 1970s being top quality, in the first half of the 1980s this percentage had come down, and barring some films, the average quality of the tracks was barely above mediocre. People tended to laud a couple of tracks and not remember most others, as opposed to the 1970s, when most of his songs in a film enjoyed immense popularity. This, as it turned out later, the first crack in the wall that should have been plastered on priority.

Public taste too had changed, and the distinction between mediocrity and class had begun to blur. *'Maine poochha chand se'* (*Abdullah*) was labelled a classic by all and sundry. In reality,

Pancham had simply rehashed one of his numbers, '*Koi aur duniya mein tum sa nahin hai*' from *Pyar Ki Kahani,* by just changing the beat. Hardly anybody had remembered the song during its time! The songs for Vijay Anand's horror (and horrific) film *Ghunghroo Ki Awaaz* (1981), which might have been considered nice a decade ago, were rejected by the audience. There were many similar stories that could be used to question the basic logic behind audience acceptance or rejection of a film, or of a song for that matter.

The early 1980s were a time of some drastic social changes that would culminate in the Mandalization of politics and society in a decade's time. Large-scale migrations from rural to urban centres resulted in a change in the audience profile in the cities, which was responsible for the eventual demise of parallel and middle-of-the-road cinema usually patronized by the middle class. The same was applicable to music. This was an environment that had started seeing films like *Himmatwala, Mawaali* and *Justice Chowdhary* rake in the moolah.

16

Earthen Pots,
Disco Dunce

Hrishikesh Mukherjee, in an interview on the radio after he won the Dadasaheb Phalke Award, said, 'Somebody had asked me why good films are not being made nowadays. I said, unless the social condition is good, unless people have a life that is worth it, how do you expect us to make good films? What you have around you nowadays are brutal murders, mass larceny, lots of scams – is this a condition from which creative output can be expected? And whatever good films are being made are hardly being seen by the masses. There are directors who are making very good films – Shyam Benegal, Adoor Gopalakrishnan, Buddhadev Dasgupta, Saeed Mirza, Govind Nihalani – but the masses hardly know about them.'

Driven by a number of economic and social factors, and rampant video piracy, the 1980s witnessed Hindi films at their worst, marked by crassness and crudity. This is generally regarded as the worst period in the history of Hindi cinema. With many of the movie moguls of the 1960s and 1970s unable to reinvent themselves and keep pace with changing times, and the new crop still to make its mark (which it would in the early 1990s), the field was left open to fly-by-night operators with little cinematic credentials. This was the era of films starring Jeetendra, Sridevi and Jaya Prada, with Kader Khan and Shakti Kapoor providing inane comic relief with their bad-guy acts. These films were easily recognizable by the overacting, loud sets and backdrops, a uniform absence of anything aesthetic, and music that catered only to the frontbenchers. Emboldened by the front bench clapping and cat calls, the infamous brigade unleashed *Tohfa* (1984), *Maqsad* (1984), *Naya Kadam* (1984), *Masterji* (1985), *Dharm Adhikari* (1986), *Pataal Bhairavi* (1985) and *Kaamyaab* (1984), which added brighter shades of purple to the garishness. A little over two rupees for one's fill of heaving breasts and gyrating hips was not a bad deal for the huge underbelly of the cities. Quite a few of these films were remade or dubbed from B-grade movies made down south.

However, this is not to say that all films from the south were uniformly bad. Pancham himself, during his stay in Madras for the recording of *Mahaan*, had watched a few Tamil films and was extremely impressed by some of the scores, especially Ilaiyaraja's, calling his music ten years ahead of its time. 'Ilaiyaraja and Pancham-da's was a mutual admiration society,' recalls singer S.P. Balasubrahmanyam.

But, what actually came to Bombay from the south were more the likes of *Fauladi Mukka* (1985), *Galiyon Ka Gunda* (1985) and *Gangvaa* (1984). These films were not representative of the best from the south, and except a handful, the best stayed down under.

The other concept that Hindi cinema audiences were introduced to in the early 1980s was disco. If '*Aap jaisa koi*' (*Qurbani*, 1980) set the ball rolling, B. Subhash's *Disco Dancer*

(1982) erupted on the screen with a loud bang with Mithun Chakraborty in the title role. He followed this up with films like *Kasam Paida Karne Wale Ki* (1984) and *Dance Dance* (1987). The common thread running through Mithun's downtown disco capers and Jeetendra's semi-urban riverside dances was Bappi Lahiri, suddenly the busiest composer in Bombay.

Suddenly, Pancham was sensing competition that was unworthy and sub-prime. 'We could have easily done disco sounds. I do not think it was at all difficult for us. However, on grounds of musical principles, we chose not to get into that rut. In fact, a lot of musicians were coming to town and landed up in nightclubs only to stick there permanently since they could not go beyond the disco sound,' says Ramesh Iyer.

'In the 1980s all the directors, composers and writers who had sophistication and class got marginalized. There was a flood of crudity and mediocrity. Look at Yash Chopra. The dip in his career graph came in the 1980s. Sophistication and class, these were not good days for them. Crude and lower aesthetics came to the forefront,' points out Javed Akhtar.

In a society that had gradually transformed from the hopeful in the 1950s to the insensitive and iniquitous in the 1980s, the contrast in tastes underlined the point. Good music ceased to be a success factor for a film. In catering to the front rows, the leading composer of the day, Bappi Lahiri, jettisoned the sincerity and sensitivity he had demonstrated in *Zakhmee* (1975), *Chalte Chalte* (1976), *Apne Paraye* (1980) or even *Aap Ki Khaatir* (1977).

There was another angle to the story. Undercutting, prevalent ever since the barter system existed, was spreading its claws dangerously. Aashish Khan mentions Pancham suffering a lot due to the undercutting employed by a composer in particular.

Pancham, in an interview in the *Times of India*, September 1985, also mentioned how prestigious projects were more prone to undercutting. On the subject of crudity taking centre stage, he agreed that Bappi Lahiri was delivering whatever producers wanted, and had the capability to turn from vulgarity to melody if he wanted to.

As good music ceased to be the determining factor for a film's success, the industry witnessed a decline in the number of composers. In the 1970s, given the receptivity to good music, even infrequent composers found encouragement. Though RD, Laxmikant–Pyarelal and Kalyanji–Anandji were the big players, small-time composers like Usha Khanna, Sonik–Omi, Sapan–Jagmohan, Shyamji–Ghanshamji, Kanu Ray and Vanraj Bhatia, among others, found a niche and logged in hit tracks. In the 1980s, this changed, with Bappi Lahiri and Laxmikant–Pyarelal monopolizing the music scene.

The advent of smut implied that the regular film-going family had to fall back on an alternative to cinema. Luckily for them, the television boom took place just then. With the Asian Games in 1982, colour TV sets became household necessities rather than luxuries. As an alternative medium of entertainment, TV offered soap operas. The popularity of Kumar Vasudev's *Hum Log* (1984), Kundan Shah's *Yeh Jo Hai Zindagi* (1984) and Govind Nihalani's *Tamas* (1987) soared. As an emerging trend, telefilms prospered too. Basu Chatterjee's *Ek Ruka Hua Faisla* (1986) was among the best in the genre.

Though the 1980s were bad in terms of music quality, it was harvest time for musicians since the demand for canned film songs, ad jingles, and TV serial theme tunes had increased phenomenally. Quantity and quality seldom go hand-in-hand, one comes at the cost of the other. The 1980s made the musician richer and music poorer.

Now that audiences had other means to watch films, video piracy also increased around the time. This burnt into the profits of film-makers. In September 1982, in an appeal to the then Information and Broadcasting Minister N.K.P. Salve, G.P.

Sippy spoke of the need for stricter control. They are all still talking about it.

2

For his part, despite his alleged choosiness, Pancham was still averaging twenty films a year. SD's advice to his son to be selective, something he had done himself throughout his stellar career, did not sit well with Pancham. Salil Chowdhury too had advised him to exercise discretion in accepting films. Maybe Pancham was suffering from the Bollywood Lemming syndrome of signing as many films as he could to stay in business. The fact is that he did not need to do that. Perhaps he was apprehensive that refusing films would result in loss of 'share of voice' with producers. In early 1983, he was simultaneously working for a number of big directors: Nasir Husain, Dev Anand, Ramesh Sippy, Shakti Samanta, Raj N. Sippy and Raj Khosla, as well as Gulzar and Hrishikesh Mukherjee. 'This business has always been like a gold rush; if you aren't overburdened with the booty, it means you are out of circulation. So, you take on a dozen films or more at a time, have a lot of nights [out] and hope you have the stamina to keep going,' Pancham said when he was asked why he was taking on so many projects at the same time. He was talking about the mechanism of the rat race, how he had often been at the top for several months followed by a blank phase when his films did not click, with the cycle repeating itself.

Pancham's prolificacy in the early 1980s impacted his quality. While his stamina held, the cycle of highs and lows that he spoke of, did not. *Hum Naujawan* (1985) could have cemented his place in the Navketan camp; the film was on his favourite subject – youth. Yet, in the end, there was very little to differentiate between Pancham's music for the film and the compositions of any other contemporary composer for any other film. Pran's son Sunil Sikand, who had worked as an intern with Manmohan Desai, turned to Pancham for his first and second films, *Karishma* (shelved) and *Farishta* (1983) respectively. These could have been Pancham's fitting reply to the Manmohan Desais of the industry. In *Farishta*, Pancham tried out the voice of a schoolboy who was trying his luck at singing, Vivek Bajaj. Maybe to accommodate the boy's limitations, Pancham came up with a music score that was quite forgettable.

By the mid-1980s, all of Pancham's horses and all his men were looking partly ragged. And the good scores suffered too.

Raj Khosla was directing two films with Pancham at the time – *Matee Mangey Khoon* (1984) and *Sunny* (1984) – and had invested a lot in the music. For *Matee Mangey Khoon*, he had invited Pakistani ghazal maestro Ghulam Ali, fresh from his success with *'Chupke chupke raat din'* (*Nikaah*, 1982), to redo his ghazal *'Awargi'*. Ghulam Ali, used to singing with a harmonium, sarangi and a tabla, was initially uneasy in front of the mike. Pancham said, 'Ghulam Ali is a terrific singer, but when Raj Khosla insisted that we record a song of his with our orchestra, we knew it would be difficult, and it was. Though his percussionist was good, performing in front of an orchestra with a mike was difficult for him.' *'Awargi'* failed to replicate the success of *'Chupke chupke'*.

For *Sunny*, Khosla had approved two of Pancham's best tunes of that time. Amrutrao recalls that the dummy lyrics *'Jaane kya baat hai'* (sung by Lata Mangeshkar), which Pancham had used during the composing session, were retained in the final take. Asha Bhonsle, who sang the non-film Bengali version of this number, has often recounted how she would sing it to Pancham in the wee hours of dawn as they sat on the benches of Marine Drive in Bombay. Recorded in Madras during the background score of *Mahaan*, '*Aur kya ahd-e wafa hote hain*', rendered by Asha Bhonsle and Suresh Wadkar, had Pancham using the geet format.

However, for all the effort pumped into *Sunny*, Raj Khosla went on to say in an interview that everything apart from direction had gone wrong in the film. Public statements like this do go against the technicians who work in a film, the music director included.

Dev Anand's films had been doing badly since the mid-1970s. Barring *Des Pardes* (1978), the others – *Swami Dada* (1982), *Anand Aur Anand* (1984) and *Hum Naujawan* (1985) – did not bring home the booty. Pancham's lustrous score in *Anand Aur Anand* – complemented by Kishore Kumar's deep, resonating vocals in '*Mere liye soona soona*' and '*Hum kya hain, tumne jaan liya*' – was hardly the darling of paan shops.

A similar fate awaited the films of Shakti Samanta, who now seemed to be caught in a time warp, fiercely determined to resurrect Rajesh Khanna's stardom, even at the cost of his own financial viability. He lined up two films with Kaka, *Awaaz* (1984) and *Alag Alag* (1985), touching upon the time-tested elements of love, song and tragedy.

Anurodh was the only film in which Shakti Samanta worked with Laxmikant–Pyarelal. And then it was back to the old team of Pancham and Kishore Kumar. Apparently, Kishore did not accept any remuneration for his work in *Alag Alag* since he was singing for his friend Rajesh Khanna's home production.

Pancham played safe with *Alag Alag*. With most of the songs based on simple keharwa rhythm and the dholak functioning as the lead instrument, one missed the uncluttered Pancham sound despite the fact that the album did good business.

Though Nadeem Khan, cinematographer of *Alag Alag*, was full of praise for Shakti Samanta's sense of visuals, the film hardly had any heart. It was no *Amar Prem* or *Kati Patang*, not

even an *Anurodh*. Rajesh Khanna's heavy shawl grazing the
grass of Kashmir didn't augur well for him. *Alag Alag* ended up
a super 'sweeper' flop. The cleaning staff chose to sweep the
empty auditorium with their backs to the screen even as the
movie played. Pancham, once again, was at the wrong end of
the firing line. His strategy to please public taste with dholak-
based songs had come undone.

Another film-maker who swore by Pancham was next up for
hara-kiri. *Manzil Manzil* (1984) and *Zabardast* (1985) were
back-to-back films that Nasir Husain directed after *Zamaane Ko
Dikhana Hai* (*ZKDH*). *Zabardast* had been part of Husain's plans
since 1977, when he tried to rope in Dilip Kumar for the main
role. The 1985 version had Sanjeev Kumar in the role once
envisaged for Dilip Kumar. Though both films were replete
with Pancham's experimentation with sounds, instruments and
rhythm, the tracks were, like many of Pancham's scores in the
mid- and late-1980s, more technique than feeling. Surprisingly,
Kishore Kumar sounded fresh and sharp in *Zabardast*, thanks to
which most of the songs managed to have a long shelf life.

Nasir Husain had once remarked that Mohammad Rafi was
the best singer of his generation, and his loss could not be
compensated for by Shailendra Singh, who was the chief male
voice in *Zamaane Ko Dikhana Hai* and *Manzil Manzil*. Why
Kishore Kumar was missing from the list of singers in the two
films whose music was composed by Pancham is hard to guess.

But the sap had dried for the Nasir Husain formula too.
Sachin Bhowmick's story and screenplay for *Manzil Manzil* and
Zabardast lacked the tautness of *Hum Kisise Kum Naheen*. True,
lead actor Sunny Deol had the looks, but then, so do most TV
newscasters.

Rahul Rawail, who persisted with Dharmendra's elder son,
had mixed fortunes. After the success of *Betaab*, *Arjun* (1985)
was released to a fair reception, mostly in metros and cities. The

music was characteristic of the RD of the '80s – a few mediocre songs riding on a stunner – in this case *Duniya maane bura toh goli maaro*. The song recreated the ambience of *West Side Story*, with Pancham increasing the dramatic impact manifold by employing awe-inspiring rhythm patterns on multiple instruments and recording it spectacularly on stereo.

Saagar was Ramesh Sippy's opportunity to rekindle the magic of *Sholay*. It was a dream project for many. For Dimple Kapadia, it was her second chance at stardom after the disintegration of her marriage. For Pancham, reeling under a tsunami of films that had tanked at the box office, it was an opportunity to get back into the groove. For Kamal Haasan, the star of the film, it was probably the vehicle that could cement his place in Hindi cinema.

'The first song I wrote for Rahul Dev Burman was "*Jaane do na*" for the film *Saagar*,' Javed Akhtar recalls. 'There was another tune which he had composed for the film which I took to Khandala for writing the lyrics. Unfortunately, I forgot the tune and wrote the lyrics on my own, without any specific metre. I came back, met Ramesh Sippy and RD, and spilled the beans. "No problem," said Pancham, after which he saw the lyrics, and within a few minutes, started singing "*Chehra hai ya chand khila hai*" in the tune it was finally made in. I mean, it was so effortless; it came so naturally to him. Aise aadmi ko aap kya kahenge? Yeh aadmi agar focused hota toh kya karta?'

'*Chehra hai ya chand khila hai*' was also commended for the gorgeous guitar prelude by Ramesh Iyer and Sunil Kaushik on A-minor scale, with a delectable use of notes and arpeggios on the E-seventh chord.

Veteran singer S.P. Balasubrahmanyam admits to being nervous about singing '*Yun hi gaate raho*'. 'It was not a live recording. I had to mix my voice after Kishore-da had sung his piece. I expressed my anxiety about being able to match Kishore-da's depth and robustness. A little annoyed, Pancham-da said, "Leave the voice balancing part to me. That is my job. Bloody fellow, just go and sing." After the take was okayed, Pancham-da played the full track to me in the auditorium after he was through with the sound mixing. "Kyun re? Thik hai na? Love your voice?" he asked. The way he had balanced the voices was amazing.'

While the interlude of 'Yun hi gaate raho' with Dimple in her long swirling skirt may have been reflective of the music of *Can-Can* (1960), the picturizaton of the intro piece of '*Sach mere yaar hai*' which shows Kamal Haasan on a rooftop was an unmistakable tribute to Norman Jewison's *Fiddler on the Roof* (1971). This song also used the resso resso to an extent unheard of since '*Mere saamne wali khidki mein*' from *Padosan.*

The tune for '*Saagar kinare*', according to Bhanu Gupta, was an old find. 'During the time of *Saagar*, we were discussing its music at Pancham's place. Pancham had pulled out an old spool player and was playing some tunes which he had composed around the late 1950s or the early 1960s. Ramesh Sippy was there too. After hearing a number, he stopped Pancham and told him: "I want this number for *Saagar*."'

This tune, which Ramesh Sippy literally snatched from Pancham, was in fact inspired by the SD number '*Thandi hawayen*' (*Naujawan*), which was itself inspired from the film *Algiers* (1938). Pancham had used the tune of '*Saagar kinare*' a few years ago as '*Hamein raaston ki zaroorat nahin hai*' in Asha's voice in the film *Naram Garam*. Till it was resuscitated by TV channels, this luminous song was forgotten within days of its release. Speaking on the Doordarshan programme *Phool Khile Hain Gulshan Gulshan*, Pancham had divulged that Roshan too openly admitted to Dada Burman that he (Roshan) had been inspired by the *Naujawan* song to create '*Rahe na rahe hum*' (*Mamta*, 1965).

Roshan had used the tune before too, in the film *Chandni Chowk* (1954). The story of a song serving as the base for several other songs is not new in the annals of Hindi film music, but this probably takes the cake. Another notable inspiration (not intentional, perhaps) in the same metre is Madan Mohan's '*Yehi hai tamanna*' (*Aap Ki Parchaiyan*, 1963).

More than the six songs, the pièce de résistance in *Saagar* was the *jalpari* theme – the sequence where Rishi Kapoor spots Dimple Kapadia taking a plunge in the sea in the early minutes of dawn, her beautiful long hair falling over her shoulders. There is a dreamlike quality about the scene, which is accentuated by the flugelhorn-based background score.

'The *jalpari* sequence had been filmed earlier,' Rishi Kapoor recalls. 'It was decided that it had to be accompanied by a song, at least some good music. Pancham was asked to do it. Imagine, he had to create a song as a background score. That made the task even more difficult. It was Pancham's sheer wizardry.'

Pancham described the *jalpari* theme as a song which he sang with a different voice. It imparted a hazy, romantic soul to the piece. He admitted: 'I was inspired by Pink Floyd for that bit.'

The influence of Pink Floyd on Pancham had been visible for quite some time. This particular portion was inspired from '*Shine on you crazy diamond*'. Pancham had previously used the loop for the tandem song '*Aaja mere pyar aaja*' in *Heeralal Pannalal* (1980), and later developed it into a full Bengali duet between Pancham and Asha Bhonsle, '*Tumi koto dure*'. This was composed on the blues scale, often using pentatonic progression. The tune also found inspiration from '*Concerto for one voice*' by French composer Saint-Preux.

Sunil Kaushik corroborated the fact, adding that this loop was used in other songs too, with minor alterations, such as in the prelude for '*Aye saagar ki lehron*' (*Samundar*, 1986), a composition marked by frequent changes of chords, especially in the prelude, with one particular change pointing to a chord progression (G–D7–E–Am) used by Salil Chowdhury.

Notwithstanding Pancham's buoyant score, *Saagar* sank. Subsequent ventures like Raj Sippy's *Sitamgar* (1985) and *Jeeva* (1986), Bharati Raja's *Savere Wali Gadi* (1986), Rahul Rawail's *Samundar* and Shakti Samanta's desi version of *Omar Mukhtar*, named *Palay Khan* (1986), were not commercial successes either. The failure of these films – and consequently their music as well – was tough on Pancham, and depressing too, especially considering that songs like *'Roz roz ankhon tale'* from *Jeeva*, *'Din pyar ke aayenge'* from *Savere Wali Gadi* and *'Mausam pyar ka'* from *Sitamgar* have since been counted among his finest compositions spanning decades. *Sitamgar* was possibly Pancham's best work for producer Dharmendra and for director Raj N. Sippy.

Pancham's health too was beginning to deteriorate. He had a heart attack during the background recording for Shakti Samanta's *Aar Paar* (1985). This pushed him out of the race in the mid-1980s. Also, there were music-dominated films which suffered due to more reasons than one, like *Namumkin* (1988) and *Libaas* (1991).

Hrishikesh Mukherjee's unlikely tale of love, betrayal and revenge, *Namumkin*, began filming in 1982, but the release, ages behind schedule, meant that the songs, poignant and reflective, lost out. Gulzar's *Libaas* too had commenced in 1982, but five years later it remained half-clothed. As a result, *'Seeli hava choo gayi'*, a delectable composition in the suspended fourth (one of the few songs where Gulzar wrote to Pancham's metre and not the other way round), and *'Khamosh sa afsana'*, an orchestrator's delight, did not get due appreciation. Other arresting compositions like *'Main thak gaya hun'*, in Jabbar Patel's *Musafir* (1986), dropped out even before release. *'Kaise dekhun in ankhon mein'*, a sonorous duet between Kishore Kumar and Lata

Mangeshkar, composed towards the end of 1982 for the film *Bharosa* started by Meeraj, was never released as the film was shelved after a few reels.

What Pancham brought to work in these songs was a gift most composers had lost in the 1980s – delicacy of thought and subtlety of expression.

But delays in releases and lack of commercial success meant that things were reaching a state where Pancham faced the choice of either yielding to the demands of the day or losing his hold in the industry. Adding to his woes was the cancellation of large productions like Romu Sippy's *Tala Chabi* with Amitabh Bachchan in the lead and *Aar Paar*, another multi-starrer, which was started by Shakti Samanta for producers Mushir–Riyaz (not the *Aar Paar* he made in 1985). Caught in the dilemma of successfully matching art and commerce, Pancham's compositions became capricious – great one day and lacklustre the day after.

Producers' pressure tactics were also something Pancham was not immune to. Not able to take a stern stand became his Achilles heel at times. Ramesh Iyer recalls one such incident: 'We were composing a sad song for a well-known producer. The producer, even after being given several options, was not clear about what he wanted. After hearing the tune, he started making comments like, *"Pancham, jam nahin raha hai. Pancham, rona nahin aa raha hai."* Pancham would gradually lose patience with such silly demands where the requirement itself was not clear, and maybe his work suffered too.' Amit Kumar chips in: 'Often, the best tunes Pancham created would be rejected by the producer. Pancham would predict, "Look, Amit, the producer will reject this tune."'

However, Pancham played it safe while talking to the press on the issue of catering to producers' shopping lists: 'There's no escaping that. You cannot forget the metre of the lyrics and the shot division, flashbacks and fadeouts in the script. Still, I maintain a degree of independence, insist that I'll do it this way, and have detailed discussions with producers in my music room. When I am told to imitate another composer's hit song, I put my foot down. Also, when a producer narrates his story and I can see he's quite indifferent about the music, I turn down the offer. Fortunately, there's been a tuning with more than sixty per cent of the film-makers who have come to me. They respect my judgement and I respect theirs.'

Given his stature as a composer, Pancham could have been more vocal and that might have ultimately helped him. In the 1940s and the 1950s, producer–directors did not interfere in the process of music creation. Naushad maintained that direction and music direction were two separate domains and composers never let the director enter into their domain. Pancham failed to stick to this golden rule, and suffered for it. The songs '*Kabhi bekasi ne maara*' from *Alag Alag* and '*Aaj tu gair sahi*' from *Oonche Log* (1985) are examples of Pancham copying tunes of popular Pakistani songs. These were perhaps instances where the producer insisted on having the final say. But this does not absolve him of his responsibilities as a composer. This was not the first time that Pancham had used the metre of a Pakistani ghazal as the base for his composition. The mukhra of '*Meri tanhaiyon ko*' (*Rusvai*, 1985) was inspired by Mehdi Hassan's '*Dekh toh dil ke jaan se uthta hai*', a ghazal which supposedly introduced songstress Noorjehan to the world of Mehdi Hassan.

Pancham was either running out of ideas or unable to invest the quantum of time required for his compositions.

Guitarist Soumitra Chatterjee, a member of the team from 1985 to 1989, and witness to the bad days in Pancham's career, says, 'Though the music was certainly good, given the standards of those days, earlier, the Pancham sound was fresh. Even vague films like *Hifazat* (1973) had interesting scores, where a mere shift of the chord from major to minor within the same line could colour the song like a rainbow, like in the number "*Yeh mastani dagar matwalee wadiyan*", which probably very few people have heard.'

Over and above his skills in rhythm and melody, Pancham's key differentiator from other composers had been his people management skills. He had managed to get the best out of them by making them feel important, never slighting them, connecting with them by calling them over for meals and drinks and socializing with them. This kept the morale of the team high. His proximity to his team won him their goodwill, trust and musical contributions.

Sometime in the early 1980s, a distance crept in, probably without Pancham even realizing it. Bhupendra, whom Pancham affectionately called the 'Guzzler' for his love of spirits and his decision to step back into the world of ghazals, quit the team in 1983 (probably after *Mahaan*). Basu Chakravarty, the elderly, almost fatherly figure in Pancham's group, who was looked upon for advice during times of crises, left Pancham, preferring semi-retirement to being ignored as he was.

How much these factors contributed to Pancham's miseries is debatable, but the end result was more than a dozen flops in a row in the mid-1980s. This in turn made producers doubt if Pancham could still be a card that they could play blindfolded. Their misgivings were somewhat reinforced by films like Ravi Tandon's *Ek Main Aur Ek Tu* (1986), where it appeared that Pancham was gradually letting go of his core strengths and had started relying more on frills rather than on building blocks like tune, rhythm and emotion. '*Yeh wada raha*', the title track, was what he should have been doing more of. In the intro music, the bass guitar leads the way before giving way to the rest of the instruments. In the second antara we hear an abrupt shift from a Western beat to folk, followed by the Western beat again. Percussions span from a predominant dhol in the antara to the bongo, and one can sense sounds made by coarse sandpaper to delicate aluminium foil. The song had the finesse of rare hand-crafted artefacts. The investment of time, effort, thought and innovation is clear, but compositions like this were becoming rare and were increasingly replaced by predictable rhythm structures. Pancham now appeared to be unsure, stretching a number unnecessarily. This was one more departure from his strength. He should have stuck to his winning strategy of keeping the length of the tracks teasingly short.

However, there is another angle to the story. Something is a failure only when it is labelled as one. It is here that Pancham could have managed perceptions better. He made the vital mistake of lamenting his string of flops to the press.

Also, the flops were not *his* flops. A film may fail for any reason. Clangers like *Awaaz* and *Alag Alag*, *Zabardast* and *Manzil Manzil*, *Swami Dada* and *Anand Aur Anand* wouldn't have fared any better than they did with any other composer at the helm. Raj Khosla may have lamented about everything barring the direction being bad in *Sunny*, but the final cut of a film is made as per the director's discretion. If everything was bad, the direction couldn't have been any good. The truth is that these film-makers had gone past their sell-by date and had been caught trying to peddle off age-old ideas. They were unable to see that the new era called for fresh stories and new techniques of film-making. If anything, the music was the saving grace of these duds. Pancham, in all sincerity, seemed ready to take up the unnecessary blame of the collective failure on his shoulders.

A chain is only as strong as its weakest link. Amitabh Bachchan kept his superstardom intact through the 1970s and the 1980s despite multiple failures. Dev Anand has had just eight hits in the last forty years. No more than twenty films come to mind when one thinks of Naushad's successes in the last sixty years. Yet all of them retained their financiers and sponsors. Shrewd operators shrug it off and walk away from failures as if nothing has happened. Pancham was anything but that. Ironically, he was the one criticizing his music most.

3

In the winter of 1985, Pancham eagerly awaited the India release of his international album *Pantera*, an experiment carried out at the behest of his friend Pete Gavankar, maternal nephew of recordist Mangesh Desai.

Pancham had spoken at length about the album in an interview to *Filmfare* in June 1984. The idea had germinated in 1975 when Pancham had met Pete in Las Vegas and the latter had suggested that he go international. Pancham was apprehensive that distancing himself from Bombay would marginalize him in the industry. An album in the US with Pancham's tunes was planned instead. In 1981, Pete took fifteen tunes from Pancham, and his sister shared the same with Jose Flores, an upcoming musician in San Francisco. Flores liked some of the numbers, and in subsequent trips, seven songs, out of which four were Pancham's compositions, were recorded. The tracks were purely experimental. The lyrics, one of the cornerstones of Indian film songs, played a minuscule role in the entire set-up. Pancham and Jose may have used gibberish lyrics as well, since scatting was an area where Pancham had experimented. The album was released in the US in 1982 under the Roco International label to mixed response.

Pancham was very excited about the album, since it might have been his first step towards creating a rock group. *Pantera* was released quite late, in 1987, in India, with Shammi Kapoor doing the honours. Released during a time when Latino music was not the *in* thing, the album was one of those enthusiastic ventures which got snubbed.

In hindsight, the tunes were enthralling. The title song *'Pantera'* might have been created while jamming to *'O diwano dil sambhalo'* (*The Great Gambler*). It was later used as a song in the film *Gardish* (1993). *'Carnaval'* was woven out of the antara of *'Yeh din toh aata hai'* from *Mahaan* (1983) and was given a Spanish spin while the original had an Arabian and gypsy essence. The original from *Mahaan*, replete with scatting, was an indicator that Pancham, if given the freedom, could have earned his kebab and single malt simply as a scatting star.

Pancham talked about the failure of the album in an interview in the *Times of India*, Bombay, dated 9 November 1989. 'The musicians in San Francisco are highly influenced by South American music since many of them are immigrants. Perhaps that's why the album did not have a universal appeal. It sounded more like Carlos Santana's music. Besides, we were also swindled by a guy involved in the project. In India, the album was released after a gap of nearly five years. It sounded outdated.'

Pancham's reasoning is hard to swallow. Till the advent of the electronic boom, a five-year lag with the West was commonplace. So that could not have been why *Pantera* did poorly in India.

One of the primary reasons behind the failure of the album was that non-film music in Hindi, barring ghazals and the occasional Anup Jalota bhajan, was yet to catch on in India. And music channels like MTV, a popular platform for non-film albums, were yet to make an entry into the Indian scene. Even high-profile albums by reputed rock groups did well only in patches in metros. Lastly, the lyrics of *Pantera* bordered on the juvenile, and this could have been another reason why it did not catch on even with the hip crowd.

The failure of *Pantera* halted Pancham's westward trudge though he did work with Boy George subsequently. Back home,

his demand had, meanwhile, waned. He had seven releases in
1986 and nine in 1987 as opposed to the nineteen in 1985. The
albums were not noteworthy either. Being labelled renegade at
times imposes limitations. Pancham did try to prove his
detractors wrong, succumbing to the rules he might not have
believed in, and subsequently stopped experimenting beyond a
certain point. *Pantera's* failure could have been one of the reasons.

By 1987, Pancham was confronted with the possibility of
having to take a second hiatus in his eventful career. The first
one, during 1961–65, was that of an untested maverick. This
one was thrust upon him by the change around him. In the
early 1960s he did not have a reputation at stake. The early-
1980s were when he was basking in his personal winter sunshine,
the warmth of which few in the industry had ever enjoyed. He
had created an entire cult. From here, the only options left were
to stay on top or slide down.

There were patches of success too. Gulzar's *Ijaazat* was under
production, and *Dil Padosi Hai*, a private album with Gulzar
and Asha Bhonsle, took him back to his glory days of yore.
'*Chhoti si kahani se*' in *Ijaazat* was intelligently inspired from one
of his own compositions (one could find the notes of '*Aye mere
bete*' rearranged), while '*Khali haath shaam aayi hai*' had the
Bhairavi notes of his father's Bengali song '*Malakhani chilo*', and
the opening bars of '*Qatrah qatrah miltee hai*' were based on Jeff
Wayne's '*Horsell common and the heat ray*'. Nevertheless, the
strength of the album was the way the songs fit into the script.
The blank verse of '*Mera kuch saamaan*' even prompted Pancham
to ask Gulzar if he might, one day, ask him to write music to
the front page of the *Times of India*. Another incident related to
this song goes thus: Asha, Pancham and Gulzar were in the
sitting session when Asha nonchalantly hummed the phrase
'lauta do'. Pancham latched on to the phrase, elaborated on it
and composed the metre for the song.

Gulzar relates another well-remembered anecdote: 'I wanted to sit with Pancham while he was composing *"Chhoti si kahani se"* as otherwise I would not have been able to picturize the sequence. But Pancham kept postponing it, saying, "I don't know when I will sit down to compose." Finally he called me to the recording studio, which is where I got to hear the song while it was being recorded in dual tracks. He said, "Here is your song. In two tracks. Now you can go and picturize it."'

Pancham said of his involvement with Gulzar to Pavan Chawla in the *Independent,* October 1992: 'With Gulzar, I would sometimes need a day or two to understand the significance and beauty of his lyrics, and then he would take a couple of days to appreciate my tune.' In another interview in the *Observer,* 31 May 1992, Pancham said, 'Gulzar is another director with whom I have enjoyed working enormously. Take, for instance, *Aandhi* or *Parichay.* Another favourite film of mine is *Namkeen.* *Kinara* was also wonderful. More recently, there has been *Ijaazat.* Gulzar has been a great inspiration to work with.'

Gulzar and Asha Bhonsle won National awards for the film. Pancham was, once again, glossed over.

There was, however, a disconcerting facet to his music of this period. Pancham was increasingly falling back on recycling tunes, borrowing from his father's tunes, and even using long passages inspired from the West for his best scores. Earlier, instances of him citing scores which were born out of inspiration as 'great' were rare. Sure, insecurity is an overwhelming emotion in tinsel town.

The private album *Dil Padosi Hai,* born out of his partnership with Gulzar, had shades of the class one associated with Pancham. Recorded in two phases, the album was released on Asha Bhonsle's birthday in 1987, at a grand function in the Taj Mahal Hotel, with Sunil Dutt as the guest of honour. One can't help but observe that had the album been conceived a decade earlier, however besotted Pancham may have been with Asha's vocals, Lata Mangeshkar would have featured somewhere. And had it come a decade later, a time when non-film music had really come of age, it would have been a much bigger success than it was at the time.

Pancham did point out to the media that *Dil Padosi Hai* was a creative outlet. But creative outlets do not always translate into popularity or money. The songs were neither proper geets nor ghazals. They were something in between, more reminiscent of Hindi modern songs, a term not coined in the 1980s. Pancham might have been pinning his hopes on the acceptance of the album by the perceptive minority. This happened, albeit a few years later.

The album was largely experimental, but Pancham did rework some of his Bengali songs, like '*Jete dao amaye deko na*' (1969) into '*Jaane do mujhe jane do*'. It is apparent that the lyrics, at least of the mukhra, were a translation of the original. The Bengali song was noteworthy for its arrangement, the syncopation, and the use of the sanchari, a stanza with a different tune inserted between the two antaras. The Hindi counterpart merges the sanchari into the antara, and the wonder that a sanchari creates, courtesy its short but significant use, is missing. According to Bhanu Gupta, Pancham rarely used a sanchari in his career. Bhanu had asked Pancham why that was so. In response, Pancham played the sanchari of Salil Chowdhury's composition '*Na jeona*' ('*O sajna*' from the film *Parakh*) and said, 'The day I can compose a sanchari like this, I will.'

'*Jete dao amaye deko na*' was one instance when he did.

Pancham also used Subal Dasgupta's composition sung by SD, '*Katha kao dao sara*' for '*Umeed hogi koi*'. Though he orchestrated it brilliantly, he certainly did not deserve credit for recycling his father's song in an album supposed to be original.

Credit, if any, should have been given to Pancham long ago for
fleetingly using the notes of the second line of 'Katha kao dao
sara' to fashion the second lines of the mukhras of 'Kaun si hai
woh cheez' (Jaise Ko Taisa) and 'Ai khuda har faisla' (Abdullah).

But the orchestration of Dil Padosi Hai wedded technology
with tradition, to the extent that Pancham even used the
flanger notes in the sitar in the prelude of the haunting 'Raat
chup chaap thi'. One also finds Pancham using a three-part vocal
harmony in 'Koi diya jale kahin'.

Pancham was also very quality conscious during the making
of the album. Ronu Majumdar recalls: 'This was the first album
where I was given arrangement responsibilities. I had arranged
"Bheeni bheeni bhor aayi". The kind of taans used in the song was
my speciality. I remember being abroad when the song "Saaton
baar bole bansi" was being recorded. It had sarod pieces by
Zarine Daruwala. She is a brilliant player, but once I was back,
Pancham-da insisted that all the sarod pieces be dubbed by my
flute pieces since the lyrics were about the flute.'

Given the standards of the second half of the 1980s, Dil
Padosi Hai would have comfortably made it to the 'excellent'
category. Ramesh Iyer describes the recording of Dil Padosi Hai
as a fun-filled experience for sixteen-odd days where he and
Bhupi – who used to be part of the team, occasionally – tried
out interesting chords, while Pancham would encourage the
experimentation despite the traditional nature of the album.
Ijaazat, likewise, was satisfyingly different to the ears from the
fare that was being peddled around. But the scores appeared to
have been created out of trepidation, as if he was a little unsure
of what exactly he was planning to do.

In the meantime, more members of the group had left
Pancham. Sunil Kaushik, known for his sensitive guitar riffs,
left the team in 1986. Uttam Singh, a key member of the string
section, moved away in 1988. 'Important team members definitely

have their influence. And their absence does leave some void. During his heyday, he had a very strong team which was very talented and which ably supported Pancham,' says Javed Akhtar.

'He had a permanent group of people who knew his soul and heart. The style was decided at the stage of composing itself. He is the one who started recording when the song was being composed. Bharat Ashar used to sit with a four-track recorder while composing. The style of the song and the colour of the rhythm used to be decided right there,' points out S.P. Balasubrahmanyam.

'Frankly, some of us lost interest post 1987 as there was nothing new in the arrangement pattern,' says Manohari Singh.

Fate too dealt a hard blow to Pancham as Kishore Kumar, his musical alter ego, so to speak, breathed his last on 13 October 1987. 'My kind of music is finished now because Kishore-da is gone,' Amit Kumar recalls Pancham's words on the singer's passing. 'There was alchemy and matching of stars between Kishore Kumar and R.D. Burman. The kind of compositions that he made my father sing were of a very high quality and only Kishore Kumar could do justice to them,' states Amit.

4

After Kishore Kumar's death, Pancham entered what was probably his worst phase. Not only tunes, his orchestration too suffered. The inconsistent quality of his music became glaring. Scores in films like *Zalzala* (1988) and *Aag Se Khelenge* (1989) were so unlike Pancham that the legitimate question arose as to how the person who composed '*Mera kuch saamaan*' could create '*Batata vada*' (*Hifazat*). Was it Pancham who was composing? Or was it his assistants doing it for him most of the time, except for critical scores? If rumours are to be believed, he had lost interest in his work; the producers' demands had drained his creative urge.

Pancham did try to regain lost ground by establishing Amit
Kumar as the voice of the era, and in the process gave Amit
Kumar one of his best songs, 'Rama o Rama' (Rama O Rama,
1988) which was the first song Amit recorded after his father's
demise. 'I had gone to Mahabaleshwar for the New Year when
I received a call from Pancham-da asking me to come back for
a recording,' Amit recalls. 'Adesh [Srivastava] played the drums
and "Rama o Rama" was recorded.' Amit sang the song the way
Pancham would have sung it, giving it the guttural feel one
associates with Pancham's voice.

But the 'Rama o Rama's were now exceptions. Pancham had
now entered a phase similar to the mid-1980s, where people
who had confidence in him left. 'Maybe he became a bit careless'
is Javed Akhtar's observation on one of the possible reasons for
the slump.

'It was practically Sapan-da who did everything now. Pancham
would leave everything to him with a summary "Tu dekh le",
ignoring the work himself. He had become so dependent on
Sapan. The teamwork that existed at the time when Bhupi-ji,
Bhanu-da, Maruti-ji were there was scattered now because of
Sapan-da. Sapan-da used to get into composing also,' says
Yogesh. 'If he could compose, why did he not become a composer
himself?' he adds.

A few others, while agreeing that Sapan passed off Pancham's
tunes as his own, disagree that Sapan ghost-composed on
Pancham's behalf. Sapan, however, is rumoured to have distorted
Pancham's creations by applying his own interpretations so
that the final song ended up being a crooked shadow of what
Pancham had envisaged.

Vidhu Vinod Chopra sees Pancham's misery as a result of low
self-esteem during that period: 'Lack of self-confidence. People
close to him, including Asha Bhonsle, left him. He began
thinking that he lacked the ability and burnt out. This was

untrue, but he somehow got swayed by other people's opinions and ended up losing his belief in his music.'

5

Gradually, Pancham was brutally axed by his professional partners who had once ridden to success on his music. Dev Anand dropped him after *Hum Naujawan*, effectively ending a thirty-five-year-old relationship with the Burmans. In any case, Dev Anand had always explored other options. Despite the successful music of *Hare Rama Hare Krishna* through to *Bullet*, Dev had signed up Rajesh Roshan for *Des Pardes* and *Lootmaar* (1979). *Jaaneman* (1976), a remake of the 1954 Dev Anand classic *Taxi Driver*, went to Laxmikant–Pyarelal though one would have expected it to have gone to RD since SD had scored the music for *Taxi Driver*. 'Well, except the lead character, *Jaaneman* was not really a remake of *Taxi Driver*,' claims Dev Anand. 'And I signed up Laxmikant–Pyarelal [for *Jaaneman*] just for the heck of it!' says Dev. Ramesh Sippy ended his association with Pancham after the failure of *Saagar* and signed on Laxmikant–Pyarelal to compose the score for *Bhrashtachar* (1989). Not that it did anything for the film. At least one remembers the music of *Saagar* till date. Romu Sippy too parted ways with Pancham after *Jeeva*. Shekhar Kapur had already left him after *Masoom* and *Joshilay* – which was still under production – and moved on to Laxmikant–Pyarelal for *Mr India* (1987).

In between, Pancham received an offer from Subhash Ghai for a film named *Ram Lakhan*. Subhash Ghai, named the Showman after Raj Kapoor, already had a steady working relationship with composers Laxmikant–Pyarelal. His commercial clout was undeniable. Though he made nothing more than basic masala films, he did ensure some sophistication within the framework.

Pyarelal, in an interview, said that Ghai had asked for Pancham-style music in *Karz* (1980), and thus were born songs like '*Om shanti om*'. Ghai had never worked with Pancham. Whether he liked or disliked Pancham's music is immaterial; it is evident that he could not help being influenced by it.

Around the same time as *Ram Lakhan*, Ghai was involved in formalizing his dream project *Devaa*, his first with Amitabh Bachchan. The music for *Devaa* was being composed by L-P. A song for *Devaa*, '*Pyar mohabbat rog hai dil ka*', sung by Manhar and Ila Arun was filmed too. Unfortunately, the Ghai–Bachchan bonhomie lasted only a few weeks. The film was dropped and Ghai poured all his energy into *Ram Lakhan*, produced by his brother Ashok.

Reportedly, Pancham had almost finalized the tunes for *Ram Lakhan* when the news was broken to him that he had been summarily dropped from the film. 'Till the evening before, we were composing for *Ram Lakhan*. Next morning we got the news that we were not in it,' recalls Manohari Singh.

'Till 1985, everything was fine. After that came a particularly bad patch. Twenty-seven films of mine flopped, and though some songs did become popular, they did nothing for my career. Around this time, Subhash Ghai signed me for *Ram Lakhan*, and Laxmikant–Pyarelal for *Devaa*. *Devaa* was an ambitious project and Ghai was paying more attention to it. We never really got down to discussing the music, but I had tentatively kept a few tunes ready. Then one day I heard that *Devaa* had been shelved and that Laxmikant–Pyarelal were doing *Ram Lakhan*. Mr Subhash Ghai didn't even have the courtesy to tell me this himself. I have never felt so humiliated in my life,' Pancham said in an interview to *Filmfare* in August 1992.

Mild-mannered all along, such outbursts were uncommon with Pancham. In sharp contrast to this outpouring, in an interview in the *Sunday Observer* in May 1992, Pancham was

more generous to Ghai as a director: 'Ramesh Sippy is a
fantastic director. His eyes are like viewfinders and he is
tremendous with music. In fact, only people like Subhash Ghai
and Sippy are left now, people who can compare with Raj Kapoor.'

6

Already on the edge due to multiple failures, being so
unceremoniously dropped from *Ram Lakhan* proved to be the
last straw. In an interview on Times Now on 14 March 2006,
Asha Bhonsle said that Pancham had his heart attack after *that*
episode. She was diplomatic in not mentioning the name of the
'big banner producer–director'.

However, Sachin Bhowmick refutes Asha's claim of this being
the reason for Pancham's heart attack. Pancham had a heart
attack in May 1989, and *Ram Lakhan* had been released by then.
Discloses Sachin Bhowmick: 'I told Subhash to consider Pancham
for *Ram Lakhan*. Ghai called him and asked him to do the film.
RD was very happy. Later, I saw that L–P had been signed up
instead. I asked Subhash Ghai why. L–P had told Subhash that
if he signed up Pancham, they would not henceforth work with
him. This hurt Pancham greatly, but the heart attack came
later.'

'We told Subhash Ghai that if he signed up Pancham, we
would not work with him thereafter,' confirms Pyarelal Sharma.

In an interview with the *Times of India*, 29 September 1985,
Pancham talked about the camaraderie that had once existed in
the industry. 'I miss the old atmosphere when composers like
my father, Naushad and Roshan would get together, discuss
each other's achievements and failures threadbare. Today, we all
work in isolation. Sometimes a composer even tries to undercut
the others' price to get a prestigious project. But I'll concede
that Laxmikant–Pyarelal are terrific. Pyarelal specially is a very
accomplished musician. If I were the producer, I'll tell each

party to do three songs each by L-P and RD.' Unfortunately, Pancham's sentiment was not reciprocated when things boiled down to petty commerce.

Guitarist Soumitra Chatterjee, who was there during Pancham's heart attack, remembers Pancham carrying his sense of humour during the critical period. But this humour was short lived, as time would tell.

The instances of composers 'stealing' tunes from Pancham around this time were increasing in frequency. They were taking advantage of the loosely framed intellectual copyright legislations.

The story of '*Aise na mujhe tum dekho*' (*Darling Darling*, 1977) being pilfered and turned into another song by a rival composer wasn't as serious. As the problem escalated, Pancham spoke about one of his experiences in an August 1992 interview to *Filmfare*: 'I remember an incident. A few days ago, Ilaiyaraja played for a producer a selection of tunes he had originally composed for his south Indian films. Imagine his plight when the producer turned around and said that the same tunes had already been "composed" by so-and-so music director for Hindi films. I've also had a similar experience. One of my arrangers, who also works for another music director, was present while I was composing a song. At the recording a few days later, when I handed over the notation to the musicians, they said, "But we played the same tune just the other day." Today, the music business has become akin to prostitution. There are no scruples whatsoever. Grab whatever you can and call it your own. However, music piracy is not a new phenomenon. It was there in the past too, but only five per cent of the tunes were copied.'

S.P. Balasubrahmanyam recollects an incident in the same context: 'On one occasion when Pancham-da was mixing sound at Film Centre with the unique "R.D. Burman at work – No Disturbance Please" board outside the studio door, I approached him. A young composing duo had come to meet him as well. Pancham-da asked the gatekeeper to "ask Balu alone to come inside". Later, when asked the reason for this, Pancham-da, taking a drag of his cigarette, stated point blank to me: "Even if they listen to just eight bars of my composition while I'm mixing, it will be immediately 'imported' to their song tomorrow. They will anyway do it after my song is released, but I don't want to give it to them right now."'

Kishore Kumar, in his distinctive way, had once tried to console Pancham when he complained about tunes being leaked from the studios: 'You should be happy that people are following your style.'

No significant theft has ever happened anywhere without the hand of an insider. It is believed that Pancham was constantly surrounded by self-seekers. A shrewder person would have smelt the storm clouds ahead of time. Musicians quitting, producers turning away, no new breakthroughs ... there was something seriously wrong within the camp. Pancham was an acknowledged genius. But geniuses make it a point to surround themselves with intelligent people. More importantly, they hold off schemers and operators. Music arrangement and assistantship, a critical back-end activity to the final output of a song, was now being managed by people who did not bother about the trust composers placed on them.

It took Pancham ages to figure out what was happening around him, so removed had he become from reality. Ultimately, in the 1990s, he did let Sapan Chakraborty and two more assistants go. But the gangrene had set in by then.

He suffered another personal loss when his friend Ramesh Behl died of jaundice on 5 January 1990. Ramesh, Randhir and he had been very close in their professional and personal lives. Manu Pal, Sudam Jana and Ramesh Maharana were really the only other 'family' that stood by Pancham all through.

'From a time when he would record at Film Centre, Pancham-da had slid to recording at a small studio in Khar. He would urge me to go to Anand–Milind and Rajesh Roshan as he did not have any work to give me,' recounts Abhijeet. Shurjo Bhattacharya also recounts that Pancham had moved to Madhur Dhwani Studios for smaller and regional stuff.

The recording studios and their acoustics made a lot of difference to the output. Digital recording, the highlight of *Dil Padosi Hai*, appeared as an intrusion into the main melodic flavour at times because the songs had been recorded at HMV studio which hardly had the facilities an R.D. Burman song required.

'I had recommended Pancham to a few people I knew since the people who had been close to him had left him one by one,' recalls Javed Akhtar. 'Even musicians stop coming to you. This industry is like that,' laments Yogesh.

Remembers singer Sivaji Chatterjee of what Pancham told him once: 'My evenings used to start at midnight and cars belonging to producers used to be lined up outside Marylands. Look today. My evenings start at six in the evening and there are no cars outside.'

With such drastic changes in his fortune, Pancham's luck seemed to have finally run out. According to Baba Desai, 'Luck runs alongside the whole team. When the team splits, the luck gets split too.'

Till an admirer shared some of his own.

7

Fresh from his songless success, *Khamosh* (1986), Vidhu Vinod Chopra had planned *Parinda* (1989), one of the earliest films set in the Mumbai underworld. A self-confessed Pancham fan who grew up singing his songs on shikaras on the Dal Lake in Srinagar, Chopra requested RD to compose the music for the film. Chopra's love for Pancham's music was immense – apart from the use of *'Ruk ruk'* (*Warrant*) in *Murder at Monkey Hill*, his diploma film project at FTII, he even had the inmates of an asylum chanting *'O mere dil ke chain'* in his first feature *Saza-E-Maut* (1981).

Good film-makers make a decisive difference to song picturization, and to the way songs are edited in a film. Chopra's use of a fuzzy brownish filter gave Bombay a hazy texture in *Parinda*, making the city a cauldron of crime, where life was suspended by a thread, thin and weak. The film had a lot of high crane shots by Binod Pradhan, and there were the occasional wide-angle and the fisheye-lens views. Often, there was a stillness in the shots that created an eerie feeling, and Vinod Chopra ably extracted the best from the composer he loved most.

'I had grown up listening to his music and had always been a big fan of his. I went to him with *Parinda* hoping he would say yes to it. There was a crisis in the casting which stalled the production even before it started. The recording schedule was planned but I went to him a day before the schedule and said, "You will have to cancel the recording. I have no money to proceed as the star has backed out." Later that day, he called me to say that he would be at the Film Centre studio the next day for a recording of his and told me to meet him there. When I went there I discovered that he had started recording for *Parinda* with his own money.'

For the song *'Tumse mil ke'*, Pancham took the opening bars of Leo Sayer's *'When I need you'*. Contrary to his style of just being inspired by the first line, he used the reprise of the song as the mukhra. The similarity ended there. Like a jazz musician, he built up the entire song on waltz. Lately, he had found immense potential in the voice of Suresh Wadkar, who ably complemented Asha Bhonsle's voice which had matured like old wine. *'Kitni hai pyaari pyaari dosti hamari'* was Pancham's extension of *'Ek din hasana ek din rulana'* (*Benaam*), and had present-day singers Shaan and Sagarika singing, albeit out of tune. *'Pyar ke mod pe'*, perhaps the best composition by Pancham in a long time, was shot in two parts – the Asha Bhonsle portion was filmed with the sun sinking into the sea as the background, while the portion sung by Suresh Wadkar was picturized on the hero returning to his sweetheart. Pancham's use of a flugelhorn instead of the trumpet and the sax augmented the cry of conflict so poignantly underlined in the script. His falling back on the joiner tune between the antara and mukhra of *'Aaye re aaye re'* (*Doosri Seeta*), reused as the joiner in this song too, created the feeling of numbness, so fundamental to a lullaby, yet profoundly poignant, evoking a feeling of tearful craving. The outdoor version, shot by Sanjay Bhansali, used many solid colours – orange, white, cream and black – and the use of filters and polarizers enhanced the concentration. For the tune, Pancham used both the Ni-s, but ended on the base note, Sa, creating an atmosphere of hope despite the Catch 22 situation the characters Karan and Paro (Anil Kapoor and Madhuri Dixit) were in.

'After the recording of "*Pyar ke mod pe*", Renu Saluja, Binod Pradhan and I went down to the street crossing and were trying to recall the tune of the song,' Chopra recounted. 'At that moment I saw Pancham-da driving away in his little Fiat and waved him down. He spotted me, got out of the car and walked over to us. Seeing me so moved by the melody, Pancham-da joined in as well. Now, since Pancham-da was going through a rough patch at the time, he wanted us to move out of the streets so that the crowd that gathered around us didn't start thinking that he had turned into a street performer. He commented, "Yaar, tu toh road pe hai, ab log sochengay ki mai actually road pe utar gaya hoon."'

The background music of *Parinda* used several motifs from Western classical music. The use of a short Carnatic piece to fan Anna's (Nana Patekar) pyrophobia was one of the building blocks of the film. Aaron Copland's song '*Fanfare for the common man*' was used in the titles. The same piece of music would also be used by Steven Spielberg in the multiple Oscar winner *Saving Private Ryan* (1998). Pancham's involvement in the background music of *Parinda* was, however, limited since he was mostly away for his operation, says Manohari Singh.

Other important films started coming his way: Vinod Mehra's *Guru Dev* (1993), Rajkumar Santoshi's *Ghatak* (1996) and *Ajay* (shelved). *Ghatak* was initially signed with Kamal Haasan in the lead. Inordinate delays led to Kamal walking out, making way for Sunny Deol in a script rehashed to suit Deol's persona.

Along with the films he was doing, Pancham signed a contract with Gulshan Kumar and Anuradha Paudwal for a pop album. He also chose S.P. Balasubrahmanyam, Kumar Sanu, Shailendra Singh and Danny for the album. S.P. Balasubrahmanyam had heard Pancham sing the Bengali version of the *jalpari* theme at a Puja function in Kolkata and had used the tune in a Telugu film, thinking that he would never be able to sing it in Hindi or Bengali. Pancham surprised him by asking him to sing the composition which was named '*Aja meri jaan*'.

'This number is indeed a special one for me,' remembers S.P. Balasubrahmanyam. 'Pancham taught me the song on harmonium at around 7.30 p.m. Then he and Manohari-da played the music track. My apprehension about the music track was that the intro portion was totally ad-lib. When the track was being recorded, there was a violin [to support the musicians] which was not recorded. So it was blank, and only the chords and bass guitar were there. As there was no rhythm, I didn't know how to come into the same chord singing the lines. I recorded that portion and kept rewinding and listening to it. For the first harmony, I was coming in all right but in the second one, I was either a little early or a little late. The track was on a thirty-five mm tape unlike today's digital ones. You could not punch in and punch out at any place you liked. Then I went to Pancham-da and told him that I was finding the ad-lib portion very difficult. The answer to that was a four-letter word followed by "That's why I've called you all the way from Madras. You can do it!" When I listen to it even today, I feel as if Pancham is singing it; though honestly I never tried to imitate his voice. But my voice in that song sounds typically Pancham-da!'

Ketan Anand, who filmed the video for the song, liked the title so much that he used the name of the song as the title of the film, *Aja Meri Jaan* – a crime thriller, based on *Teesri Manzil*, produced by Gulshan Kumar.

8

On 21 September 1989, Pancham had a bypass surgery at the Princess Grace Hospital in Devonshire, London. 'He had been a long-standing diabetic [for twenty years] and was on oral drugs,' remembers Dr Mukesh Hariawala, the cardiac surgeon who performed the bypass surgery on Pancham. He had been on insulin since the late 1980s, and the heart attack the year before had led to complications. 'Out of his two heart attacks, one was an ischemic attack and the other a full heart attack,' discloses Dr Hariawala.

Initially terrified at the very prospect of a bypass, Pancham periodically lapsed into depression and had to be cajoled by doctors. The operation rejuvenated him to the extent that he rediscovered the confidence that had ebbed away in his pre-hospitalization days. He also claimed to have started composing in his dreams.

'He had an uneventful recovery. No problem during and after surgery. He was asking me, "When can I start drinking?" He was fit enough to resume life the way he wanted to. Once he invited my family and composer Biddu for dinner in London. He asked me, "Doctor you're a Gujarati. How come you chose the name Mitali for your daughter?" I replied that I like Bengali names. He also presented fourteen CDs and a CD player to me,' says Dr Hariawala.

In London, Pancham came across a French pop group, one member of which knew quite a few of his songs. Being noticed and recognized in a foreign land by another musician was a great booster for a man who had lost belief in his abilities. He was also invited by BBC as the chief guest for one of its music programmes.

Asha Bhonsle's prolonged absence from London, startling as it was, was something Pancham had been used to in recent years. 'My wife Asha Bhonsle was there initially. Unfortunately, she had to leave after a fortnight. She had commitments; she had concerts in America and the Scandinavian countries. But I have a large part of my family, from my father's side, in London. They were with me, always by my bedside, till I boarded the aircraft home,' Pancham told the *Times of India* on 9 November 1989.

Dr Hariawala recounts: 'In hospitals, we can identify the bonding between the patient and his spouse; in the way they sit next to each other, in their body language, in the expression in their eyes, etc. In Asha Bhonsle's case, the bond was not visible. She was like any other visitor. There seemed to be some kind of formality in their relationship.'

It was generally assumed that Pancham was in financial distress during the late 1980s. This was untrue. 'He never used the words "money" or "finance" with me. He funded the entire surgery himself. About 22,000 GBP. That was the package. He could afford it. He never felt any strain paying the bills. He never asked for a discount, which I could have given had he asked. And he did not have any medical insurance. He paid the amount out of his pocket, cash. I remember that clearly. He had rented a luxurious apartment close to Oxford Street near Princess Grace Hospital. He was there one week before the operation and four weeks after surgery,' reminisces Dr Hariawala.

Back in India, he had films to complete. Among the old-timers, only Ramesh Behl with *Indrajit* (1991), Rajesh Khanna with *Jai Shiv Shankar* (1992) and B.R. Ishara with *Police Ke Peeche Police* (shelved) had stood beside him. Gulzar's *Libaas* had not progressed much. Two more songs were recorded for *Libaas*, the first being *'Kya bura hai kya bhala'*, his last duet with Lata Mangeshkar, modelled on SD's song *'Saite pari na bola'*. By this time Lata's voice was nowhere as mellifluous as before, and the results were expectedly unappealing. The other song to be recorded, the Lata solo *'Phir kisi shaakh ne'*, was definitely one of the most poignant tunes to be created in the late 1980s, and might have been a classic if Lata had sung it in her prime. Had it not been plagued by financial insecurities and ill luck throughout, including Gulzar's inability to promote the film for a proper release, *Libaas*, and not *Ijaazat*, might have been the musical benchmark of the 1980s.

On the personal front, Pancham had become quite lonely. He had few friends left. 'He would come over here or go to Ramesh Behl's place,' says Amit Kumar. After Ramesh Behl's death, few had time for him.

Sivaji Chatterjee talks about the loneliness and exclusion Pancham faced once he had lost his place in the sun: 'He had become extremely lonely. He had discarded both his assistants Babloo and Sapan. Of his sitting members, only Manohari Singh and Bhanu-da would come to his place every day. Among the singers, he was only close to Manna Dey and Amit Kumar.

I remember a poignant incident during autumn 1992. Pancham-da wanted to invite Amit Kumar to his house one evening. When he called, he was told that Amit had gone to a birthday party of a well-known film star. I was shocked that Pancham-da, in spite of being the senior of the two, had not been invited.'

Says Dr Hariawala: 'Burman Saab used to be kind of alone. Some of his questions were the sort lonely people would ask. When talking, he wouldn't say "Bombay aa jao, dhamal karenge", instead, "Aap aao, humse milo, spend some time with me; take out some time for me." These are signs of insecurity.'

'Pancham's driver Aslam had left him for a job in Dubai as there was not much work here. He got a new driver [Ramesh] but would drive himself despite his illness. He was highly diabetic and had to take insulin regularly. He used to feel lonely as even Asha-ji would not come to see him often. He used to call me and play me tunes on his harmonium,' recollects Sachin Bhowmick.

But Pancham was expecting a comeback. He had been forced to change his lifestyle and become a more disciplined person. He admitted to having been depressed before and to letting the quality of his work slide, but he was looking forward to what the new day had to offer. And there was another change for the better on the horizon.

After what seemed like ages, a film rode to success on the back of genuinely good music: Nasir Husain's son Mansoor Khan's film *Qayamat Se Qayamat Tak* (1988), featuring Nasir's nephew Aamir Khan and Miss India 1984 Juhi Chawla. Mansoor Khan decided not to carry on with the Pancham legacy in Nasir Husain films and signed up Anand–Milind instead as composers, though Nasir did take the final nod from Pancham. A sprightly Khan, jiving with a guitar at a college farewell, crooning his dreams aloud, announced the first blip of hope that melody may still be alive, after all. '*Papa kehte hain*' from *Qayamat Se Qayamat*

Tak could have easily been the anthem of the 1980s' youth. Between 1988 and 1992, melody reclaimed further lost territory with films like *Ashiqui* (1990), *Maine Pyar Kiya* (1989), *Jo Jeeta Wohi Sikandar* (1992) and *Dil Hai Ke Manta Nahi* (1991). Veteran sailors Kalyanji–Anandji, guided by Viju Shah with his EMU SP1200 keyboard, scored a return to business with *Tridev* (1989). Actors like Aamir, Salman and Rahul Roy were the new faces representing a fitter, younger nation. They looked comfortable in jeans and T-shirts and did not need blazers to hide flab. They could dance well, and looked cool and credible when they claimed to be college students. The goggles were genuinely for shading the eyes from the glare of the sun and not to hide middle-aged crow's feet. The men avoided white shoes and the women eschewed earthen pots to punctuate group dances. The new heroines were smart and urbane, and a majority of them had taken to acting as a logical progression to a career in modelling.

Youthful, elegant romance was back.

Mani Ratnam's *Roja* (1993) brought A.R. Rahman to focus; the dubbed Hindi version with its phenomenal influence made listening to south Indian music a fad in the early 1990s.

The lost era of Hindi music was making a comeback in the early 1990s. In the late 1960s, Pancham was beginning to take control of the steering wheel, ready to accelerate. In 1992–93, he was trying to revive a powerful engine, albeit one gone cold. Vinod Chopra brought him *August 1942* (renamed *1942: A Love Story*) and director Priyadarshan offered him *Gardish* (1993).

Pancham, at this point, was probably poised at a fork in the road. Despite being equipped to match the technique that the new breed in Bombay and Madras had skipped in with, he had negligible assignments in Bombay. In Calcutta, his last Puja album for HMV was in 1990. Named *Ga Pa Ga Re Sa*, it had received a lukewarm response, like the one in 1988, leading to

Pancham being sidelined by HMV. Around 1992, he was contemplating accepting an offer proposed by Biswanath Chatterjee of Concorde records.

It was time for him to decide how he wanted to proceed: look at the glitzy superstructures of technology and flair, or delve deep within for the emotional core of music. It was a critical choice, one that would enable him to get back onto the track that was suited to his style of driving.

Epilogue

THE PANCHAM LEGACY

'Time is the critic that discovers the masterpieces. Before their lasting powers are proven to us, we must experience them with mind and imagination. We must go through disillusionment with them, even hate them periodically. When we have been thrust away from them, we are in a better position to appreciate why they have drawn us back.'

– Neville Cardus

26 April 2008

On board Cathay Pacific CXP 746, from Dubai to Los Angeles via Hong Kong on 25 April 2008 was an Indian passenger. Upon alighting at Los Angeles, Kaustubh C. Pingle proceeded to ArcLight, Hollywood. He had covered more than 13,000 kilometres to watch a film. Brahmanand Siingh's *Pancham Unmixed: Mujhe Chalte Jaana Hai* was being premiered at the Indian Film Festival of Los Angeles (IFFLA) 2008 that evening at 6.30, Pacific Time.

22 February 2009

Indranath Mukherjee steered his Maruti Alto off NH-8 and onto a muddy patch of land upon sighting a dhaba. It was time for brunch. Shankh Banerjee, the youngest of the four occupants, was sick of the air inside the car and urgently needed some fresh tobacco.

JAIPUR–126 km, read the milestone. 'We should make it by 1.30 p.m.,' Indranath said to his companions. Half an hour earlier, Naresh Khattar had sped past on the same route. Dr K.K. Goel was also travelling to Jaipur from Muzaffarnagar. It was neither a business tour nor a fort-seeing trip. They were all on their way to watch a movie.

In Jaipur, music aficionado and owner of the website www.gulzaronline.com, Pavan Jha, had arranged a special screening that February afternoon of the same film that Kaustubh C. Pingle had flown over 13,000 kilometres to watch.

Of the handful of documentaries that have ever been made on Indian film personalities, Pancham is the rare representative of music directors. *Pancham Unmixed* is not one of those badly researched and shabbily handled documentaries done by some inept technician under political pressure for institutions like the Films Division. It is a film by an artist who put his heart, soul and hard-earned money to build up the plot like a collage, with narratives by people associated with Pancham, personally and professionally.

Recipient of a 'special critical mention' from the jury at IFFLA as 'a must-watch film for all', the film is a testament to R.D. Burman's unmatched popularity across continents. Director Brahmanand Siingh leaves his audience with the revelation that Pancham is the most 'remixed' Indian composer ever.

2

In the last fifteen years, the Pancham mix has spread. Not in a sudden gush, but quietly, almost unnoticed. If imitation is flattery, remixing must at least be idolization. A cursory surf of music sites shows at least two hundred RD songs remixed by singers like Bally Sagoo, Mahalaxmi Iyer, Shankar Mahadevan, Shaan and DJ Aqueel, among others. And remixes – with their popularity in private parties, corporate parties and pubs – have been a prominent vehicle for the spread of Pancham's music.

'For all us DJs looking for tunes to remix, R.D. Burman's original compositions are the first choice. His music is best suited for mixing because most of his tracks are based on a 4 x 4 beat on which it is very easy to put add-on beats that don't need much editing,' says DJ Kiran from Delhi, winner of the 2004 edition of The War of DJs, a competition hosted by Zoom and Times Music. "*Jahan teri ye nazar hai*" is my trump card every Saturday night. It makes you move,' DJ Ashok Bajaj reveals. 'R.D. Burman's party tracks are wild.'

Not that Pancham's music needed remixing to promote itself. What is important is that Pancham's tunes and rhythm sound current enough to be remixed.

Says Javed Akhtar: 'At any given time, there are successful people. They are sought after. Then they get old, fade away, exhaust their talent or die. Kuch log baad me yaad rehte hain. You are remembered if you have done something new and different, and have set a milestone. Pancham has been becoming more important with time. Earlier, he was merely successful. Now, with more distance, the contours are becoming more visible. Pancham is a milestone in music – a certain sensitivity, modulation, a certain sound, a certain beat. RD urbanized Hindustani music and brought it closer to world music. Pancham's music sounds universal and international. It is not getting obsolete. Rather, it is becoming more modern because our society is reaching the point to which RD's music had taken a leap ahead of time. It is now contemporary.'

It is not just remixes. His original compositions have been important parts of feature films in the new millennium, at times becoming chartbusters and helping the films on to success. Two movies in recent times carried the intro guitar riff of *'Aaja aaja main hoon pyar tera'* (*Teesri Manzil*): *Rab Ne Bana Di Jodi* (2008) and *Chandni Chowk to China* (2009). While the former was rearranged on keyboards as an interlude in a medley, the latter was a taped version of the original. The original track (thankfully, with the original credits) of *'Bachna aye haseeno'* made an appearance in the Ranbir Kapoor film of the same name in 2008. 'I am so proud that Nasir Saab and Pancham's tune has been scored in my son's film.' Rishi's eyes light up as he talks of the film. Farah Khan's *Main Hoon Na* (2003) uses Pancham's songs as motifs, including the medley of *Hum Kisise Kum Naheen*. In *Om Shanti Om* (2007), one hears the original tracks of *'Mera naam Shabnam'* (*Kati Patang*) and *'Hungama ho gaya'* (*Hungama*) in the background. 'What people are following now, what Rahman is doing today with so many more gizmos and recording instruments and electronics, Pancham did thirty-five years back!' says Randhir Kapoor, as excited as he was when the songs were originally composed.

'I've grown up in Calcutta in an R.D. Burman culture. And it grew on me,' declares Sujoy Ghosh, director of *Jhankar Beats*, arguably the first film in India that has the essence of Pancham's musical genius as its core theme. Its lead characters take the initials 'R' and 'D' in a slick screenplay that plaits various subplots around the backbone which is R.D. Burman's music. The background score is an appropriately tailored adaptation of original RD tracks. A lot of typical Pancham aspects had to be included for the right effect, according to Ghosh. 'The scream *"Zeeera!"* in the intro of *"Duniya mein"* was the seed of *Jhankar Beats*. It is what inspires the maker of a creative work that convinces the audience. Pancham was the inspiration of *Jhankar Beats*,' he admits.

With thirteen Pancham tracks, Ananth Mahadevan's *Dil Vil Pyar Vyar* (2002) is another film built around the ethos of Rahul Dev Burman's music. 'Viveck Vaswani had this very bizarre idea of actually using published music all over again in a different format, and he was clear that it wouldn't be a remix,' recollects Ananth Mahadevan. 'Pancham-da looked as though he had created music for generation next. This plus his melody made us opt for a retro musical with Pancham-da [over other composers],' he adds. 'Bablu Chakravarty used to keep a photo of Pancham-da, do a puja and start recording. It was Pancham-da's soul . . .' he says. A new generation's tribute to Pancham is keeping the soul of his music alive while packaging it in a new body.

FM channels have fragmented music into silos. There are metro hours, regional hours, retro hours, etc. One composer's name, however, cuts across all compartments: R.D. Burman. Like his favourite singer Kishore Kumar, Pancham is somebody who is considered as a bridge over the generation gap.

'Today's generation can do wonders with computers and all, but there is no heart, no soul. Today's songs last for two months and vanish. RD's music never vanishes. It will be there for centuries,' reinforces Amit Kumar.

'Whether it is percussion style, resso, saxophone, rhythm pattern or cello, almost all music directors have at least one sixteen-bar phrase of Pancham-da somewhere or the other in their compositions,' says S.P. Balasubrahmanyam with a suppressed chuckle.

In an interview with the *Hindu*, leading music director Pritam acknowledged: 'R.D. Burman was my inspiration, and my favourite composer as well.' Composers Jatin–Lalit, Vishal Bhardwaj, Shantanu Moitra and the trio of Shankar, Ehsaan and Loy echo Pritam's sentiments on various media platforms.

The Pancham resurgence has also been helped along by the strides made in the retailing trends in the music industry. In 1977, one remembers walking into leading music stores and having to ask for a specific gramophone album packed in cardboard boxes and stored away inside dowdy shelves. Today, music retailing, vide a Planet M or a Music World or a Reliance TimeOut, is as integral to a mall as a KFC, McDonalds or a Pizza Hut. Ranging from 200 square feet to over 10,000 square feet, these upmarket outlets arrange their collections under logical heads like Devotional, Western Rock, Indi-pop, Evergreen Hits and Recent Hits, guiding each consumer segment to their choice.

This large-scale music retailing has also encouraged audio companies to release R.D. Burman's old collections (and of other composers as well). *The Versatile Genius: R.D. Burman, Kabhie to Hasaye Kabhi to Rulaye: A Lifetime Collection, Immortal*

Duo: Asha Bhonsle and R.D. Burman, are just some of the many albums on offer. These collections, which are a bouquet of songs from various films, neutralize the hit–flop factor of the films in that collection. Pancham compilations released in the last fifteen years include tracks from *Bada Kabutar, Dil Ka Raja, Chor Police, Mazaaq, Imaan, Adhura Aadmi, Garam Masala, Adhikar* and *Abhilasha*, films which had bombed badly at the box office in their time.

Vishwas Nerurkar and Biswanath Chatterjee have been compiling music anthologies for quite some time. Their effort takes off after the *Hindi Film Geet Kosh*, a decade-wise anthology of songs from Hindi films that was popularized by Harmandir Singh 'Hamraaz' and Biswanath Chatterjee. The demand for the Pancham anthology has been such that Nerurkar and Chatterjee are releasing a new, revised edition of '*Pancham*', the anthology on R.D. Burman.

Nerurkar's anthology on Pancham, released in 1997, has also rekindled the craze for his unpublished compositions. Songs from unreleased or shelved films, if magically retrieved from some old spool tucked in a container in some vague attic, are either distributed to fans over the net, or are up for sale at prices fit for a 40-inch television.

Brand-new Vinyl albums are another commodity that has attracted attention in the last two decades. When the name on the album is R.D. Burman, prices go up considerably.

In September 1985, Raju Bharatan had written a story on the ten best musicals of all time in *Filmfare*, a selection which included heavyweights like *Guide* (1965) and *Anarkali* (1953), surprises like *Bobby* (1973), *Mere Mehboob* (1963) and *Kabhi Kabhie* (1976). Composers Rahul Dev Burman, Madan Mohan, Roshan and Anil Biswas were conspicuous by their absence. Ironically, Bharatan writes repeated obituaries on R.D. Burman today, with stories that are often dubbed dubious by music lovers who know their Pancham well. *Filmfare*, whose annual award for the best in Hindi cinema used to deviously elude Pancham, has ironically named an award — the only award in the name of a person — after Pancham. It is called the Filmfare R.D. Burman Award for New Music Talent.

As Javed Akhtar puts it, 'Time is kind to talent and class.'

Today, Pancham is a brand.

Also, something has changed in the way people look at Hindi music. Thanks to its garnished tracks and a visual frontage in the form of MTV and Channel V, Hindi music

> Barely a few months after Pancham's demise, his locker number 1045 at the Central Bank of India, Santa Cruz, which could be opened by key no. 1035, which was lying with Pancham's secretary Bharat Ashar, was drilled open under a court order. The contents of the locker, a solitary five-rupee note, made big news. Pancham's intent to buy a flat for eight million rupees in the early 1990s had gone unnoticed.

has become cool. From being frowned upon with condescending glances, it has gone international. 'Desi' is in. 'Asha Bhonsle's appearances on MTV have a twofold role to play — that of establishing a link between two generations and effectively broadcasting her R.D. Burman numbers,' says Joy Bhattacharjya. Today, the Pancham sound is revered globally, with the media outside India too getting a feel of his music. A casual Google search will return many results such as the one cited below from the blog of Phil Ramone and Danielle Evin, Dog Ears Music, which appears in the *Huffington Post*:

> Bollywood legend Rahul Dev Burman, born in Calcutta in 1939, was one of the most notable Hindi film composers of the '60s and '70s. The son of distinguished singer/composer Sachin Dev Burman, Rahul wrote his

first song before the age of 9, and grew up to score over
330 films. Burman's compositions fuse jazz, Motown
funk, and rock 'n' roll. Collaborations include Asha
Bhonsle (his wife), Kishore Kumar, Rishi Kapoor, Kajal
Kiran, Seenat [sic] Aman, and Tariq. Accolades include
countless *Filmfare* nominations and three *Filmfare*
awards. Burman passed away in 1994, but his treasure
chest of music is mammoth. Start with '*Dum maro dum*'
from the collection *Bollywood Legend (The Best of the
EMI Years)*.

Buy: iTunes

Genre: World/Jazz

Artist: R.D. Burman

Song: Dum Maro Dum

Album: Bollywood Legend (The Best of the EMI Years)

Robert   Iannopollo,   a   jazz   enthusiast   (http://
www.allaboutjazz.com/php/contrib.php?id=2652) lives in New
York. He probably eats pizzas for lunch, takes the tube every
day and watches baseball just like most New Yorkers. With a
difference. He listens to R.D. Burman and, surprisingly for an
American patronizing jazz, rates *Amar Prem* and *Mere Jeevan
Saathi* as his favourites among the 120-odd Pancham albums he
possesses. He belongs to a fast-spreading group of people of
non-Indian origin who are fans of Pancham.

'I started the site Panchamonline (www.panchamonline.com)
sometime in 1997,' says Vinay P. Jain who calls the site his
'labor of love' (the omission of the 'u' in 'labour', characteristically
American). 'And the Pancham Yahoo! group, which started on
13 January 1999 with thirteen members, has grown to over
fourteen hundred. After India, the highest membership is in the
US. There are Pakistani and Bangladeshi fans of Pancham too.
The membership reach is as wide as the Indian diaspora. Some
of his records [especially *Shalimar*] are popular in some music

circuits though, and sell well on sites like eBay. And some time back, Kronos Quarter versions of RD songs generated some interest too,' adds Jain.

The Pancham Yahoo! group has a bunch of dedicated 'Panchamanics' (as they call themselves). Leading the pack is Shashi Rao, an IT professional based in Eagan, Minnesota. Today, he is *the* repository of information on Pancham and preserves Pancham's vinyl albums like artefacts.

There are more forums patronizing Pancham's brand of music. The Pune-based Panchammagic group (www.panchammagic.org) organizes biannual symposiums on 27 June and 4 January, Pancham's birth and death anniversaries respectively. The group comprises members who not only have a great regard for Pancham but also possess deep knowledge about the technicalities of Pancham's music. Their website is as comprehensive a portal to the composer as one would like to visit. In Kolkata, the forums Euphony (www.euphony.co.in), MelodyChime (http://melodychime.org) and Amit Kumar Fan Club (www.amitkumarfanclub.com) regularly organize Pancham shows where leading associates of R.D. Burman perform.

Says David Harrington, the leader of the Kronos Quartet, the group which remixed some of Pancham's tunes in an album named *Aaj Ki Raat*, which was nominated for a Grammy: 'As an orchestrator, Burman is up there with Stravinsky; as a writer of melodies, he's as good as Schubert.'

Stravinsky's experimentation with rhythm and his theory of appreciating music simply as a motley of sounds and patterns almost finds an Indian echo in Pancham. Schubert's prolificacy as a composer in a career and life that was very short and the increasing interest in his work posthumously uncannily matches Pancham's.

Today, the adulation for Pancham has reached cultish proportions.

When did the Pancham wave begin? With the grand finale in *1942: A Love Story* – as spectacular a comeback as anyone could hope for. There is no sportsman, businessman or artist who has not gone through a period of extreme lows. But these troughs in their career graphs only underline their greatness by showing the crests in greater relief. In that phase, the best in class go back to the basics. That is where the problem invariably lies, surprisingly overlooked.

3

What were the elements in *1942* that made the wheels turn around? The answer is easy: melody and emotional content.

Ironically, Pancham might have been in a more relaxed frame of mind in 1993 than he was in 1986. Friends, associates, producers, health – he had nothing more to lose now. In a television interview around that time to Aparajita Krishnan, Pancham had stated, 'Vinod Chopra's *1942* is a period film, and it is a very big challenge as the entire thing has to go like Dixieland [Dixieland is often today applied to white bands playing in a traditional style]. There was the challenge for me to go back as we always tend to see forward. We have definitely managed to go back in time and I am happy. After listening to them, people might say S.D. Burman has composed these songs. Regarding the lull in the last eight–ten years, unless a film is a hit, [good] things do not surface, say [in] acting, composing or direction – if the film is a hit, faults do not surface. There have been instances when people have lived with my music during its production, listening to the cassette day and night. Once the film is released and the film flops, nobody listens to the songs. I used to take up fifty–sixty films earlier and also did thirty songs a month. Now I want to work with a great sense of fun so that the work is creative. I want to enjoy myself.'

His enthusiasm was back, as was his delight in his work, something that he had lost during the late 1980s and the early 1990s. 'He left London around six weeks after the surgery. He was in very good spirits. "No chest pain, mai chal raha hoon, ghoom raha hoon, Oxford Street mein shopping kar raha hoon. Aap ne pehelwan bana diya hai. I feel good, athletic," [is what Pancham said]. It's a very good sign of mental awakening and physical rejuvenation; you need a combination of both to keep the wheels turning. Without mental awakening you're still in a slump. In his case, the combination had happened,' remembers Dr Mukesh Hariawala.

Pancham started picking his kind of races to run. He was considering working with Pandit Ajoy Chakrabarty on an album that was to feature nine Ajoy Chakrabarty solos, two Asha Bhonsle–Ajoy Chakrabarty duets and a solo by Asha Bhonsle. He had started going back to doing what he was good at. He was neutralizing his fixation with Asha Bhonsle by exploring newer voices and reaching out personally to singers like Kavita Krishnamurthy and Indrani Sen.

Usha Uthup was also back in his scheme of things.

In a stage show commemorating Pancham's birth anniversary in Kolkata in 2008, Indrani Sen recalled her first meeting with Pancham: 'Even the thought of working with Pancham-da was a dream. I was getting good work in Calcutta during the late 1980s and early 1990s. It was during those times that the idea of collaborating on an album with Pancham-da was floated. I had certain issues in going to Bombay, and one day, I received a phone call from Pancham-da himself, who said that he would come down to Calcutta to record my songs. I was floored. It was a dream come true.'

'A year before he died, he and I would pick up a Black Label Royal Salute, play *Back on the Block* by Quincy Jones and drive round Vile Parle till 3 a.m.,' recalls Amit Kumar.

Pancham found more opportunities to relax and reconnect with himself.

'I asked him whether he would be interested in doing a programme on Vividh Bharati called *Sangeet Sarita* [a programme on classical and Hindi film music] which I was producing,' Chhaya Ganguli recalls. 'For the next fifteen days, he listened to *Sangeet Sarita* every day, even skipping his morning walks in the process; such was his sincerity.' At Pancham's suggestion, Gulzar and Asha Bhonsle too were included. The epic fifteen-episode programme with Pancham was titled *Meri Sangeet Yatra*, and it gave Pancham the width to take a leisurely stroll down memory lane along with two of his closest professional associates. 'They recorded all fifteen episodes in one go at Akashvani Studios, just one day before the Bombay blasts of 1993. They had decided on a general direction and had discussed which songs to include; the rest was all extempore. They were all very easy to get along with,' says Chhaya Ganguli.

While the importance of *1942: A Love Story* in RD's resurgence is undeniable, there was another album that preceded *1942* by a few months. Even though its impact was not as visible as *1942*'s, this album was as important. Priyadarshan's *Gardish* was released in September 1993 and had an average run, but its music more than made up for everything else. The tracks included S.P. Balasubrahmanyam's solo '*Hum na samjhe the*' and the fast-paced club number '*Rang rangilee raat*', officially an Asha–SP duet in which SP is used sparingly in the background. Vidhu Vinod Chopra's *1942: A Love Story* was under production when *Gardish* released. Pancham was not even invited for the premier of *Gardish* – so unlucky was he considered to be at that time.

'Pancham went about *1942* with a do or die spirit. "I need to show who I am. Just you wait till the music of the film releases,"' Javed Akhtar recalls a conversation with Pancham during the sound mixing.

With *1942*, Pancham was perhaps also planning to regroup with his old and trusted team, as Manohari Singh was back as the main arranger.

Dr Hariawala recalls a bizarre conversation: 'After his first heart attack, he stopped producing good music because maybe he started losing focus on music and started focusing on his health. He used to tell me that somehow his heartbeat was connected to the way he developed music. He told me, "Doctor Saab, thode saalon se thik nahi ho raha hai." What he meant was "music thik nahi ho raha hai, maybe because dil thik nahi hai". Now, there is no medical correlation between heartbeat and writing music. But mentally he had a correlation, probably because his music was so instinctive.'

Like that of most champions, his comeback had to be painstaking. Vidhu summarily turned down Pancham's original tune of '*Kuch na kaho*', calling it 'all crap'. The insecurity of a clouded star gripped Pancham as he asked, 'Am I still there in this film?' A relentless Vidhu replied, 'Pancham-da, don't give me your emotions. Give me your music.'

A week later they re-assembled. As Pancham played the intro bars of the alternative tune in Bengali, Vidhu listened with his eyes closed. Pancham looked up for feedback, and saw the tips of Vidhu's index finger and thumb held up in a circle – in a 'perfect' sign. Pancham had worked just as hard at another audition almost thirty years ago – for *Teesri Manzil*. He had always been just as good.

'On 31 December 1993, we threw a huge New Year's party on the sets of the movie [at the 'town square' of Film City]. All the workers and crew had gathered. We played "*Ek ladki ko dekha*" on the sound system and that was the last time he ever really heard his music, and the entire crowd cheered and clapped heartily for Pancham-da. And at that very moment, I could tell that Pancham knew that his work had been appreciated. This moved me deeply,' Vidhu remembers.

1942 was a film where Pancham went back to the old order, where tune was given the top billing. In effect, he went back in time and filled in the spaces with sounds typical to the period. With '*Ek ladki ko dekha*', he got on to the full-on mukhra–antara style that his father once pioneered in '*Borne gondhe chhonde geetitey*' (the original tune for '*Phoolon ke range se*' in Dev Anand's *Prem Pujari*), where the mukhra and the antara are merged as one. It also had a cadence that was deceptively fast in spite of the progression being very slow. '*Kuch na kaho*' found Pancham fleetingly referencing the tune of SD's '*Rongila rongila*' and giving it a totally different colour and contour, with an orchestration bordering on the symphonic. Originally recorded by Kavita Krishnamurthy, the song was dubbed by Lata Mangeshkar after Pancham's death. RD went back to Indian classical music and Rabindranath Tagore for '*Dil ne kaha chupke se*', basing it on the dual inspiration of Raga Desh and Tagore's '*Esho shyamal sundaro*', and using strains from '*Panna ki tamanna*' (*Heera Panna*) and '*Aisa kyon hota hai*' (*Ameer Aadmi Garib Aadmi*, 1985).

Sivaji Chatterjee who sang '*Ye safar*' in *1942* reveals: 'In October 1992, while teaching me the song and test-recording my voice at Marylands, Pancham-da said that he had "*Jaane woh kaise*" [*Pyaasa*] at the back of his mind while composing the song. Next day, Javed Saab and Vidhu had come there. To fill up the intro, Javed Saab penned a couplet and Pancham-da composed the music right there.'

Pancham's attention to detail extended to the use of music particular to the period in order to impart some semblance of reality to period films. He chose his period songs with caution, and did not go against the time in which the period film was set. Fifteen years ago, Pancham had chosen a Nazrul geeti ('*Kuhu kuhu bole koyaliya*') and had it translated into Hindi by Gulzar for the shelved *Devdas*. Of course, with Gulzar infusing it with his own imagery, it evolved into something more than a literal translation.

In contrast, we also had an instance of Raga Darbari being used by a present-day composer for a period film dating back to around 250 BC, the caveat being that the raga is said to have been inducted into north Indian music by Tansen only in the sixteenth century.

With the score of *1942*, Pancham had probably realized that he just needed to look within for the right metre and that he shouldn't succumb to peer pressure. He also went back to the difficult task of writing music for lyrics. 'Three of the songs were composed to metre and the remaining three he composed on my lyrics,' remembers Javed Akhtar.

'"Ab heart thik hai aur music bhi. Dekho gaadi chalne lagi hai," Burman-da [as Dr Hariawala used to call him] said once,' Dr Hariawala remembers, pointing to the link between Pancham's music, success and health.

In his farewell, Pancham had left his footprint. In the final count, his Hindi and Urdu film career tallied 292 released films and 40-odd unreleased films. His Bengali and regional films totalled thirty-nine and he also composed for mercurial director Sukhdev's documentary *Ma Ki Pukar*. Given that *Kati Patang*, the film that stabilized his career according to Pancham himself, was approximately his fifteenth released film, the peak continued till his 230th released Hindi film (approximately), *Saagar*. In contrast, out of a total of seventy films in his sixty-five-year-long career, Naushad, had thirteen films after the 1970s, all of them inconsequential. Before he parted ways with Asha Bhonsle, O.P. Nayyar had successfully composed music for sixty-five films, but that number came down to eight released and five unreleased films after the break-up. Shankar was virtually wiped out after the untimely demise of Jaikishan, with around forty failures out of a career total of 173 films. For these composers their slide was a one-way street. None of them could make a comeback.

Composers Laxmikant and Pyarelal would usually never play other composers' songs at stage shows. Nevertheless, in Dubai, on 7 May 1994, they made an exception. They played Pancham's music and Laxmikant's daughter Rajeshwari sang a Pancham number as a tribute.

Pancham, from being 'burnt out' in the mid-1980s, rose like a Phoenix to come thundering back with *1942*.

4

'Imagine what would have been his position after *1942*. Woh picture chali hi sirf music ke liye! He was the sole horse. I give him the entire credit for the film,' declares Randhir Kapoor.

Chhaya Ganguli, who won the National Award for '*Aapki yaad ati rahi*' (*Gaman*, 1978), and who is currently the assistant station director of Doordarshan, Mumbai, says, 'I don't see it as a wave of R.D. Burman coming back. He never went away. In many compositions nowadays, one can see his shades and influences. If one has to sing a ghazal, one needs to gather something from the likes of Begum Akhtar-ji, Mehdi Hasan Sahab, Madhurani-ji, Ghulam Ali–ji, etc. Similarly, one has to refer to Pandit Birju Maharaj-ji in kathak. In playback singing, for anyone to sustain, he needs to imbibe from Lata-ji and Asha-ji.' This is an obvious reference to Pancham as a benchmark for contemporary light music.

'Situation is important in film music. Pancham-da's music had a fullness to its personality. Even without the visual aid of the film, the end-to-end feel of the composition would help draw up the images – this is worthy of credit to both him and his singers. His progression of a raga-based tune would be on the interwoven chords with the raga notes being almost invisible. The chords and not the raga alone lend colour to the song. And whenever you listened to Pancham-da's purely raga-based compositions, for example, *"Bada natkhat hai"* [Khamaj] or *"Mere naina saawan bhadon"* [Shivranjani] you get the true essence of the raga,' Ganguli adds.

S.P. Balasubrahmanyam says emotionally, 'Pancham-da's legacy will live as long as music exists. His father's influence was there, but he comfortably converted it into his own style and turned it into a beautiful legacy. He is immortal.'

'In the West, composers have started using traditional instruments like violins, brass, etc., for recordings, reducing the dependency on computers. Music is natural, and live instruments connect better with the human heart. With his mixing, Pancham could arrive at a judicious blend of instruments and technology, which is why he remains the greatest in popular music in Indian cinema. He will emerge more with time when people realize his calibre. He made his own style,' Amit Kumar emphasizes.

'He could get the best out of even ordinary singers. He knew every bar of his composition and would nurture and develop his music,' says SPB.

Classical musician Pandit Ajoy Chakrabarty affirms his unabashed love for the Pancham sound: 'Today, Indian music is being recognized in the international arena. I would hate to say this, but had the setting been similar in Pancham-da's time, some of his preludes and interludes might have been potential candidates for the Oscars.'

To be endorsed by one's peer group is the greatest compliment.

Pyarelal Sharma of the L-P duo, often mistaken for a competitor to Pancham, sums up succinctly: 'He was the number one.'

Not just that, composers as diverse as a conservative yet

progressive Anil Biswas, a temperamental O.P. Nayyar, a philosophical Salil Chowdhury, or a maverick Jaikishan have unanimously converged on the same opinion: Pancham was one of a kind.

Said composer Anil Biswas in an interview with Tushar Bhatia on AIR: 'I would have touched his feet had he not been younger to me. I can say aloud that neither has there been nor will there be an all-rounder like him. And that includes his father, me and other music directors.'

5

The legacy of R.D. Burman is matched by something else, the legacy of Pancham the person.

SPB walks us through his indirect association with Pancham while singing songs from *Aradhana* at a stage show: his first glimpse of Pancham at an award function in Hyderabad, his first duet *'Baagon mein khile'* in *Shubh Kaamna* (1983) with Asha Bhonsle, the timely help to Pancham's assistant Deepan Chatterjee with the audio system during a stage performance in Madras during the mid-1970s (which was when he first got to speak to Pancham), Pancham's mispronunciation of Ilaiyaraja's name as 'Erliya' despite his admiration for him . . .

'He used to come to Hotel Sea Rock [where SPB would stay when in Bombay] around 10.30 p.m. and would call out, "Hey, Balu!" I would rush to him, we would settle in my room, have a couple of drinks and exchange jokes . . . I was not present during his last rites. So I was bent upon doing a show as a tribute to him in Hyderabad,' SPB says. Balu's homage to his Pancham-da in the form of a show titled *Yeh Shaam Mastani* has been telecast by Sony TV on multiple occasions.

'Pancham was very different from any of his peers. He never cared for money. Apart from paying musicians who were sick for prolonged periods of time, I have also seen him paying musicians out of his own pocket when producers refused to pay on time. In spite of being cheated and back-stabbed by so many people he trusted, he never complained and always went out of his way to help others. I do not think I shall ever come across such a great musician and such a wonderful human being,' Gulshan Bawra recalled.

'Once Pancham extended his recording session at Film Centre to allow me to record *my* composition for a Nepali film,' remembers Ranjit Gazmer.

Pandit Ulhas Bapat remembers Pancham's advice on humility: 'During the background score session of *Harjaee*, Pancham-da said, "I want a morning raga in *aaroha* and an evening raga in *avaroha* [akin to the experiment in '*Raina beeti jaye*']." I started off, playing Ahir Bhairav and Marwa, Todi and Yaman, and told him hesitantly, "I have tried something. It may not be quite what you have in mind." He held my hand and said, "No matter how high you go and earn wealth, remain just the way you are – down to earth." I touched his feet and promised him that I would never change.'

Polio-afflicted since birth, young Macky would be avoided by boys his age. Pancham would bring him to Marylands where the boy would sit by himself and watch TV with Meera Dev Burman. For Maqdoom (Macky) Ali, son of Mahmood, Pancham's home gave him what he missed elsewhere – acceptance.

Doel Gupta says, 'He had the vision to see beyond the usual. Every day, he would have additional people for lunch. People used to barge in, mostly unannounced. He never said no to anybody. All and sundry were welcome to the fine dining experience of Rahul Dev Burman. Pancham Kaku had also gifted a flat to Manu Pal, his cook of twenty-seven years.

Pancham Kaku's culinary skills were remarkable too. We did not like to eat vegetables, and he somehow used to make vegetarian dishes taste like non-vegetarian ones. He made my father eat bitter gourd, a vegetable he detested, by stuffing it with chicken nuggets.'

'His simplicity was his asset. With him, you would never feel that he was Rahul Dev Burman. He would help you with household work, cooking, almost everything. He would sleep on the floor, open the car doors for people and carry packages on others' behalf. He would also eagerly be looking for prospective brides for his men Fridays Sudam and Ramesh,' recalls Mili Bhattacharya.

'Let's call the gang. Bring Rishi too. I'll call Asha. Let's have dinner together. We'll have a sitting again,' Pancham had said to Randhir Kapoor.

'That never happened. He died within two days of that invitation. Asha did call us for dinner later, saying it was his last wish. We gave food and drink to his photo. Asha said, "He would have been happy that all of you have come for dinner,"' remembers Randhir.

'I bought a Johnnie Walker Blue Label for him in October 1993 on the way back from the US. I meant to go to Bombay to give him the gift. That never happened,' recounts Sivaji Chatterjee.

A poignant fan mail written by a middle-aged lady – whom Pancham remembered as a little girl ('Woh Bulu jo frock pehna karti thi') – to Pancham runs thus:

Dear Pancham,
    ... I don't wear a frock any more ... Neither have I grown up as far as you are concerned ... In April 2009, some invisible magnet pulled me to 15th Road, Khar ... Didn't they know that it was *your* house and should be

preserved like 'Dove Cottage' or 'Anne Hathaway's
Cottage'? ... More when we meet in Heaven,
   With love,
   Bulu (Anindita Roy nee Chakrabarty)
   31/05/2009

Ms Roy, now in her fifties, left for Singapore two days after
handing over this handwritten letter to her younger sister
Anasua in Rajendra Nagar, New Delhi. The taste of the mangoes
they were caught stealing in Pancham's garden in 1964 and the
slabs of chocolate they got as a 'reward' for that act still
lingered.

'On 3 January 1994, he told me to pick up a collection of
songs on the way to my office the next day. "But give me a call
before you come as I will be going to Pune to see the location
for a Marathi film," he had said. The next morning around 4
a.m., Bharat Bhai called me. He said, "Pancham-da chale gaye."
I replied, "Achcha Pune chale gaye? Koi baat nahi, main nahi
aaongi aaj." He clarified, "Nahi nahi woh guzar gaye,"' reminisces
Chhaya Ganguli.

In Hrishikesh Mukherjee's film *Anand*, the man with a big
heart, who is destined to a short lifespan, presents balloons to
children by the seaside and walks away singing a song about
the puzzling ways of sorrows and joys.

Pancham's last Bengali song that was recorded in Bombay was with Usha
Uthup, and it was titled '*Aagami shishura*' (the children of tomorrow). Perhaps
prophetic.

'On 2 January 1994, he came to my Dadar flat and gave me
a cassette with his songs. He saw some children playing in the
compound and handed out New Year greeting cards to all of

them with signed messages like "Music is Life",' recalls Chhaya
Ganguli.

Pancham, in these cards which he handed out just two days
prior to his death, seemed to have bequeathed his musical
legacy for them to carry safely in their young hearts in his
absence.

General Index

Song Index

Acknowledgements

Many people who were either associated with Pancham or have been followers of music and cinema in general offered generous help and support to us at the research stage. We would like to acknowledge their contributions and thank them.

Our understanding of Pancham's music was greatly enhanced during our discussions with the following musicians who spared many hours for us (in alphabetical order of first name):

- Amrutrao Katkar, Bhanu Gupta, Homi Mullan, Kersi Lord, (Late) Manohari Singh, Ramesh Iyer, Ranjit 'Kancha' Gazmer, Sunil Kaushik and Viju Katkar

The following musicians, poets, singers, film-makers, actors, technicians, media persons and friends also offered valuable insight into the nuances of music and trivia associated thereof (in alphabetical order of first name):

- Arati Mukherjee, Aashish Khan Debsharma, Abhijeet Bhattacharya, Pandit Ajoy Chakrabarty, Alka Yagnik, Amit Kumar, Baba Desai, S.P. Balasubrahmanyam, Chhaya Ganguli, Dipankar Chattopadhyay, (Late) Gulshan Bawra, Ivan Muns, Nandu Chavathe, Pritam, Prince Rama Varma,

Prodipto Sen Gupta, Pyarelal Sharma, Pandit Ronu Majumdar, Shikha Biswas Vohra, Shurjo Bhattacharya, Sivaji Chatterjee, Soumitra Chatterjee (guitarist), Susmit Bose, Pandit Ulhas Bapat, Usha Uthup, Uttam Singh, Yogesh

– Ananth Mahadevan, Bindu Jhaveri, Brahmanand Siingh, Dev Anand, Javed Akhtar, Ketan Anand, Madhu (Bubbles) Behl, Randhir Kapoor, Rishi Kapoor, Sachin Bhowmick, Samir Chowdhury, Shammi Kapoor, (Late) Shakti Samanta, Sujoy Ghosh, Tarun Majumdar, Vidhu Vinod Chopra

– The Bhattacharya family, namely, Badal, Mili and their daughter Doel for regaling us with tales of Pancham and for also sharing their fascinating photograph collection

– Abhijit Gupta, Anindita Roy, Anasua Banerjee, Birajmohan Das, Chandrahasan, Dr Mukesh Hariawala, Polly Gupta, Sanjeev Kohli, Sromona Guha Thakurta

We are indebted to the following people who are not associated with either the film or the music medium directly, but without whose help the book could not have taken the shape it has:

– Archisman Mozumder who escorted M.L. Lahiri – Pancham's erstwhile local guardian – to Marylands on 4 January 1994 and who shared the details of the fateful day with us. We also owe to him most of the discussions in the book revolving around the influence of Indian classical music on the Pancham sound. He also shared with us his vast collection of songs.

– Devdan Mitra, Nilanjan Lahiri and Bobby Mudgel for photographs of record covers

– Dr Shakti Ray of ABP who made articles on R.D. Burman available to us

– Parthiv Dhar for sharing books and making available songs which were proving very difficult to find

– Vishwas Nerurkar for sharing photographs from his dazzling photo collection of Pancham

- Amitava Chakraborty and Jai Shah for sharing photographs from their collection
- Rajat Gupta for sharing a rare picture of Ali Akbar Khan, Subhasis Poddar for sketching the portraits of Samta Prasad and Brojen Biswas, and Amal Kumar Banerjee for the photographs of Pancham's schools and residence in Kolkata
- Vinay P. Jain for the stories of Panchamonline.org and the Pancham Yahoo! group
- Sudipta Chanda for introducing us to many of Pancham's close acquaintances and also for sharing his film posters and booklets with us
- Shankh Banerjee and Indranath Mukherjee (New Delhi) for their help in research and compilation, and for suggesting changes at various stages
- Somraj Dutta and Debabrata Barua for helping touch up old photographs

We also wish to thank the following people for their passion/ engagement during the research and for their good wishes in the launching of the book. There is no way we can hope to repay the debt we owe them:

- Anindya Bhattacharya, Anindya Roychowdhury, Arghya Dutta, Arnab Chakraborty, Arundhati Bhattacharya, Ashok Bajaj, Atanu Chatterjee, Atanu Ray Chaudhuri, Biswajeet Dutta, Balai Bose, Basab Moitra, Bedanuj Dasgupta, Dr Binayak Sinha, Debopriyo Chakraborty, Dixit Arya, Gautam Choudhury, Dr Haimanti Banerjee, Jayanti Bhattacharjee, Joy Bhattacharjya, Kanchana Vishwanathan, Kinshuk Biswas, Dr Kamal Kant Goel, Kathakali Gupta, Kaushik Bhaumik, Kaushik Maitra, Kausik Dutta, Kaustubh C Pingle, Kiran DJ, Kusum B., Madhav Ajgaonkar, Naresh Khattar, Pankaj Sinha, Partha Bhattacharya, Dr Partha Sarathi Bhattacharya, Pavan Jha, Pawan Jalan, Paul Mukherjee, Priyodorshi

Majumdar, P. Raghu, Pritam Pritu, Dr Probal Moulick, Rajarshi Majumdar, Rajib Chakraborty, Rajsekhar Saha, Raju Nag, Ritu Chandra, Robert Iannopollo, Robin Bhat, Samarjeet Acharjee, Santanu Majumdar, Sauyma Kanti Sengupta, Shankar Iyer, Shashi Rao, Shibnath Lahiri, Siddhartha Das Gupta, Dr Siddhartha Ray, Sonali Chowdhury, Soumendu Datta, Soumik Sen, Subhashini Jalalabadi, Sujay Basu, Sunil Pandey, Sushobhan Mukherjee, Srijit Mukherjee, Sudhir Kulkarni, Sujata Shinde, Dr Sukanya Datta, Supratik Gangopadhyay, Dr Tanuka Ghoshal, Tapojyoti Sarkar, Vinay Jaiswal.

– G. Sethu and Mrs Radha Sethu, Vashi, Navi Mumbai, for the food and shelter, and for bearing us out despite our weird work hours

– Hari Om, the taxi driver from Vashi who once drove us to Bandra (West)

– Vijaya Mary, Ziya Us Salam, and the *Metroplus* (*The Hindu*) family

– Mr N. Ram, Editor-in-chief, *The Hindu*, and Mr Mukund Padmanabhan, editor, *Metroplus*, for granting us permission to reproduce some of the articles contributed to *Metroplus*

– To all our colleagues and well-wishers from The Royal Bank of Scotland, PwC and IBM for the encouragement and for sharing our enthusiasm

– To the members of the Pancham Yahoo group, the Pancham Orkut group, Sangeet Smrithi (Delhi/NCR), Swar Sagarika (Mumbai), The Pancham pages on Facebook and the Google-based group, Saatsur. They made the journey easier.

– To the suburban train network of Mumbai for helping us keep our appointments

Writing a book entails referencing and cross-referencing, and we had to browse through many books, films, periodicals and websites for the same. A few which we immediately recall are:

Books: *Hindi Film Geet Kosh* (volumes 3, 4 and 5) by Harmandir Singh 'Hamraaz' and Biswanath Chatterjee, *Pancham* by Vishwas Nerurkar and Biswanath Chatterjee, *Dhuno ki Yatra* by Pankaj Rag, *Mehmood: A Man of Many Moods* by Hanif Zaveri

Websites: panchammagic.org, panchamonline.com, livemint.com, ibosnetwork.com, imdb.com

Radio Programmes: *Sangeet Sarita, Meri Sangeet Yatra*

Documentary: *Pancham Unmixed* by Brahmanand Siingh and Gaurav Sharma

Newspapers and Periodicals: *Screen, Filmfare, Cine Blitz, Star & Style, Showtime, India Today, Movie, The Times of India, The Statesman, The Telegraph, Sunday Observer, The Independent, Mid Day, Ananda Bazar Patrika, Aajkal, The Illustrated Weekly of India, Hindustan Standard, Anandalok, Hindustan Times, Cine Advance, Cinema in India, Cinema India International, Swar Alaap*

Libraries: Archives & Research Centre for Ethnomusicology, American Institute of Indian Studies (Gurgaon); the National library, Kolkata; the ABP library, Kolkata

Television: BBC, Channel Four, Zee TV, Sony TV, Star TV, Times Now, Aaj Tak

Finally, to the family of HarperCollins India: Shantanu Ray Chaudhuri, Karthika V.K., Prema Govindan, Natasha Puri, Lipika Bhushan, N.S. Krishna, Shuka Jain and Shweta Nigam for their work on the cover and photo insert, Amit Sharma and Rajeev Sethi. It takes a wonderful team to launch two debutants. A special note of thanks for Aparna Sharma, for her help with organizing the Foreword by Javed Akhtar.

Anirudha's note of thanks:

I would like to thank my mother, Namita Bhattacharjee, my sons Aritra and Shaunak, and my wife Sudipta, for patiently putting up with most of my mercurial temperament, indecisiveness and Pancham-like unpredictability

Balaji's note of thanks:

I would like to thank my children, Ashapoorna and Akhilesh, and my mother Shanthi Vittal, for all the strength and support, and of course, Vandana, my wife for standing by me through thick, thin and vacuum